THE LAND OF
FEAST AND FAMINE

The Land of
Feast and Famine

BY HELGE INGSTAD

*Translated from the Norwegian
by Eugene Gay-Tifft*

McGILL-QUEEN'S UNIVERSITY PRESS
Montreal & Kingston • London • Buffalo

© McGill-Queen's University Press
ISBN 0-7735-0911-9 (cloth)
ISBN 0-7735-0912-7 (paper)

Legal deposit second quarter 1992
Bibliothèque nationale du Québec

Originally published as *Pelsjergerliv Blandt Nord-Kanadas Indianere*, copyright 1931
by Gyldendal Norsk Forlag, Oslo.
First published in English by Alfred A. Knopf, Inc., copyright 1933.

The translator and Alfred A. Knopf, Inc., wish to thank
Father J. L. Coudert, O.M.I., of Fort Chipewyan, Alberta; Corporal R.A. Williams,
Royal Canadian Mounted Police, of Fort Resolution, Northwest Territories; and
Captain James C. Critchell-Bullock for their generous and invaluable assistance
in the preparation of the first English edition.

Printed in Canada on acid-free paper

Canadian Cataloguing in Publication Data
Ingstad, Helge, 1899–
The land of feast and famine

Translation of: Pelsjegerliv blanct Nord Kanadas indianere.
ISBN 0-7735-0911-9 (bound) – ISBN 0-7735-0912-7 (pbk.)

1. Northwest Territories – Description and travel – 1906–1950.
2. Native peoples – Northwest Territories. 3. Trapping – Northwest Territories.
4. Ingstad, Helge, 1899–   . I. Title.

FC3963.I6413 1992   971.9'202'092   C92-09128-X

TO MY FATHER

Contents

Preface

SIXTY-FIVE YEARS AGO I SOLD MY THRIVING LAWYER'S practice in Norway and made for the Canadian wilderness of the Northwest Territories. For four years (1926–30) I lived as a trapper in the isolated region north-east of Great Slave Lake. I had decided to realize a dream that had always been with me: a primitive life in northern, practically uncharted wilds, in a region where the lives of the natives still largely followed their ancient traditions.

The wilderness north-east of Great Slave Lake proved to be what I had been looking for. After a long voyage by canoe, my partner Hjalmar Dale and I lit upon an enormous stretch of land with forests and tundras, extending to the Arctic Ocean in the north. A few groups of Indians, of Chipewyan stock, had their hunting grounds here. They were known as the Caribou-Eaters, a name they had received because their lives were utterly dependent on the caribou. At that time there were still great numbers – probably several hundred thousands – of caribou in the Northwest Territories. But the migrations of the caribou herds are mysterious. The Indians have a saying: "They are like ghosts; they come from nowhere, fill up all the land, then disappear. " When thousands of these animals poured over the land, the Indians and the few white trappers there were filled with joy; when the animals disappeared, hunger and famine followed in their wake – at times, people starved to death.

These were years of many long dog-sled journeys through forests and over the Barrens – they took me to the upper Thelon River and to other uncharted regions. The trappers were convinced that there were more wolves, more white foxes, in the far-off distances on the blue horizon, that it was there that the greatest riches were to be found.

We lived off the land. Practically all of the caribou was eaten: meat, fat, marrow, brain, liver, kidneys, blood – sometimes we ate the contents of the stomach as well. I did well on this entirely meat diet and never missed bread, potatoes, salt, or sugar. I was never ill during the long winters, and my teeth were perfect.

For a year I lived with a group of Indians ("Caribou-Eaters") in the inland forests, and I was the only white man there. I often think of these people with whom I shared everything for so long, and who became my good friends. It felt strange to become part of the world of the Indians, where so much ancient tradition was still alive. I imagine that most of these Indian friends of mine are dead by now, but I shall always remember them. The year I lived with them was not quite an easy year – but even though there were few caribou, we managed quite well, thanks to the Indians' skills and their principle of the hunt: the catch was shared by all. But the fate of three men who spent the year north of us was tragic – they all starved to death.

Forty years later a Canadian friend visited me at home in Norway. He showed me a Canadian map, and to my great surprise I saw that a small river south-east of the southern part of Artillery Lake had been named after me. I had lived alone with my dogs in these parts by the very

PREFACE

edge of the Barrens for a year, hunting and trapping wolves. From my tent I only needed to walk up a hill to see the endless Barrens. This was a good year, with plenty of caribou. And I had music almost every evening – on the hills around the wolves used to howl, and they were soon joined by the howling of my dogs. Quite an orchestra ...

Today, the foreboding which I describe on the last page of this book has come true: civilization has invaded the Northwest Territories. When I was there, air traffic was only just starting. During all the years I was there, I saw only two small planes – today there are planes everywhere, there are oil wells, there are mines, there is commercial fishing and much else connected with modern life. At Snowdrift, that beautiful place by Great Slave Lake where the Hudson's Bay Company had a small trading post and where we trappers raised our tents together with the Indians, enjoying the light summer after the hardships of a long and cold winter, there are many houses now and alcohol is a danger. The polar dogs are largely being replaced by noisy snowmobiles. I am glad to have been born at a time when silence reigned in the wilderness, when dog teams and canoes were the only means of transport.

There was yet another Canadian surprise awaiting me. More than half a century after this book had first been published, I received a letter from Philip Cercone, director of McGill-Queen's University Press. Praising the book, he stated that he wanted to republish it. I was happy to know

[xi]

PREFACE

that it was at last to appear in the country which had meant
so much to me. It had been a best-seller in Norway, and
new editions are still being published. It has also been
translated into many languages, and has appeared in most
of the European countries and in the USA; in the Soviet
Union, two hundred thousand copies were printed.

It was to be my fate to return to Canada in 1960, but the
purpose of this journey was an entirely different one. I
had decided to investigate the coasts of Newfoundland
from the sea and the air, in the hope of finding traces of
the settlement built by Leif Eiriksson, the Norseman who
discovered America about five hundred years before
Columbus.

A few words about this project are appropriate in the
preface of the present book, since all I had learned during
the years I lived at one with the Canadian wilderness and
the Indians was to stand me in very good stead in my
search. These experiences were of great value not only for
my interpretation of the sagas' descriptions of Leif Eiriksson's sailing to the new land which he called Vinland but
equally in understanding and assessing the land I saw
along the coasts of North America.

Where is Vinland? The Saga of the Greenlanders contains fascinating items of information about Leif's voyage
from the Norse community in western Greenland to the
new land in the west, but it is not easy to interpret these
passages. Scholars have been working on the Vinland
problem for almost three hundred years. Most of them
thought that Vinland must lie far to the south, in the
regions where wild grapes grow, such as Massachusetts,
New York, Virginia, etc., but no Norse traces were found
in these southerly regions. I was of a different opinion and

[xii]

PREFACE

published detailed arguments for it: in my view, Vinland must have been in Newfoundland.*

My investigations along the coasts of Newfoundland led to the discovery of faint traces of dwellings in a place called L'Anse aux Meadows, a beautiful green meadowland on the north coast. To me, those traces held great promise. During the years from 1961 to 1968 seven archaeological expeditions with international participation excavated the site under my leadership. Anne Stine Ingstad, a trained archaeologist, was in charge of the archaeological work throughout.

The ruins of seven houses, all built of turf and some of them large, were uncovered in the course of this work. All the buildings were of the same type as ancient buildings in Iceland and Greenland. One of them was a smithy, where iron was produced from bog-ore. Other fascinating finds included a soapstone spindle whorl and a bronze ring-headed pin of Viking Age type. A series of radiocarbon analyses have dated the settlement to about A.D. 1000, the very time when the Vinland voyages took place according to the sagas. These finds and dates, in conjunction with other significant factors, leave little doubt that the settlement is not only Norse but that it is identical with Leif Eiriksson's "large houses" in Vinland.

UNESCO has included the settlement at L'Anse aux Meadows in its "World Heritage List" as one of the most valuable historical monuments in the world.

Helge Ingstad
Oslo, 1991

---

* *Landet under Leidarstjernen*, Oslo, 1959; *Land under the Pole Star*, London and New York, 1966.

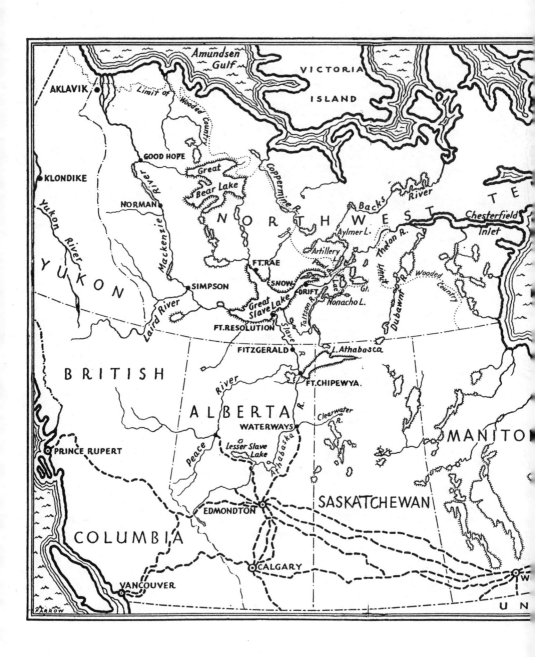

MAP *of the Territory* *covered by the Author of* THE LAND OF FEAST AND FAMINE

MILES

50   0   100   200   300   400

TERRITORIES

HUDSON BAY

QUEBEC

ONTARIO

NEW BRUNSWICK

QUEBEC

MONTREAL

OTTAWA

Lake Superior

PEG

UNITED STATES

L. Erie

THE LAND OF
FEAST AND FAMINE

The River

HJALMAR DALE CAME FROM THE MACKENZIE RIVER, I from the forests farther south. We met in Edmonton.

Here is a city to which a man may come straight from the wilderness, an overgrowth of beard on his face, moccasins on his feet, the seat of his pants blazing with patches, and walk down the street without having a single soul turn round to stare at him.

In spite of its modern construction and its population of over seventy thousand, Edmonton is still a pioneer town. It dates back to the rough-and-ready days of the early fur-traders and has written the chapter of Canadian history dealing with the opening up of the west; today it is the chronicler of a new episode, and perhaps the greatest of all: the conquest of the Far North.

Hither come the wild and restless souls who have found civilized society too tame for them and who have therefore come to seek adventure in the wilderness. Here they all congregate: trappers from the Barren Lands and the great forests, gold-diggers from Alaska, river captains from the Yukon, cowboys from the prairies, men with furrowed faces and unflinching gaze. Their varieties are many, but their type is one. All express the same spirit of swashbuckling independence, the same unshakable feeling of self-confidence, found in men accustomed to doing for themselves.

To these fellows Edmonton is the " City." She it is who beckons to them as they struggle onward through blizzards behind their dog-trains, or, worn out and starving, tramp across barren wastes in quest of gold; she it is who shines in their camp-fire dreams in the depths of the sighing wilderness. It is she, their Mecca, who, with a gesture, will find for them again all which they have lost. In her arms a mighty celebration will be theirs — and a speedy farewell.

Dale and I sauntered about and visited with a number of people. He was an old hand down north, had many to look up and much to talk over. Of all the people we encountered, one class in particular distinguished themselves from the others: the trappers from the Far North. Just how this difference manifested itself is pretty hard to say; perhaps it lay in a certain bluntness of manner. In their dry, everyday sort of talk, they hashed over various matters having to do with the " Country," which was their name for the northern wilderness. There were reports of long journeys by canoe and dog-sled, of a hand-to-mouth existence, which demanded the ability to act quickly and a knowledge of how to handle a gun. There were tales of Indians who still pursued their ancient nomad hunter's life, descriptions of the endless stretches of forest and plain where fabulous herds of caribou streamed forth across the barrens, pursued by packs of wolves.

With that, Dale and I decided to set out for the north.

Our plan was to go by river as far as Great Slave Lake, follow this east to Fond du Lac, take whatever water route offered itself, and then, alternately as necessary, paddle and portage our equipment as far north into the treeless plains as we could before the waters froze. That meant a canoe trip of 750-odd miles. At the end of it we would be

[4]

well up into caribou country. The blank spaces on the map, thank the Lord, showed many a region where no surveyors had gone tramping round before us.

A trapper's initial outfit for such an expedition as this is surely no ten-cent affair; this we discovered at the very start. We dug down deep into our pockets simply to procure a canoe, rifles, ammunition, and a few other essentials. These were no more than sorry preliminaries to a long though conservative list of equipment. So we decided to eliminate as non-essential all articles we could not under any circumstances afford and which were painful even for a moment to think about, and to put these out of our heads immediately. Other articles we figured we might be in a position to acquire later on, provided we could pick up an odd job or two along the way. But that would depend entirely upon fate.

Our purchases made, we had just enough cash left to get us by train to the rail-head and to buy us a glass of beer apiece. After drinking our beer, there was no longer any real reason why we should continue to remain in Edmonton, and early one April morning we started north for Waterways, so named because several rivers meet near there.

There was something quaint and naïve about that northbound train. Sedately it rattled along through the country, taking each up-grade at a leisurely pace and pausing long enough at each station to rest up. There was very little variety of landscape — swamp, woods, and stretches of water alternating in a slow and endless rhythm. Here and there was a pioneer settlement grouped about an open square, where Indians stood and stared. Thereafter we had the wilderness all to ourselves. A moose, stalking furtively through a forest of poplars, was the only sign of life.

Our fellow-passengers were all people who had one
thing or another to do with the Northland. With us rode a
Roman Catholic missionary with a youngish face and a
long beard, a number of trappers and fur-traders, and the
inevitable " Mountie," sitting there stiff as a poker in his
dashing red uniform. Everyone had something interesting
to say, and always, in one way or another, it dealt with the
" Country." The tone of voice employed by the speaker
was always loud and singing, for up here each man is no
worse than the next.

After a full day and a night on the train, we arrived at
Waterways, the end of the line, on the banks of the Clearwater River. The town consists of no more than a few rough
shacks. Here is the place where South meets North, where
the rails leave off and the rivers begin. With the exception
of a stretch of rapids between Fitzgerald and Fort Smith,
there are about fifteen hundred miles of continuous waterways all the way down to the Polar Sea.

The completion of the railroad in 1925 was civilization's
first advance against the North. Fur-trading, for all practical purposes, was, until 1931, the Northwest Territories'
principal means of livelihood, yielding a revenue of some
two millions of dollars per annum. But now the country is
being opened up, and the untold resources of radium, other
minerals, forests, water-power, fish, et cetera prepared for
exploitation. When one takes into consideration the fact
that this territory measures 1,310,000 square miles, thus
more than one third the area of the United States, whereas
its population is not even 12,000, of which only 1,000 are
whites and half-breeds — the balance Indians and Eskimos
— one has gained some impression of how unproved the
whole thing is, and of the enormous possibilities there are
to be reckoned with.

THE RIVER

The ice had not as yet broken up, so for the time being we would have to wait over and look around for something to do. We tramped down the river several miles to the "town" of McMurray, composed of two modest rows of houses, facing each other across a road. Aside from a Chinese barber-shop, the town's chief attraction is a saloon. The latter distinguishes McMurray from the commonplace, lends it prestige in the eyes of the wilderness folk.

As it happened, the river boats were just about to undergo their big spring overhauling. As laborers were much in demand, we landed ourselves jobs, and, together with a half-dozen Indians, we set to work immediately.

High up on the bank of the Clearwater River stood the old steamer *Northland Echo*, a tragic sight indeed. She was a flat-bottomed affair with cabins which rose from her decks to inconceivable heights. Two enormous bright-red paddle-wheels completed the impression of something quite naïve and helpless. But then, what river boat ever did appear imposing hauled high and dry on a river-bank? With scrapers, hammers, and brooms the six of us attacked the *Echo*. We scraped her and we scrubbed her, polished and painted her until she gleamed like a sunbeam. When that was done, we moved up the river to repair the scows which the steamer always pushed ahead of her on her voyages.

Of late years the scows had been used to transport living cargoes: buffalo. These animals had been brought up from Wainwright Park, Alberta, to a preserve west of the Slave River where the stock was running low. There are now some ten thousand of these animals there. We were to have no buffalo aboard on our trip, however, and we greatly regretted this, for, as the half-breed John used to say: "Buffalo, good cargo, walk aboard, walk ashore. Bags

[7]

and boxes hell of a cargo, got no legs to walk on, heap of work."

Our new place of employment was a scene of idyllic beauty. Back from the river-bank was a clearing in the poplar forest. Down by the river lay the scows, and strewn about them were the sorry remains of what at one time must have been a stern-wheeler. Back at the edge of the woods stood a cosy log cabin, and that was where we lived.

Our job was to calk the seams of the scows. From early morning till late at night we were busy with hammers and calking irons. This required a special sort of knack, but after a time we were able to master it and then we made steady progress, even when we had to lie on our backs beneath the scows.

One day the river began to growl. The ice was breaking up and had begun to flow downstream. Block crashing against block, they would both leap into the air and collapse as one, only to continue their feuds up over the river-banks, where they would sweep away earth and rocks and trees. For twenty-four hours the battle raged and then it was over; there flowed the river, like yellow grease, through the forest.

We shoved our canoe into the water and one evening, toward sundown, we paddled off to see if spring really were on the way. There was no mistaking it. In through the tall columns of the poplars which lined both banks of the river shimmered a pale green mist of buds, and hosts of wild ducks were paddling in among the reeds. Here and there a muskrat scurried or swam about, only the tip of his nose showing above water, his tail, like a rudder, trailing along behind him. The Indians could decoy these creatures with a call. They would purse their lips and produce a sucking sound. This was more than the muskrat could resist. Quite a distance away he would turn sharply round and swim as fast as he could straight in our direction until, scenting danger as he approached to within a few feet of us, he would lift up his tail and dive with a splash. On the way home, as the canoe fairly danced down the river, Jim, the Indian, began to sing a mournful, monotonous song. This was his manner of giving expression to his highly pleasurable mood.

" All hands clear! Let her go! " The *Echo* was given free rein, cantered down her greased track, and dove into the water with a grand splash. It was no such easy matter to launch the scows. When the moment arrived for them to begin gliding forward into the river, they did not so much as budge. We eased the way for them with bucketfuls of green soap, we coaxed them and dug at them with wooden poles, twisted them bow and stern, went at them with block and tackle, but the scows stayed right where they were. After we had fooled round a full day and had succeeded in moving one of the scows no more than an inch or two, the skipper went up in the air and said to the pilot, Dan: " Go on and get the *Echo*! " She arrived on the scene and, with a brutal display of strength, got her stubborn brood into the river. A proper launching indeed!

Then began the loading of the cargo. There was a motley array of goods to go aboard, all the way from hens' eggs and pants buttons to cedar beams many inches thick, requiring seven of us to carry — in short, all the things which folks down north would be needing to last them an entire year.

We worked at our job in the best of spirits, for the faster we worked, the sooner we should be finished and the sooner we could get away. Skipper Alexander was a splendid chap to work for. He took off his coat, made himself one of us, and didn't give us hell more often than was necessary.

Among other things he might say: " Come on, we'll make quick work of this pile of goods, then call it a day." And, with that, we would quicken our pace. There were other occasions when we were obliged to work on after quitting-time, and there was no way out of it. But we would make up for this by sneaking out into the galley while the skipper was in the mess-room and stuffing ourselves with apple pie, which we washed down with black coffee. For days and days, after an expedition such as this, the cook would be full of thunder and lightning.

The crew was made up of Cree Indians, with the exception of one whom we dubbed Jim, who belonged to the Chipewyan tribe. He had a more alert mind and was more willing to work than the others, but he was an odd chap at best. One day he abruptly left his work, came over to me, and, in his broken English, said: " My father die, now I a poor shit." Having eased his heart with this confession, he immediately went back to work.

For the most part, though, he was a man of few words, and the reason for this lay in the tense relationship which existed between himself and the other Indians. There was one strapping big hulk of a fellow in particular who never let an opportunity go by to taunt him. Jim, phlegmatic chap that he was, bore it with unruffled calm until the day when the Cree, as if by accident, allowed a steel cable to fall on Jim's toes. Quick as a cat, Jim leaped in, grabbed his tormentor by the hair, and refused to let go. The Cree clutched one of Jim's ears, and then things began to happen, as is usually the case when two Indians decide to settle accounts with bare fists. The Chipewyan gave the Cree's head a good half-twist. The latter retaliated by screwing his adversary's ear. At the same time they kept kicking each other's shins and flailing about with their free fists.

Their brown faces were distorted by grimaces, but they hung on with suppressed fury, for here an old grudge was about to be settled. We expected any moment to see Jim's ear twisted off and the other's dark mop of hair torn out by the roots. But things didn't go that far; the skipper stormed up on deck and ruined the rest of our entertainment.

. .

One morning an Indian came paddling up the river with the news that Lake Athabaska was open to navigation. The ice had broken up and was drifting eastward. At once a feverish activity broke loose aboard the *Echo,* whilst we made her ready for sailing. We must be under way at all costs before the Hudson's Bay Company's steamer, *Athabaska,* for she was the rival we were determined to defeat decisively in the annual race for the north. Which would be the first ship to reach Fitzgerald? That was the burning question.

The race is repeated each year and is always pursued with the same tense interest, experienced not least by those who witness the final dash — the people down north, who throughout a long winter have been practically without contact with the outside world. They make up a grand sweepstake, the winner being the one who can most accurately figure out the time the first steamer of the year will arrive.

The *Athabaska* cast off and began splashing down the river, pushing her deeply laden scows on ahead of her. We followed several hours later. Toward lunch-time we passed our rival; she had grounded both scows on a mud bank, and there she was, hard and fast. Her people were moving about like whipped puppies, and the voice of her captain went thundering out over the river. Our own skipper viewed the mishap with huge indifference, whilst we others hung over the rail, hugging ourselves with delight. But it wasn't long before our own turn came. Our scows plowed into a shoal, and there they stuck. For hours we sweat to get them loose. The *Echo* churned the water into muddy foam, and in the end every known form of river strategy had been tried. We had already reconciled ourselves to the prospect of spending the night shifting cargo when suddenly, and for no good reason, the scows floated free. Such are these flat-bottomed brutes — mean, incalculable.

Our skipper was not to blame for the fact that we had run aground, or that we were to repeat the performance on later occasions. He had gained his experience navigating the waters of the Yukon, and few others had mastered, as he had, the art of " reading " a river by the color of its waters, the formations of its banks, and the changing nature of its surface ripples. But the Athabaska River is capricious; it is full of silt, and the channel shifts from year to year. Even the wisest of navigators can err in their course.

We continued our way north. At first we had banks of tar sand on either side of us. Mile after mile of dark bituminous strata rose from the river's edge. There had been much talk about exploiting these deposits, but everything is still in an experimental stage. Thereafter we sailed through a country of undulating woodland and low flat swamps; then the river branched out into a maze of lesser passages, and there, ahead of us, lay Lake Athabaska. We made fast the *Echo* and paddled on ahead in order to plot the channel, which is tortuous here and extremely difficult to follow. Long sand banks covered with masses of drift-logs stretched in all directions. And what bird life! Ducks, swans, and geese, swarming and mingling their flocks. Far off to the east the ice-pack gleamed white, but ahead of us the channel was clear.

On the other side of the lake we made our way in between islands of red granite to Fort Chipewyan. Indians came paddling out to us in their small canoes, and ashore, dressed in their Sunday best and anxiously awaiting our arrival, stood the entire population of the place. On the slope were a small group of buildings belonging to the Hudson's Bay Company and a handful of houses — these were all.

Fort Chipewyan is a place with a tradition dating back to the virile " Hudson Bay days." It was from here, too, that men like Sir Alexander Mackenzie and Sir John Franklin set forth on their expeditions into the north. Hunting and fishing now engage the local inhabitants, and in these activities they fare splendidly. Lake Athabaska is the home of many fish and wild fowl, farther to the east lie winter ranges for the caribou, and in the immediate vicinity are numberless rivers and lakes abounding in muskrats.

We were unloading sacks, cases, drums of petroleum, and planks at a steady pace, every now and then casting an eye in the direction of our rival, the *Athabaska*, already in sight, plowing across the lake in the distance. Just as she came abreast of us, we finished unloading, cast off, and began splashing northward again. Soon we were in the Slave River, a broad stream with a swift current.

Now it was pleasant indeed on board. I loafed on deck in the shadow of a life-boat, puffed on my pipe, and watched the land as it slipped by. The river meandered along, first narrow and swift, then wide and cosily littered with islands. The wilderness pressed close to the river on either side, with an occasional rift in the forest through which the sunlight poured. Forward on the deck of one of the scows lay our dogs, stretched lazily in the sun. Everything was peaceful. Only the steady beating of the paddles and the monotonous cries from the Indian who stood up in the bow of the leading scow and measured the depth of the river with a long pole. " Five feet, six feet, eight feet! " he would call.

But we would have to shake off our drowsiness and be ready for a good snappy job each time we arrived at a wood-pile. The river boat burned wood in her grates, and a fuel-hog she was indeed. Two gang-planks were laid ashore, and in a long line we would tramp back and forth, our shoulders sore from those knotted chunks of wood, our faces smeared with sweat and resinous dust.

One night we were rudely awakened. The boat lay alongside the river-bank; in the forest stood a shed bursting with goods which had been stored there since the previous year. We were to bring them aboard " right snappy "; those were our orders. We rubbed the sleep from our eyes, and fell to good-naturedly, for, after all, it was pleasant to be awake on such a mild moonlight night. Our muscles felt strong and springy as we tossed sacks and boxes over our shoulders, convinced that we should get over this job in a hurry. In and out among the trees the shadows of men slipped through the moonlight. We laughed and joked, and the Indians joined in with songs which resounded far and wide through the night. But after we had dragged along into the gray hours of the morning, our high spirits gradually wore away. Our shoulders ached, and it seemed as though there would be no end to that pile of goods. As the sun came up over the tree-tops, it was a silent line of men that tramped back and forth between the forest and the ship.

We passed one place by the river where a broad-shouldered giant of a Swede had made his home. He was the farmer-pioneer type if ever one existed, with good sense enough to clear a place for himself in the very heart of the wilderness. He had a potato patch, two cows, some hens, and the loveliest wife imaginable. Already three little ones were playing about the hut, somewhat brown of skin perhaps, but with Norse blue shining eyes. Here he planned and managed exactly as he wished, and far and wide he was master of all these forests, through which he roamed in the winter on hunting expeditions with his dog-team.

One last curve in the river, and there lay Fitzgerald. The roaring of the rapids sounded in our ears. Quietly we sailed up to the bank, which was black with people. Just as we were busy making our ship fast, the *Athabaska* appeared upstream, steaming at top speed. But she had very little to be proud of, as we had been " the first boat north " by almost ten minutes.

We went ashore at Fitzgerald. A short distance below the town begins a series of rapids, so turbulent that not even a flat-bottomed river boat can navigate them. In the old days it was a practice to shoot the lesser rapids in scows steered by huge oars, or sweeps, balanced outboard over the stern; down the more dangerous stretches these scows were tracked by means of ropes. Today all freight is transported via a sixteen-mile-long dirt road to Fort Smith. From there the river becomes navigable again. The only living thing to feel reasonably at home out there where the river breaks into a gallop and, in bursts of spray, hurls itself over jagged rocks is the pelican. As long as men can remember, it has inhabited these rocky islands.

Neither Fort Smith nor Fitzgerald is a place to arouse the visitor's enthusiasm. There, for the millionth time, one encounters the scourge of the Northland — the mosquito and the bulldog fly. Before long the newcomer looks as though he were suffering from a bad case of boils. Nor are these places much to attract the eye. Everything about them smacks of itching, scratching, boring half-civilization.

We hung round down by the river for several days, revelling in our new freedom to do as we wished with our time and saying good-by to skippers, wood-toting, and all that sort of thing. The Hudson's Bay Company had just begun the construction of a heavy eighty-foot cargo barge, and a whole gang of men under a roaring boss were frantically at work. We lit our pipes, found ourselves a couple of stumps to sit on, and with keen interest watched them at their gruelling toil.

That evening, after work, there was a general gathering of the clans, out in front of the barracks. Boxing-gloves appeared, whereupon the men paired off and went at each other, all taking their share of punishment. One chap with a mop of light hair and I happened to be matched together. With all the ring knowledge we could muster up, we lit into each other, the spectators roaring their enjoyment and shouting: "Knock him cold! Step on him!" After experiencing several close calls, it suddenly occurred to me that I owed it to my native Norway to come out of this combat with a foreigner with at least some honor to myself, and this thought caused me to put up all the fight I had in me. It is hard to say which one of us finally got the worst of it, but I can swear that that lad with the light hair was a real tough customer. Afterwards, as we stood wiping the blood and sweat from our faces, I fell into conversation with my opponent, and it was his speech which gave him away: he spoke English with a Kristiansand accent!

Our leisure was shortlived. We needed a hundred and fifty dollars for my trapper's license. Nothing for it, then, but to look around for a new job. There was still no hurry about continuing north. The month of May had hardly begun, and it would be July before Great Slave Lake would be free of ice and navigable.

A man named Dick was the owner of a little saw-mill a short way down the river. He asked us if we knew anything about mill work. We replied that we were both pretty handy with a saw, and it was lucky for us he didn't ask us what kind of saw we meant. Hired, we packed up and moved on to begin work for three dollars a day and keep.

The mill was a quaint affair reminding one of James Watt and the infancy of the steam engine. At a little bend in the river, which flowed quietly between banks of reeds and rat-grass, was a clearing in the woods. A pipe-like smoke-stack rose from some rusty wheels in an attempt to make the place look factory-like. Back in the trees stood a shack, painted up after a fashion. I paid but little heed to decorative effects just then, however, absorbed as I was in fighting off the mosquitoes. The muskegs round about were their El Dorado, and the scent of human blood seemed to set them wild.

We began to rid the furnace flues of wild ducks. They must have alighted on the smoke-stack to rest, lost their balance, and tumbled down inside. When we had completed this job, we took a pail in each hand and spent half a day running back and forth between the river and the mill. In that way we filled the boiler. Before long we had everything shipshape, save for the fact that the machinery wouldn't budge. We were able at length, however, to overcome even this obstacle. When the saw was ready to turn, we went up the river to a place where logs had been piled along the bank. We were to roll these into the river and float them down to the mill. Splendid, straight spruce logs they were, from eight to twelve inches in diameter.

This was the beginning of a period rich in incident. I made the acquaintance of the cant-hook, that mysterious tool with which a lumber-jack can accomplish everything, a greenhorn nothing. I had my first experience running over floating logs. To hop about on a raft of moving timbers seems simple indeed when someone else is doing it. When, however, you have to do it yourself, it seems like an entirely different matter. It is not merely that one's foothold gives way beneath one, but that it gives way in *all* directions!

Boldly and full of confidence, you start out from shore and come to log number one. It sinks. You hop over to log number two, which immediately begins to spin round backwards as fast as it can. While your legs work like drumsticks and you flap like a crow, you look wildly about for some means of escape. That is when you spy log number three. It appears to be a perfectly trustworthy log and you venture to leap over to it. But now you have made the acquaintance of the most deceitful of all these various logs — a forward-roller. No sooner have you set foot upon it than it begins to spin, slowly at first, then faster and faster. A clever beginner at this point would jump of his own accord into the river. But there are certain enterprising souls who prefer to hang on to the very end. And the end for them is bitter indeed. There are others who actually succeed in getting over onto log number four which slowly and inexorably tilts up on end. A further change of steeds is out of the question. The manner in which you come to rest in the river depends entirely upon which log you choose to accomplish the trick. In any event, you take immediate leave of your dignity.

When bathing of this order in the ice-cold water of the river has continued on through a day of hard work, it begins to seem less amusing. And when a red-headed fellow-workman takes huge delight in your difficulties and gives vent to his feelings in howls of brutal laughter each time the mishap is repeated, even the most patient of men grows bitter in his soul.

At last all the logs were gathered together into a raft, which we steered down the river with an enormous oar. All went well until we swung off from the main stream into a narrow side channel, for here the whole business naturally got jammed. Then we had a grand time for the rest of the day, splashing about in muck and sweating over our poles, with the mosquitoes literally chewing us up. At length, out of sheer spite, we drew aside the boom and let the logs drift loose, whilst we paddled on ahead for our lives, dragging the log-chain behind us. Down by the mill we lost no time in hauling it athwart the stream. The result was that Dick missed no more of his logs than he deserved.

The milling of the logs began. We were each given a particular job to perform, and upon me fell the heaviest of all. For that is the custom down north — the meanest tasks are allotted to the newcomer. That is the school he must go through. In any event, it was a tough job I was put to — one intended for one horse and two men. Not only was I to keep the saw clear of boards and planks; I also had to sweep the sawdust aside, heap it up in a big piece of sail-cloth, and drag it down to the river. I thanked the Lord when a hungry Indian came paddling up the river. The odor of food deadened his normal disgust for work and he took his place beside me. That was some help, of course, but even so, no bed of roses was mine, for we had to work ten hours a day and keep up a terrific pace.

Up at the steel-table raved Dick, who was a tough one, broad of shoulder and stooped, his face grimy with sweat and sawdust. He managed the saw, tirelessly, inexorably. Couldn't afford to waste a second, for his workmen had to be paid, and the harder he drove them, the more he could get for his money. Steadily the stream of logs rumbled up; a swing of the cant-hook, one log rolled off, the next, the next. With a rasping song, steel chewed through wood, sawdust spurting from the wound, whilst planks and boards flowed by in a flood, and the pile of sawdust grew. On and on we worked.

In the door of the cabin Joe, our cook, used to take his station, his legs spread wide apart, his hands held under his kitchen apron. He enjoyed watching other people work and gave authoritative advice on just what should be done. Cooks down north are as alike in that particular as they are in most others. As a rule their names are Joe — that is, unless their names are Jim. They are all to a like degree fattish, they are all to a like degree disagreeable in the kitchen, and jovial talkers outside. But when it comes to the hotcakes, that's where they begin to differ, and it is on this basis that the worth of a cook is established. Joe occupied a high position in our esteem. Unimportant traits of his character we were happy to disregard in favor of his one all-important talent: namely, that of making class-A hotcakes.

As week after week went by, my fellow-worker, the Indian, became more and more reticent. In the evening he would go down to the river and sit by himself, smoking his pipe and staring off into the woods. Then one day, right in the midst of work, he suddenly dropped with a clatter the planks he was carrying and walked down to his canoe. " Where are you going? " I asked. " Hunt moose," he replied, hopped in and paddled up the river out of sight. Such are these children of the forest. Steady work means nothing to them. They get a job only when driven to it, and go their way when the life of a hunter beckons, even though it means an even greater amount of toil and privation. In the wilderness there is freedom, and that is everything to them.

One night I felt Dale's fist punching my shoulder. It couldn't have been that I was snoring, for in such matters we were so well trained by habit that a mere shout from one of us would cause the other, without even waking up, to roll over on his side. Foggy with sleep, I sat up in the mosquito-netting. " Listen! " he whispered. I could hear a mighty splashing down in the river. Beaver! In a flash we were out of the tent. Down there among the drift-logs we caught a glimpse of a dark head, silently gliding back and forth in the water. Longingly we stared at it, paying little or no attention to the mosquitoes swarming about our bare legs. Closer and closer came the beaver, until suddenly, on catching scent of us, he slapped the water with his broad tail as a warning signal, and with that he disappeared.

We agreed at this point that we had had enough of plank-lifting, sawdust-toting, toil, and drudgery — the wilderness had beckoned to us, and it was time we were on our way.

The following day we loaded our goods and dogs into two canoes and struck off down the river. Rounding the first curve in the stream, where we watched Dick's lumbering hulk up by the saw-mill disappear, we seemed to have left all life's cares behind us. We lighted our pipes, paddled a bit, drifted a bit, and, for the first time, felt like human beings, our bare legs hugging the sun-heated gunwales, our shirts wide open in front.

We passed the mouth of the Salt River. From the districts round about it the Northland has, since olden times, derived its requirements of salt. Here we took aboard three of Dale's dogs: Trofast,[1] Spike, and Nigger, which an Indian had been looking after during the time their owner was south in civilization. We were drifting through stoneless country. The river had cut its way through clay, and the banks rose so sharply that it would have been a pretty hard job to climb ashore. Here and there the water had sheared off huge chunks of earth; these with uprooted trees formed islands lapped by the swirling current. At other spots there were stretches of overhanging banks, on the point of collapse. Sometimes the bank would cave in under our very eyes, with a resounding boom and a cloud of flying particles. In this section of the country more than one trapper, returning in the autumn from the hunt, has looked in vain for his cabin.

Our pleasant days paddling down the Slave River passed all too quickly. Here is a record of one of them:

Barefoot and in our shirt-sleeves, we paddle lazily along. Sometimes we are borne rapidly down a swift current close up against the bank, with a canopy of poplars above us, sometimes we glide in among leafy islands where a glorious stillness reigns. There is no end to the twistings of the river, to the forest that surrounds us, and to the flood of sunshine above us.

[1] *"Trofast"* is a Norwegian word meaning "trusty," "faithful." — TRANSLATOR.

THE RIVER

On the shining white drift-logs sit rows and rows of wild ducks staring at us in amazement. Here and there we see muskrats swimming upstream for all they are worth. They are out scouting for their supper, though one would imagine from their haste that they were at least bound for some important meeting or other. Some are already at their meals. In secluded spots along the banks they are sitting up on their haunches, cramming rat-grass into their mouths with their fore-paws. They glance up only as we pass abreast of them; then they calmly resume their gnawing.

The dogs are dozing as they lie curled up in the bottom of the canoe, all save Trofast, who is resting his muzzle on the gunwale and through half-open eyes is watching the land slip by. There is a dog worth having! He feels it his duty to keep watch, feels himself responsible for the safety of us all. But the sun is scorching hot, and Trofast is so horribly sleepy that he simply cannot keep his eyelids open any longer. The matter is entirely beyond his control. But with a sudden twitch he wakes up and looks sheepishly in our direction.

Just as we are passing through a narrow stretch of river, Trofast suddenly starts up wide awake and sniffs, meanwhile staring sharply ashore. There beneath the trees stands a bear. It has neither seen nor heard us and is busily engaged in scratching up a root. With both fore-paws it is digging in the ground so that the dirt flies out behind, stopping every now and then to sniff and snort in the hole. We stealthily raise our rifles. . . .

By evening the bear has been flayed. A mighty bonfire of piled drift-logs rises like a column of flame in the forest. Round about us in the brush the dogs, stuffed full of meat, lie curled up fast asleep. On spits in front of the fire the paws of the bear and several fat ribs are roasting. The odor which drifts in our direction is delicious and we can hardly wait until dinner is ready. But at length we are at it.

Out come our pipes. We smoke in silence and stare out across the river, which winds off into the pale night. Small voices murmur and gossip in the gurgle of the river, now and then a shower of sparks blows over our heads. . . . But over in the shelter of a tree-root old Nigger lies talking to himself in his sleep.

Great Slave Lake

It originates, way over by the trading store belonging to the Hudson's Bay Company, in a long-drawn-out, sorrowing wail. All at once it swells into a chorus, augmented from every side. The air trembles beneath a tempest of sound which rises and falls in endless and painful discord.

There is no spot where some dog is not howling, and no howl that is like another. Back at the edge of the woods the sound rises, for the most part, in a deep bass, whilst over by the Indian village it cuts in with a blood-curdling treble. A little puppy which has not as yet learned to howl properly, but which, none the less, wishes to be one of the party, contributes all he can in a thin falsetto. Even so, his voice breaks and he has to help things along with a series of short yelps. Our own dogs do not hold themselves aloof. They squat by the water's edge, tilt back their heads, and give way to lusty lamentation. Then, as if by magic, a deathlike silence prevails.

This is Fort Resolution, the place where the dogs of the Northland rule.

When one awakes for the first time in his tent to discover that he has been robbed of frying-pans, snowshoes, stockings, and bacon, he is unable to solve the mystery. But one soon learns: nearly everything can be laid to the door of those hungry Indian dogs. Their cunning and audacity know no bounds. They gnaw their way into tents where men lie sleeping, claw their way up scaffolds calculated to be proof against any dog on earth, assemble in piratical droves, swim out to anchored boats, board them, and plunder them. Their purpose is to·make a clean sweep. I do not insist that they devour *everything* they carry away, but such an implication would not be far from the truth. In any event, it goes against their grain to leave untouched anything that can reasonably come to rest in a dog's belly.

Night is their time for marauding. During the day they skulk about in small bands, looking for a chance to fight. The affair begins with a preliminary. Two of them make a sudden lunge at each other, wrestle head over heels in the dirt, battle for their lives. The first sound of fighting is a signal in Fort Resolution for a general gathering of the clans. As though they had sprung from the earth, dogs come racing from behind cabins, tents, and sheds and ecstatically throw themselves into the battle, all piling themselves on top of the original two. When one dog has so maimed his rival that he will for a long time be unable to drag a sled, he immediately turns on his nearest neighbor, and then the battle is on along the entire front. Back and forth the conflict surges in rhythms of savage fury; dog flings himself upon dog in a general mêlée — a snarling, snapping, straining struggle. When at length the combatants abandon the field of battle, it is certain that many will be seriously injured and will limp away uttering howls of pain. Then only may the human inhabitants resume their accustomed activities.

On the shore of Great Slave Lake, several miles west of the river's delta, we have pitched our camp. Just above us lies the place with the pompous name of Fort Resolution, a few stores and a handful of small houses scattered about on a strip of level ground. Down by the water's edge a little city of tents gleams white against the lake, where a canoe is gliding past, loaded to capacity with swarthy Indians — men, old women, and curs all packed in together. They are coming from a place farther east.

The fort is full of animation. Trappers and traders are busy with their transactions. Men laying in their equipment, loading up their canoes, paddling off on their way. Small boats arriving from the south, bringing in new supplies of goods, fresh bits of news. Acquaintances greeting each other: "Hallo! How are you?" Perhaps they have not seen each other for a full year or two. Some have kept themselves going in the land of the Eskimo, others in the forests farther south.

There is one trapper who, together with his Eskimo wife, is on his way down the Mackenzie, bound for the mouth of the Coppermine River. He must have made a coup with the white fox, for he is the owner of a brand-new schooner. She is named the *Hayohok*. He boasts of his wife's seamanship, and other virtues as well. He explains his marriage as follows: "Her husband was dead and she was left alone with two children and there I was, for my part, monkeying around year after year on the ice. We needed each other, so we simply got together — you see, we were both so lonely." Some years later I learned that his schooner had gone to pieces somewhere in the Arctic and that he himself was dead.

Another white man, named Cæsar, is married to an Indian girl. For him marriage has not produced the same satisfactory results. Filled with bitterness over the world's injustices, he unburdens his heart to us: "One fine day my wife's people and her people's people blew in, made themselves at home in our tent, cleaned up every crumb we had in the place, quarreled, and used their jaws a-plenty. That was the custom, and when my old woman sided in with them, what the hell was a poor bastard to do! "

One man after another here keeps hinting about the discovery of gold. Alaska Janssen has heard about it, and others have heard the same. Perhaps there is something in it this time and it is not one of the usual rumors which in the past have caused folks to poke around far from home and stake their claims in barren country. There is gold in the Northwest, that much at least is certain. That the Indians know of many a deposit is also a foregone conclusion. But it is impossible to get a word out of them. The yellow metal will bring misfortune upon moose and caribou; that is what they imagine.

We run into a couple of fur-trappers hailing from parts whither we are bound, the country east of Great Slave Lake. We hear about the caribou and realize more and more how these herds mean everything to the people of the Barren Lands. Will they appear this season? Nobody knows. A year or two ago they swerved from their usual course and didn't turn up at all. The Indians starved and dogs lay dead along every sled-trail. We inquire about the country off there in the east, but there isn't much information we can pick up. It is so endless and there are only ten or twelve white trappers who have penetrated its depths and who really know its natural phenomena well. There are two things, however, about which we are given clear advice, and they are these: first, we must go some if we are expecting to reach the Barrens this year, and, second, it is mighty cold up there.

Peace dwells over the Indian village. No activity there. Outside the tents squat filthy young ones digging in the sand and we are met by snarling curs. The tepees are pitched in groups. Here dwell the Chipewyans, there the Dogribs, the Yellowknives, and the Slave Indians. Some of them come from Hay River, others from Fort Rae and the tracts in the vicinity of Great Bear Lake, still others from the eastern shores of Great Slave Lake. All have dark-brown skin and straight black hair, and their features are uglier than those of the southern tribes.

The occasion for this meeting of the tribes is the paying off of treaty money. Each Indian who decides to co-operate with the Government receives annually the imposing sum of five dollars. Once each year, on Treaty Day, the Indians assemble to receive this Government dole. It is not the money, however, that attracts them from far and near; it is the fact that later they can go back and say they have been to Resolution, where they appeared before the white man as persons of consequence, embroidered moccasins on their feet, and red silk kerchiefs about their necks.

We take a walk through the Indian village and pay a visit here and there. The larger tepees are literally bursting with hunters, lying about on deerskins, smoking their pipes, and talking a jargon so outlandishly guttural that it is utterly impossible for us to distinguish one word from the next. Old Black Basil, who later became one of my very good friends, is among them. He knows a few phrases of English. We ask him about the country to the east, and with great difficulty he sketches on a piece of bark a maze of strange irregular lakes and mysterious rivers. " Old canoe route! " he says. I put the map in my pocket, though somewhat skeptically, for it is well known that many Indians consider it grand sport to fool a white man by sending him on a wild goose chase. And Black Basil wears such a crafty smile on his face as he sits there!

The squaws, for the most part, keep to themselves, smoking, chewing tobacco, and gabbling. Our main interest lies in them. We are in need of caribou coats, mittens, and moccasins, and to get these made we must turn to the fair sex. It is no easy matter, however — not like going to a regular tailor to have something made. Delicate negotiations are of a prime necessity, and the main point is not the question of payment, for this is taken for granted, but whether or not one finds favor in the eyes of the squaw. If one fails in this respect, one is licked at the start, for when a squaw says no, she means no!

We ingratiate ourselves as best as we can, but realize full well that to begin with we must simply call at the various tepees and pass the time of day. No one is anxious to work. We make preliminary presents of bacon, sugar, and raisins. This helps. Such advances are likely to prove extravagant where these people are concerned, however, for, as a rule, their desire for work vanishes as soon as they have eaten up the payment. Nevertheless, we take this risk.

With our lean purses we visit the trading post to lay in further provisions, but the money we have is like a drop in the bucket down here in the north, where prices are out of all proportion. A hundred-pound bag of flour costs fifteen dollars, a box of ammunition three dollars. In civilization these prices average about four dollars and a dollar thirty respectively. It is even worse at the remoter outposts, where a hundred pounds of flour sometimes cost as much as thirty dollars, and a similar amount of sugar fifty dollars. One can readily imagine, thus, how many white-fox pelts a hunter would have to secure merely to cover his original outlay.

In the old days the skin of the beaver was the commonly accepted medium of exchange. One still hears mention of that time when the price of one flint-lock gun was a pile of beaver pelts as high as the gun was long, and the older Indians remember the day when a cup of tea cost " one skin." Nor was it many years ago that, for example, one hundred martens had so low a value that a trapper found difficulty in paying the cost of his expedition. Barter is still practiced extensively, though at the larger trading posts the dollar has taken the place of the beaver-skin as the medium of exchange. The Indians exchange their furs for merchandise; in fact, they will swap anything they own — their dogs, their watches, their canoes, and even their wives. But when they are not *obliged* by circumstances to make a trade, they must be in the mood for it, or all barter is out of the question.

Having arranged matters with the women and having bought us another canoe from the factor at the post, we still found ourselves in need of another dog and a pair of snowshoes. Our only salvation was to try swapping with the Indians. We carefully went through our possessions to discover what we could least painfully part with. At length we pulled out two watches, a set of fox-traps, and my brand-new, tailor-made suit which I had bought on the blue Mediterranean from the leading tailor in Nice. We considered, from a business standpoint, that the best plan would be for me to appear among the Indians dressed up in this suit of mine and all decked out with both watches. The fox-traps were hardly appropriate to such ballroom attire!

The first watch brought us one emaciated dog. This stroke of business came off without a hitch, as soon as I had convinced a half-breed that the watch had eighteen jewels. The first thing an Indian investigates when he is bargaining for a watch is the number of jewels it has. My second watch didn't have a chance. It had only seven jewels and was rejected with disdain. When I brought out the fox-traps, I was greeted with howls of derisive laughter; I was given to understand that there was no snow on the ground *now*. When the fox had begun to grow his winter fur, then let me come back. Things that could not be used the same day had no interest for them.

As for my fashionable suit of clothes, a complicated situation indeed arose. There were customers for both coat and trousers separately, but for the whole suit there was only one serious customer and he was too short. This inertness of trade was difficult to understand, for the suit had otherwise created a distinct impression. Neither had I failed to advertise it. It went strongly against my grain to separate two such natural companions as coat and trousers, but since by so doing I had received two excellent offers, presto: a pair of snowshoes, a pair of moose-hide mittens, and, into the bargain, a pail of dried meat and fat. I gave in. . . .

. .
.

Late in July we received reports of favorable ice conditions and made ready to depart. Before us lay Great Slave Lake, that enormous sea of fresh water up in northern Canada. It is 325 miles long and has a water surface of 9,770 square miles, about equal to the water area of Lake Erie. The stretch that lay ahead of us from Fort Resolution to Fond du Lac, the eastern extremity of the lake, was a little over two hundred miles. This distance we should have to row. The trip by water was merely our first step, however; our most difficult stage would still lie ahead — our journey into the interior.

But our problem was not one of physical strength alone.

Much depended upon fate, for Slave Lake is treacherous. I have seen it lying there smooth as glass one moment, and five minutes later roaring and tossing with breakers lashed by the wind. There is not the long even roll in these waves that there is in the waves of the sea; they leap in mad confusion. It has happened that trappers have been marooned for weeks out on the islands, and more than one has risked his life in the thickest of the storm. The more often a man has crossed the lake, the more cautiously he behaves. "A man gets wise pretty quick," as an old-timer once said to me, "after he has clung to his keel a couple of times with his winter's supplies floating all around him."

Three canoes, one in tow, head out into Great Slave Lake. Amid a confusion of sleds, tents, traps, snowshoes, and sacks piled high in each canoe, there is hardly any room left for the men who row them. And yet somehow they do. Bracing their legs against a sack, they heave on the oars. At each stroke, there is a sharp jerk on the tow-line, as the trailer unwillingly follows on behind. In the bow and in between the rower's legs, lie half a dozen dogs packed in together like sardines in a tin. Now and then one of them shifts his position in order to lie more comfortably — " Lay down, you — — — ! " The voice echoes far out over the lake, and the dog slumps down again, the heavily loaded canoe rocking perilously meanwhile, its gunwale level with the surface of the water. About them lies the lake, endlessly broad and blue. And the men row on; day after day, week after week, past steep cliffs, in between wooded islands, over open stretches, steadily eastward, eastward. . . . Dale and I on our way up the length of Great Slave Lake.

We made good progress the first few days and had

passed the Slave River delta. Late one evening, just as we were looking about for a snug spot to spend the night, we spied the light of a camp-fire in the woods. " Hallo! " we called. " Hallo! Where are you going? " came the answer. White folks thus, and not Indians who would plague the life out of us with their begging. We rowed inshore and discovered a solitary trapper and his dogs; down by the water's edge lay his canoe loaded to capacity. The stranger was headed across the lake for the mouth of the Yellow-knife River, he said. Aside from this remark, he was taciturn, and sat most of the time staring into the fire, his curved pipe hanging down over his beard. He was a " lone hand " in the wilderness, and such folks are not inclined to talk about themselves.

We continued eastward, first to Stony Island, the traditional camping-place for everyone traveling these parts, and from there across a stretch of open water to the Taltson River. On an island outside the mouth of the river we pitched camp. Here it was that my black Indian cur twisted his head out of the chain, swam three quarters of a mile to the mainland, and disappeared. He had scented the Indian camp inshore.

The Indians at the mouth of the Taltson River would be well off indeed, were it not for tuberculosis, which plays havoc with them. Their hunting-grounds extend to the east — a wild and heavily wooded stretch of country, well supplied with beaver, muskrat, mink, lynx, fox, and many other varieties of animals. Every few years, too, the caribou migrate south as far as this point, though less frequently now that forest fires have laid waste enormous stretches to the northeast.

The Taltson River is one of the best fish-streams that

[34]

flow into Great Slave Lake. At certain times of the year whitefish, conies, and suckers are on their way upstream, and there is almost no limit to the numbers a person can catch. The waters are so teeming with fish during these periods that, by simply rowing back and forth along the net, one may haul in as many as physical strength will permit. In certain smaller streams one can scoop them up with a dip-net, a performance not at all uncommon in these parts. Huge numbers of fish occur throughout the North, in lakes located in the very heart of the Barren Lands, even where glacial gravel prevails and plant life is scarce. They are used to feed man and dog alike, and the importance of this can hardly be underestimated when one considers that here the inhabitants must, for the most part, live on what wild nature yields.

The most important of the different varieties of fish is the whitefish, whose rich firm flesh makes delicious eating. Presumably there are two distinct variations of the species, each prevailing in a separate region: the smaller and more common variety, which weighs about two pounds, and the larger, whose weight sometimes runs as high as ten pounds. In certain waters it becomes exceedingly fat — " just like meat," as the Indians say. The deeper streams with stony bottoms are rich in trout. Fish of this species weighing as much as fifty pounds have been caught, and a ten- to twenty-pound trout is not at all uncommon. As a rule, they are tender and oozing with fat; their flesh varies in color from white to deep red. Next there is the cony, a kind of salmon, which, strictly speaking, is called *inconnu,* since at first no one was able to classify it. From a scientific standpoint it is of especial interest, as it is found nowhere save in the streams of the Mackenzie watershed. It resembles in many ways the whitefish, save that it is considerably larger and that it sometimes attains a weight of over thirty pounds. Its meat is not tasty and is used principally as provender for the dogs.

There are other species of fish as well. The spiked sucker, — which is a close relative of the whitefish — the bluefish, the slimy loach, whose liver alone is edible, and the pike, which spends most of its time preying on smaller fish and grows so immense that I would never venture to guess its maximum weight. Last of all, I mention a freak herring to be found in Great Bear Lake. . . .

We continued along the mainland, now rowing by night, sleeping by day. The toil of pulling on the oars hour after hour under that scorching sun was taking too much out of us. It seemed almost incredible that this could be a land of snow and ice, experiencing eight months of winter and temperatures as low as 60° below zero.

One morning as we were gliding in between some islands looking for a place to camp, we were greeted by the howls of dogs in agony. These were the animals left behind by the Indians who had been unable to find room for them in their canoes on their journey to Fort Resolution. On their return several weeks later, the owners would stop to pick up as many of their animals as were left alive. And there surely would not be many! Such is the life of an Indian dog: starved and thrashed in the harness during the winter, only to be cast aside, abandoned to a harsher fate, when summer renders him useless.

We encountered one of these poor devils. His back stood up in a hump, so emaciated had he become, and his legs caved in under him every time he tried to walk. Step by step he managed to crawl up to where we were camped, toppled over, and lay there looking at us with large plead-

ing eyes, begging as sweetly as he knew how to be taken
along with us. From the other islands round about came
the hysterical cries of dogs suffering a similar fate.

From the mouth of the Wolf River we cut in through the
islands which lie in a long chain to the northeast. What a
delightful fairyland! We creep through narrow sounds
which appear to have no exit, apparently surrounded on all
sides as they are by woods and grassy ridges. Here and
there cosy little coves, edged with chalky white sand, indent
the island's contour. The water is transparently clear and
has a peculiar greenish cast. So deep down it hardly seems
possible, we see the bottom, and occasionally a lake trout,
hovering above the stones. Suddenly we see a narrow opening ahead of us, and beyond it against the horizon a bluish
streak that seems to come from nowhere.

A forest fire is raging somewhere to the northeast. The
wind shifts and the billows of smoke blow straight in our
direction. It lies like a canopy over the water as far as the
eye can reach. All things seem to lose their reality. A long
row of low islands at once becomes a fleet of ships sailing
a foggy sea. Hot puffs of wind blow in our faces, and show-
ers of sparks fly high over our canoes. They start new fires
on shore. From woodland to woodland the flames eat their
way, hot on the trail of the sun-parched undergrowth and
crackling up through the tops of tall trees. High over the
islands plays a sea of bright flame. . . . But in the wake
of the conflagration all is a blackened ashy ruin, broken
tree-trunks glowing like fiery serpents in a flickering half-
light. . . .

Enormous stretches of forest lands in northern Canada
are laid waste by fire every year. And for a long time this
burnt-over land remains dead. It takes years before vegetation will again take root in the scorched soil, and animal

life always shuns these regions where all is black and
where upturned trees lie in a tangle to block the trails. The
Indians are usually to blame for the damage. Irresponsi-
bility dwells in their blood. They never stop to realize that
with the destruction of the forest comes the destruction of
their hunting-grounds. From the burnt-over land the young
aspen will shoot up in time, and with it will come the
moose, and meat is all that counts, they figure.

Our dogs were none too well pleased with their maritime
existence. They lay there cramped and sullen, deprived of
their simplest pleasures. They were forbidden to rise up
and sniff the air, growl, quarrel, or even shift their posi-
tions, though Lion, for example, found himself with his
head resting on the back of Trofast, his arch-enemy! Iron
discipline was necessary, for the weight of the dogs was so
disposed as to counterbalance the weight of the rest of the
cargo, and it would take very little moving about on their
part to ship water into the canoe.

The eternal problem of the trapper is to obtain feed for
his dogs, but we experienced few worries on this score during our voyage down Great Slave Lake. We kept trolling-
lines out most of the time and, as a rule, had a splendid
catch of trout every morning when we stepped ashore. But
it was not until after we had left the islands behind that
the trout began to bite in earnest. Then there was really
something doing! Great big fellows, weighing from fifteen
to twenty pounds, were on the line in a flash. Ingenuous
creatures were these, too, lacking utterly the *kultur* which
distinguishes our trout back home in Norway. The finer
points of discrimination between the divers types of flies
were utterly unknown to them. Nor did they insist upon
gut leaders and such; they would snap at a tinfish fastened
directly to a thick line, and if they failed to hook them-

selves the first time, they would try it again just as eagerly as before.

The weeks passed and our hands grew callous with rowing; we kept up a steady pace along the mainland, threaded our way through islands, and spurted for dear life across stretches of open water. Some nights we covered from twelve to fourteen miles, some nights we made no progress whatever. But we rejoiced to the depths of our souls each morning we safely landed our equipment in a haven closer to our destination. Whilst planning our expedition, we had permitted ourselves to dream innocently of hoisting a sail and sitting back to loaf, with foam seething in our wake. What a sorry dream that had been! One day only did we have the wind behind us, and on that occasion there was so much of it that we had had enough of sailing after the first couple of hours. Otherwise, we had no reason to complain of our luck. Several times we were within a hair's breadth of having it forsake us, and thanked our stars when matters turned out as they did.

One night, when we were far out in open water, a storm broke over us. We pulled for the shore with waves splashing over our gunwales only to find sheer cliffs rising ahead of us — a steep unbroken wall extending in either direction as far as we could see. But, just when things seemed blackest for us, we stumbled across a narrow inlet and lost no time availing ourselves of this refuge. To put it mildly, however, it turned out to be a perfectly wretched shelter, as the storm still came beating in upon us. Nevertheless, after felling a number of tall spruces across the mouth of the cove, we were able to break the force of the waves. We were obliged to haul our canoes ashore, patch them, and calk the seams. A part of our cargo needed drying, besides, but other than this we suffered no damage.

[39]

And there was plenty to outweigh the toil and trouble we endured — peaceful hours on a beach, our camp-fire flaming out over the water, our dogs about us, a last slow pipe as the embers of the fire burn low. And then, dead tired, to creep in under the mosquito-netting and simply fall asleep, entirely unconscious now of three canoes which still have such a long, long way to go. . . .

Gradually the character of the landscape began to change; it became more rugged. To the east sheer granite cliffs rose from the lake to a distance of a hundred feet or so. Many an eagle had its nest up there, and now and then one would come soaring over our heads. They were black, with snow-white crowns. It was here, too, that we first encountered black flies. Each time we rowed out from land, they would follow us in swarms. It was always a race when we broke our backs to pull away from them.

There was not much to indicate that human beings ever passed this way. At one spot a few tent-poles down by the beach, at another a lobstick presiding over the landscape. The latter is a tall spruce stripped of all its lower limbs by the Indians. Such markers are rather common in this part of the country and often stand as monuments to certain individuals, whose symbols are cut into the bark.

We passed through Taltheilei, the narrow sound which leads into the large east arm of McLeod Bay. The current was swift here, but not swift enough to prevent us from pressing on.

One dark morning we paddled inshore in search of a camp-site near a river mouth where, without too much trouble, we could land a few fish. Tired and hungry after many hours of rowing against head winds, we glided in with our minds set upon a hearty meal and a sound sleep. On a point of land we let out the dogs, ourselves continuing

on into the cove. Suddenly we heard Trofast barking off
in the woods. He seemed to be greatly aroused and in a
moment or two the voices of the other dogs joined in. It
must be a bear, we thought. We turned sharply, ran our
canoes up on a sandy beach, grabbed our guns, and hastened into the woods. The yelping of the dogs ceased
abruptly. We crept stealthily forward, our guns held ready,
but there lay the forest dark and still, no living thing in
sight. Never a bear in these parts, we thought.

Then two of the dogs turned up — Nigger and Trofast.
But what under Heaven ailed them? Nigger danced round
and round, rolled head over heels on the ground, meanwhile whining piteously. Trofast took a few steps, sat down
on his rump and angrily stroked his snout with his fore-
paws, then suddenly gave a powerful shake of his head —
They had been out trying a fall with a hedgehog! All over
their muzzles, inside on the roofs of their mouths, on their
tongues, and far back in their throats were masses of porcupine quills. Nigger and Trofast had surely fought an
unequal combat this time!

There went our dinner and our hard-earned night's
rest! Those quills must come out. The danger lies in the
fact that they work their way through the body tissues to
the animal's vital organs. Many a good dog is thus ruined
there in the North.

We swore at each of the dogs in turn and propped open
their mouths, with sticks thrust in between their jaws. As
I kept the patient pinned against the earth, Dale proceeded
with the operation by the light of our camp-fire. His instrument was a pair of pliers. How those dogs howled, how
they screamed, how they struggled! I had never believed
a dog could become so angry or that it could be so strong.
In spite of the fact that I lay with my full weight upon

[41]

Trofast's body and held on to him for all I was worth, he was able to throw me off time after time. It was hours before we could tire him out sufficiently to finish the operation, but at the end of that time there wasn't much left of us either!

Most dogs steer clear of porcupines after the first encounter. But not all. Take old Nigger, for example. He will go after a hedgehog anytime, any place. It is not that Nigger is stupid; on the contrary, he has more inside his skull than most dogs, but he probably imagines that if he simply keeps at it long enough, some time he'll be able to score one on that devil's own critter, whose flesh has such an appetizing smell, but which has such a sharp unlovely taste.

At length we caught a glimpse of a purplish shore off to the northeast. It was Fond du Lac, the eastern extremity of the lake. With that we pulled on the oars with added vigor. And then one evening we came gliding into a snug little cove in the shadow of spruce-clad mountain slopes, and with that it was over: after a month of rowing we had left Slave Lake behind us.

. .

We had pitched our tent down by the beach and were enjoying life in front of our fire, when one canoe after another appeared through the darkness, a short distance away from us. Before these reached the shore, the dogs were splashing in the water. When the first canoe grated against the bottom, a man sprang out, and in a moment or two a fire was blazing in among the spruces. Men, women, and children poured out of the canoes and, as if by magic, a whole village of tepees had suddenly sprung up. These were the Indians which inhabited this district — all together about a hundred of them. They had spent the entire summer on the shores of Great Slave Lake and had subsisted entirely on fish. They were now on their way up into the Barrens to meet the caribou herds migrating south from the Arctic into wooded country — for the rest of the winter they would lead a nomad existence on the trail of the herd. Their days of meat-eating were almost at hand.

During the evening a party of hunters came over to us, a troop of emaciated dogs at their heels.

" *Si tzel-twi* (Me tobacco)," was their opening remark, as one of the Indians pointed to our tobacco pouches. We permitted them to fill their pipes, which they first dug out carefully with their knives. We were easy-marks, they certainly must have thought, for one of them immediately stepped forward and asked for a sled. Another pointed to Trofast and demanded him. A third gave the distinct impression that nothing less than our entire outfit would satisfy him, and was highly incensed over the fact that we denied him such a reasonable desire. Later, when they had finished with their begging, we offered them something to eat, and with that they forgave us. A lively conversation ensued: the Indians rattled on in their language, to which we made answer in English. They on their side and we on ours illustrated the meaning of each word with an ingenious gesture, nodded eagerly, smiled understandingly at each other, comprehended not a thing.

But when the word " *e-then* " began to occur in the conversation of the Indians, we became immediately aware of what they were talking about. " *E-then,*" we knew, was their word for caribou, the all-important topic of conversation in this part of the world. The fact which interested us most we were soon able to untangle. One of the Indians put his cheek against his hand as though he were asleep, raised four fingers in the air, pointed toward the east, meanwhile repeating over and over: " *E-then thlé, e-then thlé* (Many caribou, many caribou)." No one could misunderstand this. The caribou were back on the treeless plains, four days' journey away.

We were now faced with a decision to make. We must select the route we would take into the interior. We would have to find a chain of connecting lakes and rivers in order to avoid as much as possible carrying our equipment overland. To the east lay a range of steep hills which rose from the plateau in a north-and-south direction as far as the eye could reach. We must either climb over them or find a way through them in order to reach the naked expanse of the highland. The gate to the Barren Lands is Pike's Portage, a steep and rugged pass which winds up through the wall of hills to a chain of waterways. This is the route the Indians take every summer and, as a matter of fact, is the only known canoe trail east. We should, at least, be on the safe side, were we to follow it.

But even so — had not Black Basil spoken of an " old canoe route " farther to the south, a route the Indians had used in bygone days? Perhaps this was merely an invention of his and one day we should find ourselves helplessly stuck. Or perhaps, in spite of everything, there was some truth in what he had told us. This remained to be seen. The " old canoe route," which no one ever used any longer, beckoned invitingly to us.

Portage

WE FOLLOWED THE RIDGE SOUTH AS FAR AS WE COULD, at length discovering a small river and a pile of rotting tepee-poles down by the beach. After scouting around, we spied an opening into the woods and signs of a trail leading up the slope. It was overgrown with moss, and the blazes on the trees were dark and all too few, but, judging from the width of the path, there could be no doubt about the fact that it had been laid out as a canoe portage.

We unloaded our goods and prepared ourselves for our journey inland. The first waterway lay about two and a half miles ahead, at the end of a steep climb over rough country. The pile of dunnage we should have to carry was a problem in itself, and it was immediately clear to us that we should be obliged to abandon one of our canoes. Henceforth the dogs would have to run along the shore, as we paddled our remaining canoes.

Packing involves a technique all its own there in the north. The load is piled up as high as possible on a packing-board, which is carried on the back in such a way that its weight rests upon the body's center of gravity. A broad strap attached to the board is fastened about the head. Thus the pack is forced forward whilst being supported. This produces a strain on the neck muscles, which are strongly developed in those who are obliged frequently to go in for this form of transport. Everything depends upon a certain trick. A slender Indian, with ease and comfort, day in and day out, can carry a burden which would utterly wear out a far stronger but less experienced man.

Had it not been for the dogs, it would have been hopeless to get anywhere in a reasonable length of time. Each had his own pack, weighing about thirty-five pounds, to carry. In this manner we were able to move two hundred and fifty pounds of freight each trip over the portage, entirely apart from the stuff we carried ourselves.

The dog-pack is a fairly simple affair — a broad strip of canvas made into two panniers, which are filled and then slung over the dog's back. There is a breast strap to prevent its coming off; also under the belly it is tied with a piece of string. This saddling on of the pack is of the utmost importance. It must be so accomplished as to throw the main weight forward on the dog. Ordinarily it is a far simpler matter to train a dog to carry a pack than to teach him to draw a sled. But a first-class packer is as rare and as treasured an animal as a good sled-dog.

A number of our dogs were packing for the first time and required some schooling. My dog Fox, for example, began by sitting flat down and looking first at his pack and then at me, as much as to say that this was a fine thing to expect a dignified sled-dog to do! Sport, on the other hand, did not object to carrying a pack, but he preferred to choose his own route through the forest. He decided to follow the very first moose trail we happened to cross. Lost in rapture, he rushed here and there in the woods, his pack dashing perilously against tree and sapling. Spike was an experienced packer, but he, too, had a weakness. Into the meanest brook or water puddle we might pass, Spike would plunge with enthusiasm, and if we didn't keep close watch of him, he would unscrupulously lie down on his belly in the water. It was easily understandable that an ice-cold bath was refreshing when the sun beat down on the dog's furry back, but we had the pack to consider first. In it were sugar, boxes of matches, ammunition, and many other things it was necessary to maintain in a dry condition.

After a while we succeeded in making the animals behave, and then we were able to proceed at a steady pace. Although we had to keep an eye on the dogs continually and to be prepared to deal with their slightest whim, this annoyance was nothing compared with the service they were rendering us. It was fascinating to observe with what a sure instinct they maneuvered their way through a tangle of underbrush, over soggy land, and up the steepest slopes. We would merely have to straighten up under the loads on our backs and call: " Come on! " and every dog would be at our heels in a long line of wagging tails. Trofast was at the head of the procession which followed us, his head erect, his tail waving like a plume. At the end of the line slunk Fox, forever sullen and sulky, apparently never able to get away from the notion that *he* ought to have been spared a pack!

To put one's back into it and plug along with the sweat streaming out of one's pores is nothing more than hard work. Real trouble begins when the air is swarming with mosquitoes and black flies. On our voyage up Great Slave Lake we had experienced, for the most part, a cooling breeze about us and thus, in the last analysis, had had little reason to complain. But here in the woods where the air hung hot and lifeless over swamp and glassy tarn, the insects constituted so devastating a curse that one cannot possibly conceive of it without having been there in person.

Even the Indians are not unmindful of the mosquitoes

and black flies, though they endure them with far more patience than do white men. There are times when the hunters remain in their tepees and refrain from the hunt, even though game be close at hand. And when the swarms are thickest, not even moose will roam through the woods. They remain all day long in the lakes, submerged to their necks in the water. Once, up on the Barrens I saw a buck caribou attacked by black flies. It ran in circles like a mad thing, rolled head over heels on the ground, finally toppling over a precipice into a lake. . . . After a white man has been bitten in a sufficient number of places, his flesh ceases to swell after each sting, though he by no means becomes immune from further attack. I have encountered old-timers who had been bitten by mosquitoes and black flies during at least thirty years of their lives, but whose hatred of the mosquito swarms was as spontaneous as ever.

"Well, they certainly can't get any thicker than this," we kept telling each other all day long. Oh, couldn't they, though! Fresh armies rushed in from lake and marsh, with the result that a feast of blood was held such as the mosquitoes and black flies of "the old canoe route" will long remember. If we held up one hand for ten seconds, it was black. When we tried to eat, even though we sat so close to the fire that the smoke made tears trickle down our cheeks, we noticed but very little difference. The mosquitoes continued to bite, as other hosts of them tumbled headlong into the soup-kettle. A whole layer of them floated about on the surface of the soup we were making.

The black flies were even worse. Not once did we have the satisfaction of striking an effective blow at them. Like an intangible shroud, they hemmed us in. They flew into our mouths and up our nostrils, they crawled up our sleeves and down our necks, they found their way through

[48]

the tiniest rift in our clothing. But their favorite place, where they best liked to tumble and spin, was in our ears deep down against the ear-drums. We tried smearing ourselves with oil of citron, but our sweat soon washed this away. Then we experimented with a mosquito-net over our heads, but we could not endure the heat. At last we simply tied handkerchiefs about our necks, and, arming ourselves for the most part with sheer resignation, that most important of all weapons for those who seek to penetrate the wilderness east of Great Slave Lake, we let the black flies bite.

Our first portage consumed one full week. We then paddled over a small lake and threw ourselves into the next portage. Thus we proceeded, sometimes by lake and river, sometimes by land. At every stop, one of us would go ahead on a scouting expedition, and we were forever tense with worry, never knowing whether our waterway would hold, or peter out, leaving us stranded where we were. The Indian trail continued along in the lee of that range of hills to the east, which all the while seemed to become more and more impassable. It followed a more southerly course than we had expected, but, after all, what difference did it make where we finally landed, so long as an endless wilderness lay at our command?

Busy days were these, presenting us with a variety of duties to perform, each requiring a special kind of skill. There are things which one must sense intuitively. One must, for example, " read the country," determining the most favorable route by such telltale phenomena as the formation of the mountains, the nature of the streams, the growth of the forest, et cetera; one must know how a canoe should be loaded and maneuvered in order to keep it afloat in bad weather on the lakes or down the rapids of a river; one must be handy and quick with the ax, must know how to handle the dogs, how to hunt and fish, how to prepare food, how to sew, and still have time left over. But most particularly one must be prepared to deal with every emergency. . . . After a time all this becomes second nature to one, but not until after one has had many bitter experiences.

Slowly but surely we were penetrating deeper and deeper into the unknown, and the knowledge of this fact caused us to accept each hardship good-naturedly. Soon we were gliding out of a river into a new lake which lay before us strewn with many islands and surrounded by dense forests. Onward we threaded our course, always wondering what we should find behind the next point of land. At length from an elevation we spied way off in the distance a purplish band of plain, and this egged us on.

Before the dogs had mastered the art of running along the shore and keeping pace with our canoes as we paddled them over rivers and lakes, our way was hard indeed. At first, in order to get them to follow us, we were obliged to enter each cove and inlet. But it was not long before they had gained the necessary experience. They would then gallop along the shore, eager to keep abreast of us, and would use their common sense whenever they came to a possible short cut or when they found it difficult going. They held on by the skin of their teeth ascending steep inclines and maintained a delicate balance passing through ravines where a narrow ledge was all the foothold they could find. Seeing us start out across the mouth of a swift river or a bay half a mile wide, they would not hesitate to plunge into the ice-cold water and swim along behind us.

But, even so, there were several dark evenings when, just as we were about to pitch camp for the night, we discovered that our dogs had lost us. Then, instead of sleeping, we would have to paddle back in search of them. Sometimes, too, one of the pack might have become hopelessly entangled in rocks along some steep precipice and would remain there, howling for help. On many occasions old Lion had got himself into hot water thus, but for this he had only his own stubborn disposition to thank. Always, though his life might hang in the balance, he would insist on picking his own way, independent of the pack. Death alone finally cured him of this habit. The following year I sold him to an Indian named La Loche, who later told me of the tragedy. " Steep mountain, Lion alone go, tumble down, roll, all a time roll," he said, laughing and enjoying himself hugely over his memory of Lion rolling. . . .

It was evident that it was a long time ago that the Indians had last trekked through this part of the country. Here and there we came across age-darkened tepee-poles, usually in narrow passes where the caribou had cut deep trails. In one place we found a rotten birch-bark canoe, in another the remains of some crude animal traps — heavy timbers with stones resting on top of them, contrived to fall down and crush their quarry. Occasionally we saw an Indian grave — a number of tall pointed poles, driven into the earth in the form of a circle. Here and there in the wilderness one comes across such lonely graves, sometimes several together. They always lie in locations of great natural beauty, usually on a hilltop overlooking a lake. On the very site the hunter himself might have chosen to erect his tepee on the trail of the caribou, he finds his final camping-ground whilst his soul pursues the last great trail of all. . . .

If signs of human life were few, the signs of a rich animal life were many. Here was a world belonging solely to them — muskrat, beaver, lynx, fox, moose, mink, and all

the many others. Here they pursued their silent struggle
for existence, preying and preyed upon, reproducing their
kind and dying off, entirely according to the simple laws
which prevail in the forest before man interferes.

In lake and river the muskrat was eternally going somewhere. Bits of gnawed grass lay floating on the surface of
the water, and when twilight came, dark heads began to
glide noiselessly about near shore. On the slopes the moose
cut his curious grooves where he munched at the drooping
tops of young aspens. At the edge of small pools in the river
the beaver had erected his lodge — a mound of earth covered with branches of the white birch, its image reflected
in the still water.

But, above all, here was the bear's true paradise. We
found telltale signs of him everywhere — upturned roots,
claw marks in the bark of the spruce, fresh tracks up and
down the beach. There are two kinds of bear inhabiting
the woodlands east of Great Slave Lake — the black and
the brown.[1] Both resemble fairly closely in size the bears
of Norway. The Indians shoot them only in an emergency,
because of an ancient superstition which associates the bear
with the supernatural. The whites leave the bear in peace,
save when they are short of meat and stumble fairly onto
one of these creatures. The only reason for such abstinence
is that the price a bearskin will bring is not sufficient to
warrant lugging it all the way in to the post.

Thus Bruin is free to lumber about in the forest, disport-
ing himself and doing exactly as he pleases, gorging himself on cranberries, capturing an occasional field-mouse,
strolling over to the beaver-lodge and sniffing of the fra-
grance it exudes, digging up enormous roots and licking up

[1] East of the Barrens there also occurs a species of grizzly bear (the
Barren Land grizzly), which is somewhat smaller than the species inhabiting
the Rocky Mountains.

the larvæ he discovers, at length trudging down to his customary fishing-place by the bend in the river where the
water is teeming with whitefish. With blinking eyes and outstretched paw he awaits his chance; then one wriggling fish
after another goes flying through the air in an arc of glittering silver and lands far back on the shore.

The bear is the most delightful of all the forest creatures
and I should have no ill word to speak of him were it not
for his thieving proclivities. Nothing is safe where there are
bears. They began to display a lively interest in those portions of our equipment carried on ahead and left unguarded
overnight. Therefore we soon found it necessary to sleep
apart, one at either end of the portage, our rifles within
reach.

We had been at it for three full weeks and had encountered nothing save small lakes, short rivers, and long portages. No sign of a comfortable, continuous waterway. Then
we suddenly arrived at a river which appeared to be promising indeed. Deep and smooth as glass, it wound its way
through marshy land. From now on we could simply sit in
our canoes and drift quietly on our way. Better days were
at hand, there could be no doubt of that.

At first everything went splendidly. We could boast of
no remarkable progress, of course, for the river was continually doubling back on itself. But we could at least lean
back in our canoes and paddle, and that was a triumph in
itself. . . . After we had been enjoying this luxury for a
half-hour or so, the current began to race. So we both got
out our poles and began guiding ourselves along with
these. But even this form of entertainment was shortlived
— we were soon pitched overboard and there, with ice-cold
water swirling about our waists, we tramped along, stride
by stride, as we tracked our canoes along by their painters.

THE LAND OF FEAST AND FAMINE

Thus began our "march" down the Muskrat River. It lasted five days in all. From early morning to late evening we did not leave the water, save where the rapids were too swift for us and we had to portage our outfit. In many places the river was blocked with stumps of trees and drift-wood piled together. Here we would have to hew our way through with our axes. At other places large bowlders impeded our progress, and there we would stop and clear them away.

All this time the black flies had their devil's own way with us. When a man is gripping with both hands the painter of a loaded canoe and is leaning backward as far as he can to resist the current, meanwhile giving his entire attention to the question of finding a foothold in order to prevent himself from stumbling off a ledge into deeper water, he is, roughly speaking, defenseless. . . . When, at length, we said farewell to that " promising " river, we sat down to mend our shoes. There was very little left of them.

We had come to a definite divide. Some valleys sloped north, others south. Toward the east we were hemmed in by our bugbear, that insurmountable range of hills. In spite of the fact that our way could not possibly lie beyond those summits as we had reckoned at first, we still continued vaguely to hope. Thoughts of the Snowdrift River haunted our minds. The details of the country round about had never been charted, but we had heard such positive mention of this river from the Indians, we knew it could not lie so very far ahead. And once we could locate it, we might be able to make one last swift advance into the Barrens off to the east. We strained our eyes and expected each day to spy its shining blue expanse in the distance.

Our chief diet in the past had been fish. We cast out our lines each day, and, as a rule, we were able to catch enough for both ourselves and the dogs. But with boiled fish for breakfast, fried fish for lunch, and boiled fish again for dinner, in the long run meal-time began to lose something of its glamour for us. We never used salt; potatoes belonged to a bygone day. In short, we experienced no pleasure, sitting down to that sooty kettle of ours. It was meat we were longing for. Of course, we could hunt, but that required leisure. So we got along with simply dreaming about meat.

Then one day our dream became reality. We were paddling along a narrow stream which joined two lakes together. Wild ducks were splashing about in the water, and as I came paddling along behind Dale, I took a pot-shot at them. I brought down two, but to find them was not an easy task, for the reeds were so thick that the canoe could hardly move. I was pawing around in search of my game and had just found one mangled duck, when two shots echoed across the water. The only thing which occurred to me was that Dale, impatient over the delay, had fired his gun as a signal for me to hurry along. So I picked up my paddle and moved on.

Reaching the lake, I caught sight of his canoe way off under the opposite bank. What under Heaven was he doing way over there? As I approached, my astonishment increased to see him splashing about in water up to his knees. Peevish because Dale's uncalled-for behavior had obliged me to abandon that other duck of mine, I halted some distance away and asked disagreeably just what he had meant by it. " Come on and help me skin this moose! " cried Dale. — It lay where he had shot it, in three feet of water.

We began by devouring the heart. To be on the safe side, we took care of the tongue and kidneys in the same manner. After this we quartered the moose and loaded the meat

[55]

into our already overladen canoe. In the bow we found a
place for the head, with its mighty crown of antlers. The
effect was decorative indeed. Then we paddled on till we
found an attractive camp-site at the edge of a small river,
and, with a sense of inner well-being, we spent the remainder of the evening puffing on our pipes and discussing
the unbelievable good fortune which had suddenly come
our way. But we didn't see Lion, Nigger, and Spike again
until the following morning. At the place where the moose
had been slain, they had stuffed themselves so full of meat
that they had been unable to budge from the spot.

It was not difficult for us to wait with patience the three
days necessary to make dried meat of the carcass. Since
leaving Slave Lake we had scarcely paused for breath, and
all our clothes were badly in need of repairing before it
would be too late. We cut the meat into large slices and
hung it from a tripod, under which we kept a low smoky
fire burning constantly. On striking camp we were able to
crowd most of the smoked meat into four dog-packs, so
greatly had it shrunk during the drying process.

. .
.

The autumn storms set in with heavy rains. We might
awaken during the night with water splashing about our
sleeping-bags, sometimes with our tent collapsing over our
heads. The nights grew colder, ice formed in our water-
buckets, and the black flies did not drop in for breakfast
before eight o'clock in the morning.

Tucked away between wooded slopes lay a cosy little
lake. We found it as we came paddling down a river. We
were gliding along under a birch-clad bank when the dogs,
trotting along the beach, suddenly disappeared. A short

time later we heard a sharp bark from the woods and noticed several birch-trees bending and swaying. I had just time enough to send an unaimed shot after a large moose as it broke from the thicket and hurled itself with a splash into the water, where it began to swim, with the entire pack of dogs after it. Thus the chase began. We paddled and the dogs swam. Gradually we closed in on the moose from two sides, ready to give it a finishing shot the very instant it took the shore. At length Dale was up on him. " Take a snapshot! " he suddenly shouted, at the same time brandishing his paddle and uttering a series of wild shrieks in order to scare the moose in my direction. I leaned over backward and pawed around until I found the camera, and made two beautiful shots, without pausing to turn the film — one right over the other! This maneuver on my part gave the moose an opportunity to turn his back on the shore and make for the middle of the lake. The dogs were pretty well exhausted after floundering about in that ice-cold water for half an hour or more. We could not take a chance of their continuing on after the moose, so we shot it without further efforts to drive it ashore, tied a rope around it, and hauled it in to the beach.

We had now been on the go a month since leaving Great Slave Lake. It was September, and cold days were at hand. In just what part of the wilderness we were we hadn't the slightest notion. Far off in the distance we spied a strip of blue water which we firmly believed to be the Snowdrift River. The lake in which we had shot our last moose, however, was as far as a canoe could proceed. We were locked in tight. Toward the east rose the steep hills, toward the south flowed the river over a rocky bed in a series of rapids.

Thus we were unable to reach the Barren Lands to begin with. We took our failure calmly. The " old canoe route " had brought us into a country of untold beauty where the wilderness was ours alone. When the snows arrived, the way to the barren plains would lie open before us, and, with a train of willing dogs harnessed to our sled, we should be free to roam wherever our fancy led us. . . .

But now we should have to see about putting a roof over our heads.

THE STEAMER *NORTHLAND ECHO*

FORT RESOLUTION

"WHEN THE SUN ROSE OVER SLAVE LAKE, WE PULLED IN
OUR OARS."

A NARROW CHANNEL ON OUR WAY INLAND

OUR CACHE ON MOOSE LAKE

THE CABIN ON MOOSE LAKE

MY TEAM WITH A SLAIN CARIBOU

THE LONE WOLF

INDIAN VISITORS IN FRONT OF A WHITE TRAPPER'S CABIN

WE REJOICE IN THE SUMMER AFTER A LONG, TOUGH WINTER

TRAPPERS WITH THEIR HARVEST OF WOLF PELTS

TRAPPER JOE NELSON
WITH A WHITE FOX

TAKING A REST IN FRONT OF A LARGE BEAVER LODGE

POLAR WOLVES

INDIAN CAMP AT GREAT SLAVE LAKE
IT WAS HERE THAT THE INDIANS BECAME SICK AND SOME DIED

SKØIĘREN (FUNMAKER), THE AUTHOR'S FAVOURITE DOG,
A GIFT FROM AN INDIAN WOMAN

Log Cabin

WE NAMED OUR LAKE MOOSE LAKE AFTER THE GAME WE
had shot in its waters. It was not large — was almost lost
in the general landscape, tucked away as it was, between
summits wooded with spruce and white birch. The valley
opened up to the south, and there the river flowed, glassy
and still at first, between the reeds and rat-grass which
edged both banks, then more swiftly as it followed an
endlessly winding course through a tunnel of willows and
alders, as though it were trying to disappear forever.
Numberless small lakes and ponds were strewn throughout this luxuriant valley, each one so motionless that, from
hilltops far away, one could see the fan of ripples stirred
into being by the beaver as he swam. And up where the
woods thinned out, a carpet of reindeer moss glowed with
a bluish sheen. Yes, here was the place for us to stay.

The spruce were, for the most part, stunted in growth,
and it was a problem to find a spot where good building
logs grew conveniently at hand. But at length, close under a
precipice, we spied a clump of fine tall trees which would
supply us with all the logs we might need. At a spot close
beside the lake, we paced off twenty-five feet in one direction, and twenty feet at right angles, and drove four stakes
into the ground. Our axes sang through the forest from
morning until night. Trees crashed to earth, where we

stripped them of their limbs and carried them off on our shoulders. We gathered huge piles of haircap to stuff in the cracks between the logs, as we laid one on top of another. We chopped planks for the floor, cut turf to go on the roof, knocked a door together, and prepared a place for a window. Day by day our cabin began to take form.

Sometimes we would sit astride one of the walls and swing our axes so hard that huge flocks of wild geese far up in the blue sky would be frightened away by the flying chips. Then we would drop our axes and stare off after them. There they were, plowing their way south toward sunny lands, whilst we remained behind, fortifying ourselves against the cold dark days which were coming. We were saddened and at the same time thrilled by the thought. Winter was approaching and we should have to stick it out.

Then came the proud day when we moved into our new home. We were highly pleased with our handiwork. Perhaps it was lacking in the refinements of execution, for two axes and a handful of spikes were all we had to work with; still, the cabin was solid and snug, and these are the conditions which count most heavily on a cold winter's day. Indoors it was both roomy and livable. We had built our bunks close in against one of the walls on the long side. In front of the window, which looked out over the lake, stood a table and two stumps for chairs. Against the opposite wall stood Dale's masterpiece, a round stove hammered together out of stove-pipes. Nothing could equal it for ardor when it began to glow red-hot.

There was good fishing right outside our door, but we needed a cache, or scaffold, from which we could hang what we caught so that it would be safe from thieving animals. Bears, wolves, wolverines, minks, and martens were constantly prowling about and they would make short work of any food left within reach of their claws.

We selected four trees and cut them off about ten feet from the ground. On top of these stumps we placed a framework of heavy timbers, across which, in turn, we put down a platform of logs with room enough between each to hang our fish in strings of ten. In one corner of the cache we built a little gabled storehouse covered with the canvas which we had ripped from one of the canoes. In it, as a measure of precaution, lest an accident should happen and our cabin burn down, we stored a part of our provisions. In it, too, we would store our supply of meat later on with the arrival of the caribou. The stumps which supported our cache were stripped of bark and carefully covered with tin. Now let the bear try his claws on that!

This done, we set to work fishing in earnest. Now was the proper time for it, these last few weeks before the waters should freeze. When fish are hung up to dry without first being cleaned, they have a pretty strong taste, but these do well enough for the dogs, who even seem to prefer their fish when they are slightly odoriferous. We needed several thousand fish, for we had eight dogs to keep over the winter, and it was uncertain when the caribou would come. Each dog was to be rationed two whitefish a day.

It was astonishing that in the course of a good day's fishing, even in such a shallow little pond as Moose Lake, our ten small nets would yield us as many as two hundred fish. Most of these were whitefish of maximum size, but occasionally there was a giant pike among them. It required time to fish, and the work was not always pleasant, especially when, on cold raw days, snowflakes floated in the air, and, out on the lake, we had to sit hauling in our catch with bare hands. But gradually our cache began to fill up with fish, and, with that, a sense of security began to take root in our minds. Before we were finished, we would have upwards of fifteen hundred fish, to say nothing of the several hundred we had cleaned and smoked for ourselves, so that we would have enough to keep the wolf from the door up until Christmas, at least, even were all else to fail.

Directly across the lake from our cabin was " Cranberry Hill." There berries grew in red profusion, simply begging to be plucked. I lost no time in paddling across to gather a bucketful so that we might have a bit of jam to eat during the winter. One day I was walking along deep in thought, as I shoveled up handfuls of berries and threw them into the pail. Suddenly I heard a rustle back in the brush and looked up. At the same time another pair of eyes looked up. They belonged to a bear. It stood behind a rise of ground and blinked stupidly at me. It would be difficult to determine which one of us was the more amazed. We glared at each other for several moments, no doubt each thinking much the same thought: " What the devil are you doing here in my berry patch? " At length the bear turned on his heel and slowly shuffled off among the trees. From that day on, I never went berry-picking without my rifle.

Frosty days set in and thin ice formed on lake and tarn. We then threw our guns over our shoulders, and each went his own way into the forest. It was important that we should acquaint ourselves with the lay of the land so that we should have everything clear in our minds when the time should come for us to set out with our dogs upon our winter hunting expeditions. Furthermore, we were in need of meat.

Whilst scouting about to the south, we came across a large colony of beavers. That there were beaver in isolated numbers up here at the very gate to the treeless plains, we already knew, but the fact that in vast numbers they made themselves as much at home along this modest watercourse as they might under more hospitable conditions was something new to us. Down through the valley beside the river and at the edge of small pools we found one earth mound after another and an occasional ancient, moss-grown dam. The beavers, too, were busy with last-minute autumn chores. Their houses had been smeared over with a fresh layer of clay, and under the water in front of each mound of earth lay a mighty tangle of sticks, branches, and roots of aquatic plants — the winter's food-supply.

Beaver pelts are not of prime quality until late spring. Hence we shot only enough of these animals to supply us with an occasional beaver steak. Both the dogs and we knew that this was the right thing to do. At nightfall when I trudged home to the cabin bending forward under the weight of a beaver carcass, Trofast, Nigger, and Spike would come loping up to me, sniffing at the bag I was carrying, jumping all over me and almost pushing me over. And when at length the beaver was on the table, done to a turn and delicious, we didn't have a care in the world.

The greatest delicacy in the way of beaver meat is the flat tail, which is uncommonly rich and tasty; it is covered with a thick skin, which must first be burned off. A couple of the largest tails we stored away to eat on Christmas Eve or to use for swapping in the event we were to encounter Indians. A redskin will bend over backward to get hold of one of his favorite dishes, such as an unborn caribou calf or the horns of deer in velvet, but for a beaver tail he is willing to sell his soul.

Dale's hobby was bear-hunting. During his years along the Mackenzie River he was forever matching wits with

Bruin, and his dogs bore more than one jagged scar inflicted by bears' claws. He had his own hunting technique. Immediately after the first snowfall Dale would begin rubbing his hands together and whetting his appetite for bear meat. He would go off into the woods and refuse to give up until he had tracked his game to its lair. Taking a long, pointed pole, he would poke around inside the cave until the infuriated animal would come storming out. Then Dale would pick up his gun and shoot. It was more exciting that way, he said.

One day Dale went out beaver-hunting, leaving me home to whittle out stretching-boards for lynx- and fox-skins. Some time during the evening I suddenly heard the sound of voices coming from down by the lake. Three men were approaching the cabin — Dale with a redskin on either side of him. The Indians, who were prowling about through the forest on a hunt for moose, had caught sight of the smoke from Dale's fire in the distance. It was thus they had encountered him. Their home was farther north on a lake they called *Nō-ni-e Tué* (Wolf Lake) and they had now been out several weeks. Neither of them presented a particularly trustworthy appearance, ragged and drenched as they were from head to foot. Aside from a rifle, a knife, and a handful of matches they owned nothing in the world. At night they must have flopped down just as they were, and slept in slush and muck. But they took their hardships and their empty bellies with cool indifference. They smiled and apparently were extremely well pleased with their existence.

We set before them a huge kettle of fish, which they devoured before we could catch our breath. We then let them fill their pipes from our tobacco, after which they grunted contentedly and stretched out on our sleeping-bags, mean-

while smearing them up generally with their filthy moccasins. From our conversation with them we gathered that
the caribou were still far in the interior of the Barren Lands
and that we could not expect them in our vicinity until
" small lakes all ice."

The following morning we paddled the Indians across to
the opposite shore of the lake, from whence they immediately resumed their interrupted moose-hunt. We spent the
next few nights tense with anxiety, but it was soon apparent,
thank God, that our guests had taken all their lice along
with them.

It is a tradition in the Far North that one's door must
stand open to all who happen to pass and that food must
be set before all guests. Hospitality is the law of the land,
and the man who breaks this law in the end will suffer
most. Sooner or later each man finds that he himself is in
need of a hand-out, and it has happened on more than one
occasion that the Indians have saved white men from almost certain death. There have been cases of starving and
exhausted trappers becoming lost in the wilds, and other
instances of white hunters, the powerless victims of scurvy,
being discovered indoors in their cabins. In the latter case,
the Indians would cure their patient with fresh caribou's
blood or spruce-needle tea, and they have even been known
to drive a sick man all the way in to the trading post. On the
other hand, the cabin or tent of the white man has turned out
to be the salvation of many a hungry, freezing redskin. . . .

• •
•

It is a glorious sensation to get along without a watch in
the depths of the wilderness. After a time one actually becomes one's own timepiece, and can, with gratifying exac-

[65]

titude, tell the hour any time one wishes. On the other hand, if one stoops to use a clock, one is immediately at the mercy of it.

In all we had three timepieces to consult. Each of them had its own peculiarities.

The first of these was our German alarm-clock. It had had a jaunty, free-and-easy movement, when we had wound it up seven hundred miles farther south. But the farther north we penetrated, the more sleepy it had become. When crossing Great Slave Lake, it had been necessary for us to wake it up several times a day, and later, just as we were setting off across country, it had dropped off into a sustained coma at exactly twelve minutes past eleven. For two months it had stood on the table in the cabin with its cataleptic hands indicating this perpetual hour. At last we grew tired of seeing its inert face and heaved it out through the door. It landed face downward out among the dogs and came to rest in that sad position. Quite casually I later walked past it with an armful of wood, and, much to my astonishment, I heard it ticking. Thus it was that I learned the secret of that German alarm-clock. It ran only if it were lying on its belly. Therefore we at once brought it back to work.

Next there were our two dollar watches. Mine took life quite easily, ran or stopped according to its own fancy. Dale's watch was more conscientious by nature, in so far as it had a greater tendency to run. On the whole, there is little else to be said about Dale's watch, save that it seldom gave one the slightest idea of what time of day it was. We assumed that it gained time. But just how much it made up every day in the week was beyond our power of reckoning. On Monday it might be that it was one hour ahead of Greenwich time, which we determined after our own fashion by locating the North Star and then taking a north-and-south bearing from the shadow cast by a large spruce. On Tuesday it might be three hours fast, on Wednesday it might give Greenwich the slip entirely and go off on a time scheme all its own.

We scrupulously kept all three of our timepieces going, compared the time, exercised all the mathematics we knew, and knew no more than we had before.

But then one morning during the late autumn it was my turn to get up first. It was pitch-black there in the cabin when I awoke. I struck a match and peeked at my watch. It had stopped. I walked over to consult the German alarm-clock. It lay on its back and preserved a spiteful silence. I picked up Dale's watch and held it up to my ear in order to make sure it was running, for if ever there existed a watch I distrusted, that was it. It was ticking. I glanced at the hands, which were poised at half past six. Hence it was time to begin the day. I built a fire in the stove and began frying and boiling. Then — " *Mi-su!* " [1] I cried, and Dale crawled sleepily out of his bunk. We slumped down on our respective stumps at the table and ate. Then we lit our pipes and continued to sit there in silence, as we waited for daylight to sift in through the windows. Time passed. At last I suggested that, after all, I had been a mite early with breakfast. Dale mumbled something having to do with the early bird and yawned. After a bit I went to the door and looked out. As yet no sign of daylight. In the sky the stars glittered with midnight brilliancy. I went back to my bunk and sat down. Then, assuring Dale that for my own part I couldn't possibly sleep so late in the morning, I stretched out on the bunk and immediately fell asleep. When I opened my eyes, after a long and refreshing nap, the gray

[1] Cree Indian word for food, everywhere used in northern Canada.

[67]

light of dawn had appeared through the window. Dale's watch now indicated that it was noon. . . .

. .
.

Winter was closing in on us and we had a busy time of it making our final preparations. Everything was in order and so set to go that, with the coming of the snow, we would simply have to harness up the dogs and be off. We over-hauled our tent, edged our mittens and jackets with beaver fur, patched our moccasins, rigged up foot-straps for our snowshoes, screwed together the runners of the sleds, fastened each cariole into place, fitted it out with ropes and ties.

All winter gear in the North is fundamentally of Indian design. Models developed through long generations by a primitive people are still unsurpassed for meeting the specific demands of the region.

Moccasins, made from the tanned and smoked hide of moose or caribou, are the only proper footwear. They are soft and pliable, allowing the muscular freedom essential to warm feet. Wearing a pair of duffels (blanket socks) over two pairs of long stockings, one need have no fear of frozen toes. Three or four pairs of moccasins are enough to last the average man throughout one winter. One must give them a special kind of care, however, brushing all the snow from them in front of the fire and stuffing them full of spruce needles before hanging them up to dry. The only trouble with them is that they are not waterproof, though this condition is hardly serious in a land where, practically speaking, the whole winter passes without a single day of thaw.

Snowshoes resemble, for the most part, the Norwegian

model, save that they are of more graceful design and curve upward at the toes. The frames are made from carefully selected birchwood, the inner bark of which is not removed. Their pattern is such that there is a right and a left snow-shoe, the outer frame of each being somewhat more bowed. The web is made from *babiche* — thongs of untanned cari-bou hide. Certain white trappers make their own snowshoes, but elegant design and delicate balance are secrets known only to the Indians and are handed down from father to son.

The average snowshoes are about thirty-two inches long. They are easy to maneuver through a dense forest and they plow such a deep furrow through the snow that their tracks are a great assistance to the dogs. Where drifts lie three or four feet deep, it requires a special knack to flounder along on them. Farther north on the Barrens, the Indians use snowshoes of a somewhat smaller model — about twenty-four inches long. The typical hunting-shoe is about five feet long and does not depress the surface of the snow at all. The Indians use the last type especially when on the trail of moose or caribou in the bush.

To my knowledge, skis are never used in northern Can-ada. It is doubtful that they would be of any practical use to one driving a dog-team through the forest where a path for the dogs must be broken through drifts and thickets and where one must be free to turn round at a moment's notice, sometimes wielding an ax, sometimes attending to the dogs and straightening the sled in its course.

The Indian woodland sled is called a " toboggan " — taken from the Algonquin word *odabagan* — and is de-signed for the express purpose of scaling snow-drifts and proceeding over rugged country. Its type of usefulness is quite the reverse of that of the Eskimo dog-sledge, which

is equipped with runners and is intended for travel over
the tightly packed snow of the Arctic prairies. The toboggan
consists of two flat strips of birch or hickory, tightly
fastened together and curved sharply up in front. The result
is a kind of ski, eight and a half feet long, a foot and a half
wide, and three quarters of an inch thick. The " cariole,"
wherein all goods are safely stored, is a bathtub-like arrangement made of canvas, a foot and three quarters deep,
running the entire length of the sled and held snugly in
place by an ingenious arrangement of ropes extending from
the curved nose of the toboggan to a backboard, or lazy-
back, rising perpendicularly from the stern.

Whereas the Eskimos hitch up their dogs in a fan-shaped
formation, and the Alaska people in so-called " Nome
style " — a double rank, alternating on either side of a
center trace — the Canadians harness their dog-teams tan-
dem — one dog directly behind another, in a long line.

The Indians and whites east of Great Slave Lake have
held fast to these methods of transportation, designed ex-
pressly for woodland travel. No doubt this is because
there are certain times when they are obliged to negotiate
dense forests, whether it be on the trail of the migrating
caribou or on their way south to the trading posts with the
fruits of their winter hunting.

. .
.

The cold now struck in in dead earnest. Moose Lake lay
under a mirror of ice, broken in innumerable places by
small brown domes of earth, which were the winter lodges
of the muskrats. A fine coating of hoar-frost had formed
on the reindeer moss which grew on the hilltops, and the
cranberries now dangled in frozen clusters. The small

magpies, or " whisky-jacks," which before had spent most of their time chattering and squabbling over our cached fish, now paraded about our door-yard, where it was more convenient for them to hold their banquets. Quite brazenly they hopped about among the dogs or stationed themselves on our door-sill, where they stood flipping their tails and peeking in, their heads cocked at a saucy angle.

In front of the cabin our toboggans stood side by side, ready for instant departure. Our grub was all packed, our axes freshly sharpened, and a week's rations for the dogs stowed snugly away in sacks.

The dogs were as eager as we were to be off. Each time we stepped out to one of the sleds, they would watch us like hawks, knowing as well as we, what all these preparations meant. They were in splendid condition now. We had rid them of their tapeworms, and a moderate layer of fat clung to their bones. Their thick winter fur glistened in the light, and their tails had become so bushy that they waved in the air like luxuriant plumes. . . .

Then one morning we awoke to find the ground white with snow. A new life had begun for us.

Winter

THE ICE ROCKS BENEATH OUR TOBOGGANS AS WE DRIVE across Moose Lake in the early dawn. Dale runs along testing the ice with his ax; I follow behind with the dogs. With a sudden dash we take to land on the opposite shore, the ice cracking beneath us, and water splashing about the sleds. Here our ways part. Dale sets a course up into the hills to the east, I follow the river south, for thus have we divided the country between us.

A curt " So long," and we each disappear into the woods on our respective trails. I find smooth going at first. I had been up this way earlier and had cleared a path through the woods; now all I have to do is to let the dogs run. But after a time I arrive in a region through which I had been unable to clear a way and now I find my hands full. I run ahead of the dogs on my snowshoes, fell trees to right and to left, and drag them off to one side. Sometimes a thicket of saplings stands like a wall in my way. Here I let the dogs roam, as I chop my way through, step by step. I must keep my eyes constantly peeled, judge quickly the lay of the land, and unhesitatingly choose my course. The trail I cut through must lie in as straight a line as possible and I must make a thorough job of it with the ax, for in the course of the winter I shall pass this way many times.

The character of the country undergoes a change. Ahead

lie broad muskegs covered with tamaracks. Now a swift stream bars my progress and I must build a bridge across it. Chains of broad lakes come into view. Sometimes I cross wide areas of surface water lying just under the snow. Then I must turn the toboggan over on its side and beat the ice from it with the flat of my ax. At such times one must be deft in the use of snowshoes. Nevertheless, there are occasions when I cannot avoid the water, and splash about in it up to my ankles. Right then and there I must change my moccasins and stockings as quickly as possible, for they will otherwise freeze as hard as a rock.

Each day brings its own new excitement. Unsuspected rivers and lakes appear, each advance being in the nature of the conquest of a new land. The wilderness, stretching so endlessly white in all directions, is the broad page of a book on which creatures, large and small, have written their names and told their little stories.

Here a moose has broken through a thicket. A light sprinkling of loose snow lies in front of each hoof mark, so it wasn't so long ago that the big fellow went wandering by. In amongst a thick stand of spruce much has been going on. Tracks made by neat little paws, in pairs, each oblique to the other, lie here and there in the snow like a bit of delicate embroidery. The tracks of a mink or an ermine, were they not so large. Perhaps it was a marten which passed this way. A whole colony of them have apparently settled in this region. The marten is gregarious, and large numbers of this animal congregate in tracts where conditions are favorable to their existence. Sometimes family after family of them live side by side through long stretches of forest, and a clever trapper can, without difficulty, bag from fifty to seventy-five skins during the course of one winter. On the other hand, the martens may suddenly vanish completely.

According to the Indians, they migrate to far distant parts of the country.

I swing down onto the river where it broadens out and where, for long stretches, the ice is solid. The whole way I find myself following the trail of a mink. Sometimes it skirts the edge of the bank, sometimes it cuts diagonally across the river, sometimes it disappears entirely under rocks and tree-roots or where there is a crack in the ice. The mink is an accomplished hunter, like its cousins the marten and the ermine, and a bloodthirsty rascal it is, too, leaping lightning-like upon its prey and hanging on to the very death with no thought of fear for itself. It will gladly enter into combat with an old and experienced muskrat, even though the latter be of equal size and a terrible spitfire in his own way, too.

Suddenly my eye falls upon a strange sight; running down the steep bank of the river is a smooth, sloping groove in the snow. It looks exactly as though a child had been playing there by sliding downhill. But it is the otter which has been out having a good time. As a matter of fact, it is nothing out of the ordinary to find an otter sliding downhill on its belly. The tracks reveal the fact that this one has clawed its way up the bank to repeat the performance again and again. Down along the river a broad furrow lies in the snow where the otter has brushed the snow with its belly as it hopped along on its stumpy legs. The otter does not occur in large numbers in any known region, for its broods are small, a pair of young being all that it rears each year. It is a wary creature and is extremely difficult to capture. Nor does one ever know where to look for it; the otter is a wanderer and is forever *en route* to some distant place.

The river broadens out into a large lake, the surface of which is littered with snow-covered muskrat houses. They are built of earth and reeds over holes in the ice, and are known as " push-ups." Farther in toward shore there are a number of larger domes, whose foundations are laid on the very bottom of the lake. These were the homes of the muskrats before the waters froze. Then these creatures were not afraid to come out into the open, despite the constant menace of owls, minks, and otters. If worst came to worst, they could always escape into their huts, which have entrances under water. But in winter it is otherwise. Then the muskrat remains for the most part indoors, taking an occasional swim beneath the ice and in such a manner proceeding from house to house or diving to dig up reeds from the bottom. He suffers no discomfort, for his pelage is thick and warm, and there is plenty he can find to eat; inside the house he has his cozy bed of grass and reeds where he can loaf to his heart's content. But it so happens that during the course of certain winters the waters rise up over the ice and flood the house. Then the devil alone is to pay. The muskrats have no place to hide, and many of them perish at once. Certain ones take refuge in their summer lodges inshore, others scramble out onto the ice. But the latter do not live to grow old, for when fox and lynx and mink and owl and all the other wild things are on the look-out for prey, it is not so pleasant for one who wears a coat of brown fur in a land of white snow.

Many years have now passed since the muskrats have experienced such a disaster, and their race abounds in these parts. Whenever a high point is reached, each lake and small stream is literally swarming with rats. A trapper, if he is lucky, can bag a couple of thousand skins, provided he keeps at it and doesn't waste too much time on his flaying.

Hares are in a poor way up here this year. A few tracks

here and there in among the tall timber are all I come across. Every seven years the forest is overrun with hares, and everything within reach is nibbled as clean as though by a swarm of locusts. Then, in the course of two or three weeks, the race all but dies out completely. Where millions throve before, one now seeks almost in vain to find a single creature. . . . The rabbit of northern Canada is called the " snowshoe hare " and is somewhat smaller than the " jack-rabbit " of the prairies or the polar hare found up on the Barrens.

Close beside the rabbit tracks lie the marks of a broad paw which has hardly depressed the snow a single inch. The lynx on the trail of its prey. Hard times are upon the lynx these days, for it is upon the hare that it sustains its own life. It must roam through the wilderness on an empty stomach, seeking night after night in the moonlight for the tracks of some stray hare. Many lynxes perish and their race dies down until such a time as the hare again is plentiful.

This periodic fluctuation of stock is not confined to musk-rat, hare, and lynx — it affects all the wilderness animals, though to a somewhat less degree. There are certain years when the Indians find dead beavers in the beaver-lodges and dead wolverines on the Barrens. There are times when the wolves thin out. In certain cases, it appears as though a common disease has afflicted these creatures of the wild. In the case of the muskrat, the hare, and the cari-bou the symptoms of this disease are a series of abscesses just beneath the skin. Under these conditions the animals' powers of reproduction are of interest: they are greatly reduced at the beginning of such a period of decline, later increasing until the litters not only become more hardy, but also increase in number, as in the case of the muskrat and hare. The basic cause for this racial cycle which the animals undergo is far from obvious at present, but it seems to depend mainly upon the question of nourishment, which exerts an ever-widening influence up through the entire animal kingdom.

As I continue on down the river, the dogs suddenly prick up their ears, raise their muzzles in the air, and begin sniffing. Coming out onto a lake, I catch a sudden glimpse of gray shadowy shapes which, in a long humping line, are scurrying into the woods. Wolves. A short distance offshore a pair of huge antlers are seen protruding through the snow. I swing over in their direction, and there I discover the sorry remains of a moose. The snow all around it has been packed down hard. Off to one side the snow is streaked with blood. Quite easily here one may read the story of what has taken place. At this point the moose started out from the woods; at this the wolves surrounded it. Here they fastened their teeth in its throat and hocks, hamstringing it, and bringing it to earth. But it scrambled to its feet again, shook off its gray tormentors, ran a few steps, and again fell beneath their assault. Now the end comes quickly. It struggles up, lurches forward, stumbles again. In one last panicky burst of strength, it flounders about on its forelegs, dragging its rump on the ground as the wolves rip open its belly with their teeth, so that its blood and viscera stream out onto the snow. . . .

I cut from the carcass as much meat as the wolves have left me, for one can never have enough food for the dogs. After driving on a short distance I come across a solitary set of tracks, somewhat similar to those of the wolf, but a trifle flatter, the distance between footprints indicating a broader straddle. Here the wolverine has been snooping around, waiting for the wolves to eat their fill, so that it too

may have a taste of their banquet. Now I'm going to have a
fine time hunting furs, I think to myself. For the wolverine
is the worst thief in the forest. Systematically it goes about
robbing the traps, and it can drag off half a caribou carcass,
without wearing itself out in the least. It eats as much as its
belly will hold, then buries the rest — not, however, before
it has rendered the whole thing so filthy that neither animal
nor man can come near it on account of the stench.

A fox has been prowling about a muskrat house, has
crawled up on the roof, where it stood sniffing the sweetish
vapors rising from below. Whether it was a red, cross, or
silver fox I cannot very well determine. At all events, it is
a different breed of fox from the one which, some distance
farther back, had left his delicate footprints after him in
the snow. Blue foxes are somewhat scarce in this part of the
country, so it must have been a white fox.

Then perhaps these tracks indicate that the white fox will
come this year! There are always small packs of them out
on the Barrens, and an isolated few of them south in the
timber. But when the white fox *comes*, that is a different
matter. Then they swarm like the hare, and it is no ac-
complishment whatever to trap a hundred or so. Thus it
was in 1924. Hordes of white foxes found their way south
as far as Great Slave Lake. They were so thick that one
trapper bagged nine hundred during the course of the winter. And that was the same year he had found a dead whale
washed in on the shore of the Arctic!

The number of white foxes living all year round on the
mainland is comparatively small. Their natural habitat is
on the islands and drift-ice of the Arctic, where they either
eke out a living by eating the scraps from the polar bear's
table or seek their own banquets in the bird rookeries.

WINTER

When the drift-ice presses up against the coast, the white foxes find their way into the interior of the Barren Lands. There they follow the wolves south and put to good use whatever the latter leave in the way of freshly killed meat, or track their own game in the form of field-mice, hares, and lemmings. " When the lemming migrates, the white fox will come in droves," is an old saying of the trappers.

On we go, and for a long stretch the only tracks we find are those of the ermine. Occasionally a ptarmigan starts up under the very noses of the dogs; high up among the branches of the spruce sit noisy squirrels. Here in the snow I run across tracks which give me a sudden shock. A skunk has passed this way — a rare inhabitant of tracts as far north as this. Aside from the porcupine, the skunk is the most shunned of all the forest creatures, because of the delightful odor of hydrogen sulphide with which it endows its victim. Fortunately it is a sweet-tempered brute and lets fly only when it gets into a tight place and then only after it has given ample warning. When one sees its tail beginning to rise, one had better be moving on.

The skunk, following the example of the other fur-bearing animals, is steadily retreating into the north. According to tales told by the Indians, it was formerly totally unknown in this part of the country. Today it is constantly increasing in number, especially around the mouth of the Taltson River.

As I drive along, I catch sight of a fox crossing a lake far off in the distance. I reach into the sled for my gun and send a shot flying off in the direction of the fox. But the animal trots merrily along on its way, finally disappearing into a thicket, and I am thoroughly convinced that the animal I have just missed was a silver fox. However, this is no time to pause for chagrin; I must break a way through the wilderness and lose no time about it, either. Furthermore I have traps to set each time I come to a likely spot.

It is no simple matter to entice animals into one's traps. The white fox and marten present no stupendous problem, as both are rather thick-witted. But when it comes to bagging the red fox, wolf, otter, or wolverine, the trapper must know something about his business, if he expects to have anything left for himself after he has paid his debt to " Hudson Bay." Each animal has its peculiarities, and it takes years for a trapper to learn them all. Take, for example, the lynx. At times it is so inquisitive that a small piece of bright red rag is enough to land it in the trap. On other occasions it is so blasé that not even a special delicacy, like a half-decayed fish, will lead it to investigate. The wolf I shall not even discuss; it sniffs about through the deep snow and occasionally, out of sheer deviltry, will put its paw under a trap and push it off to one side.

Each fur-hunter has his own method of trapping which he swears by and whereby he operates with entirely satisfactory results. For other methods he has nothing but a pitying smile. As a matter of fact, no enormous variation in technique exists, and in the long run the most powerful factors making for success are experience and intuition.

I am driving along through dense woods when daylight gradually begins to fail. I inspect the trees to right and to left and at length discover some dry enough to make good firewood. Here I stop and unhitch the dogs. They immediately lie down and begin licking the ice from between their toes. They know as well as I do that this is the place where we are to spend the night.

I chain each one to a separate tree-trunk and give each a bed of spruce branches to lie upon. Then I take one snowshoe and begin clearing the snow from our camp-site, later laying a thick carpet of brush in its place. I drive four poles into the deep snow behind us and stretch out the sled-cover between them. Thus I have a wind-break which also serves to reflect the heat from the fire, so my back won't be cold as I sit here. This done, I strap on my snowshoes, throw the ax over my shoulder, and start out to chop me some firewood. We shall need a whole pile of thick logs if we may hope to keep warm until morning. I drag in as much of the tree as possible and chop it up into shorter lengths just outside the camp.

The flames shoot up. After an hour of toil the hardest part is over. It seems so good to sit down and have a bite to eat. The tea-pot is beginning to simmer, a whitefish is on the spit, and the fish for the dogs are thawing under the snow near the fire. I stretch out my legs and begin to enjoy myself. But the time to relax has not yet come. There, the tea-pot is boiling over. There, the end of one of the logs has burned off, and I must shove the log back into the fire. The fish is beginning to scorch and must be turned on the spit. The spruce branches under me begin to ignite and I must extinguish the flames with snow. A shower of sparks blows in across my sleeping-bag and my caribou robe and must be brushed off as quickly as possible.

The dogs are curled up each in his nest in the snow and are gnawing their half-frozen fish. All save Fox, who is a privileged character. He has devoured his fish long before the others, for he knows that as soon as he has finished his supper, I will come and untie him. Now he has taken his place beside me as close to the fire as he can without singe-ing that shaggy red coat of his. Motionless he sits there gazing into the flames. Fox adores a fire.

I have finished with my labors. About me lies the wilderness, the moonlight casting deep shadows in through the forest, a faint murmur up in the tree-tops. A branch gives way, and its burden of snow meets the ground with a series of hollow thumps, a mist of loose flakes glistening in the glow from the fire. From the depths of the forest comes a distant sound of drumming. The woodpecker is at work. . . .

I crawl down into my sleeping-bag. I stuff my half-wet socks and moccasins under me and, my last pipe in my mouth, I watch the smoke curl up against the stars, as the camp-fire burns low, and small flames flicker over charred wood and glowing ember. . . . I feel something heavy settling itself down over my legs; it is Fox preparing to go to sleep. I can feel the warmth of his body penetrating even my sleeping-bag.

Morning is not always a time of joy and thanksgiving. When a man opens his eyes about six o'clock of a dark and icy morning, perhaps to find that he is partially snowed under, it is not always that he bounds with joy from his warm and cosy sleeping-bag. . . .

As time goes on I succeed in breaking trails here and there through the wilderness. Then my labors are of a less arduous nature. I can sit in the cariole and drive mile after mile behind my dogs. Coming down the slope of a mountain, I keep them running ahead at a gallop, whilst I steer the toboggan by shifting the weight of my body from side to side, as likely as not bringing up short against the trunk of some tree when I come to a sharp curve. Each time I go foul, the dogs halt of their own accord and remain rooted to the spot until I have set things to rights.

The dogs are guided by the sound of the driver's voice: " Mush " means go ahead, " You " means to the right, " Cha " to the left, and " Whoa " stop. Sport, the leader of the train, improves with each passing day. I can make him go wherever I wish, by merely calling out from the sled. Upon the lead-dog depends the entire success of a team. His spirit of willingness and the pace he sets are communicated at once to all the other dogs. But the butt-dog, too, has his own responsibilities as the dog which is nearest the sled. It is his duty to steer the toboggan, to keep it from banging into tree-trunks, and to steady it when it begins to side-slip.

To team all my dogs together was not accomplished with a simple wave of my hand. Two of them were Indian dogs and had been wretchedly trained, indeed. How I worked to get them to follow me at first when I was breaking a trail on snowshoe! They were not accustomed to dragging a sled when no one stood behind them with a whip in his hand, and they were damned if, at their age, they were going to change their ways!

If there is one thing to make a man get red-hot under the collar, it is trying to handle an intractable dog. Naturally it is wrong of a driver to let his temper get the better of him, but it is a rare individual who never forgets himself. When mile after mile of deep snow lies ahead and the dogs refuse to follow, when it is necessary to mush like the wind over rotten ice and the dogs pull up short, when a dog slips its collar late in the morning and one must spend hours chasing it before he is finally able to capture it, I suppose a man may be pardoned if he finds mere language a poor outlet for his feelings and fails to handle the situation with kid gloves.

The important thing to consider in adopting a manner of handling these wild creatures, all of which have wolf blood in them to a varying degree, is not whether one should flog them or swear at them, but that one should in some way establish the supremacy of man's will over theirs. Once let the dogs have their own way, and it is hard telling where things will end. "Dogs are dogs," as the old saying goes, and one may count upon them to shirk hard labor whenever and wherever the opportunity presents itself.

There are two kinds of dog-mushers. Some swear and lash out with their whips from morning till night. These never get all there is to be had from a team. The other type is made up of men of quiet demeanor. They say a few words when necessary, use the whip seldom, but when they do, effectively. The latter are the more successful mushers. Between them and their dogs a perfect understanding exists, and where such is the case, there is no limit of willingness to which a team will go.

. .
.

Occasionally Dale and I meet in the cabin after intervals of several weeks. Then we rest up for a day or two whilst preparing ourselves for a fresh expedition. There is always something to talk over. We are both eager to trade experiences and are forever inquiring about the lay of the land in the other's territory.

There is one matter which begins to concern us more and more: the coming of the caribou. What in the name of Heaven has become of them? Christmas is drawing near, and for a long time our diet has consisted solely of fish, a most inadequate form of nourishment on a cold winter's day. We no longer find it so easy to keep going on snowshoes, and when the thermometer drops to temperatures somewhere between 40° and 70° below zero, the cold seems sharper than it ought. Our food-supply for the dogs, too, is becoming perilously low.

WINTER

Hunger for meat again afflicts us. As we sit on our upturned stumps before the stove, our conversation inevitably
returns to the subject of juicy meat. Dale, who is the sober-
est man in the world, dwells longingly upon his memory of
a certain roast of lamb he once ate. He describes it in great
detail, tells me how tender and juicy it was, how much there
was of it. " No, there's nothing like a good roast of lamb,"
he concludes. I challenge his statement by bringing up the
matter of beaver, lay powerful arguments before him, and
sum up with the incontrovertible statement that roast lamb
is as flat to the taste as squab, compared with a nice juicy
beaver.

Of late both the wolf and the fox have been increasing
in number. This indicates that the caribou cannot be so
very far away. Strange, then, that neither of us has seen a
trace of them during our long expeditions. Each time we
meet in the cabin, our first question is: " Have you seen
them yet? " But the answer is ever the same. A white stillness lies over the forest, a thick blanket of snow, embroidered with the same small animal tracks. We wait and we
wait. . . .

Then one day we are sitting in the cabin eating our midday meal, mechanically swallowing down our fish and staring out over Moose Lake, as it lies there in a bath of sunshine. Suddenly I start up. " Isn't there something black
moving off there by the river mouth? " I make a grab for
my gun and leap for the door. . . . *There they are! The
caribou!* . . .

One by one the animals appear at the edge of the woods.
With easy playful springs they proceed out onto the lake,
pause for a time, gaze about them, then resume their leisurely march, the older ones walking with sedately measured strides, their necks stretched far forward as they sniff

[85]

about in the snow. An endless procession of bucks, does, and fawns. Ever-increasing numbers follow, and soon they are like an army invading our quiet land.

One enormous buck is leading the herd. His head is bowed beneath his mighty crown of antlers, and the shaggy mane about his neck is as shiny and white as the snow. Calves lope everywhere, dancing about with a restless energy; occasionally a pair of young bucks pause to restrain them. Nearer and nearer they come to the cabin, resting so peacefully here in amongst the trees, a plume of frosty wood smoke curling up from our chimney into the blue sky.

No more than five or six hundred feet from the cabin the leader suddenly halts, raises his head to investigate. Instantly the whole line halts. A sea of heads, motionless, staring.

We are hardly able to believe our eyes. The caribou have actually arrived! Over stretches measuring hundreds of miles the herd has wandered south from the Arctic to seek the woodlands, and here they are, strolling right past our door, just as though it were the most natural thing in the world. . . .

The forest lives and breathes with them. Everywhere there are caribou. We hear them crashing through the thickets as we drive along in our toboggans, we encounter small flocks of them asleep on the ice of each lake. The snow is carved and re-carved by a network of deep and hard-packed deer paths.

Now we have no need to complain of meat shortage. We set up two lines of spruce brush planted in the snow, about thirty feet apart, extending this lane from the other side of the lake where the caribou usually come out of the woods, all the way back to the cabin. Thus game is deflected over in our direction and, as a rule, we can kill as many as we need right in our own front yard. But after the first wave the caribou arrive in more scattered contingents, and these are more wary than the first. Therefore we adopt regular hunting methods and go after them with our dog-teams.

A band of caribou is in sight off there on a lake. I hop into my toboggan and give the dogs a word they are quick to understand. They all prick up their ears and start staring off into the distance. Then, as their eyes light upon the game, we are off. Madly we gallop ahead, the toboggan skidding and leaping, as it hisses along over the snow. I hold tight to the ropes of the cariole, throw my weight from side to side, afraid that any moment we shall capsize. Closer and closer we come to the caribou, and Sport lets out more than one gasping whine, out of sheer enthusiasm. . . . Suddenly the herd becomes aware of us. Those which before have been fast asleep on the ice are on their feet in the twinkling of an eye, and together they present a solid front against the storm of our approach. They stare, bursting with curiosity. Never in their lives have they seen anything quite so odd. But the strange phenomenon does not pause for an instant, it keeps coming straight in their direction, so perhaps they had better be thinking of their safety. A young buck begins stamping with anger, makes a tremendous perpendicular leap into the air, coming down on his hind legs first, repeats the performance — once — twice — three times in succession, then starts running off over the ice as fast as his legs will carry him. Instantly the others turn tail with a wrench of their bodies and, in a single tightly packed mass, storm off down the lake, snow flying in their wake. A sudden senseless panic has put them to flight, and there is every indication that they will keep on running until miles lie between them and our sled. Then, as is their wont, they will halt just as suddenly and will turn round to resume their staring.

The dogs are now wild with excitement and are straining themselves to the utmost. Sport, as leader, keeps his eyes fastened upon the caribou, makes after them by sight alone, paying no attention to their tracks in the snow. A pair of large bucks separate themselves from the main flock and begin trotting off by themselves in a zigzag course. Like a shot, Sport is after them. Soon we are near enough. "Whoa!" I command, and the dogs stop dead in their tracks. A shot rings out over the ice. One caribou crumples and falls.

It is not always so simple as that. There are times, especially on really cold days, when we must spend hours hunting the caribou. Sometimes it is, utterly impossible to come within range of them. When one of their number lies wounded in the snow, however, the others will usually halt and stand by; thus the hunter may without difficulty shoot as many as he needs. When the snow lies deep in the woods, the caribou are reluctant to leave the ice, even when they are being hunted. A shot fired ahead of a band will, as a rule, cause them to change in their course. In a pinch, it is possible to shoot from a moving sled, provided the dogs and the game are running abreast of each other. But even then it is sheer luck if one is able to hit the mark. When a toboggan is skidding every which way, one's shot is more than likely to go off in the direction of the clouds or straight down in the midst of the dogs.

Hunting the caribou with a dog-train has no equal for sport. It thrills the heart of the hunter. Nevertheless, it is exacting in a number of particulars. One must enjoy full mastery over one's dogs and must act quickly and with precision. If one has a dependable lead-dog, half the chase is won. With a dog that feels, even for an instant, that he can have his own way, one might just as well try to hunt with a team of wild horses. And if it happens that, out on the open plains or on the ice of a large lake, a hunter steps out of his sled and fails to keep an eye on his dogs, the merest whim on their part may mean that he has seen them for the last time. Given their freedom, they will continue their blind, insane pursuit as long as they have breath in their bodies. . . .

. .
.

Christmas Eve in the forest. On the table in our cabin stand a pot of steaming venison stew, a bowl containing two thick beaver tails saved for this special occasion, and a cup of cranberry sauce. We begrudge ourselves nothing. . . .

" Suppose we take a whack at the Barrens now," says Dale, as we sit there enjoying the evening. I agree that the time has arrived for us to find our way into that country we have from the very beginning planned to explore. It is unwise for us to set out into the unknown, when we have so thoroughly arranged for our security here beside Moose Lake. We realize that full well. But those wide barren plains are calling and beckoning to us, and we are filled with a keen unrest. . . .

The journey lasted well over a month, and when we returned, we were rich in experience, but in little else. We had seen the Barren Lands and learned what their malevolence could be like.

Bad luck was with us from the very start. Blizzards set in and our hunting went awry. Along the way we met a party of Indians who reported that they had a camp up near the northwest end of Artillery Lake. We decided to make this our first objective; there we could always get a little food for the dogs, whilst we hunted and stored up meat to last us for some time to come. I have no clear recollection of that last day crossing Artillery Lake, as we pressed on hoping to reach the camp of the Indians. The blizzard beat directly in our faces, and the dogs could hardly see. We kept on going, far into the night. At length we came to a bay. This must be the place, we thought. During the rest of that night and all the next day we saw no sign of human life. So we shared the last of our grub with the dogs and started on our way back home.

The dogs were hungry and we were hungry and we might have had a really hard time of it, were it not for the fact that we stumbled on a caribou carcass which the Indians had left there as white-fox bait. The viscera had not been removed and the meat stank horribly, but it was something to eat, none the less. We cut off as much of the meat as we thought we would need and, as payment for this, we hung on the antlers of the dead beast a little pail containing the last of our sugar. It swayed back and forth in the wind and indeed it looked forlorn! A year later I met the Indian who had found the pail of sugar and, when I brought the matter up, he beamed all over and cried: "*Nézōn, nézōn, nézōn!*" meaning that he had been highly pleased over the exchange.

. .
.

It was getting along toward spring. The pelage of the land animals had begun to lose its luster, and their hair was coming out in tufts. Their pelts would be worth nothing now, so one day we loaded all our stuff on the two toboggans and set out for Snowdrift, the trading post on the shore of Great Slave Lake. There we would sell our stock of furs and immediately equip ourselves for a new venture: the beaver season was directly at hand.

I never saw our cabin again, for the winds of fate thereafter bore me far and wide. But I can still see it shining to greet me, there amongst the trees, when, tired and half-frozen, I came driving home behind my trotting dogs. As long as I live, I shall preserve the memory of our cosy evenings indoors when together we sat on our crude stools before that round stove of Dale's and peacefully drew on our pipes.

The cabin is probably the same as ever today, and all is as of old, there on the shores of our own Moose Lake — the birchy slope where we shot the moose, Cranberry Hill, the river winding its way along through reeds and rushes, our two canoes lying bottom up on the beach, and everything else the same. We left the door ajar, so it is possible that at this very minute some wolf or some fox is prowling about inside or sniffing about a pile of old rags. And who knows but that some Indian, passing by chance on his sled, catches sight of that gable amongst the trees? If he is cold and tired, it is likely that he will peep inside. Then, after he has made a fire in the stove and stretched himself out on the bunk and discovered how cosy it is to lie between four walls, perhaps he will be gracious enough to send a friendly thought to the *téotenny*, the white men, who built a little log cabin there on the shore of Moose Lake.

Beaver-Hunting

On Great Slave Lake, in the vicinity of the Snow-drift River, there is a trading post managed by a half-breed. Here a number of Indians and a handful of white trappers have assembled at the close of the winter hunting season. The year is well on into April, and the melting of the snows has reached its most disagreeable stage. In amongst the tents, gleaming white in the clearing, there is a veritable network of gurgling brooklets. Jutting out over the eaves of the store itself is a tremendous fold of wet snow from which long icicles hang like glittering spears. Lake and forest lie knee-deep in slush.

There are five of us in our tent — four white trappers and an Indian, named Souzi. We are all planning to go out after beaver, the others two by two, I as a lone hand. Outside in the snow our toboggans are lying in a row, each simply waiting for the dogs to step into the harness. Our outfits are packed, ready to go. These consist of a gun and ammunition, an ax, matches, a woolen blanket, and any number of smaller articles. Some of the men are also taking with them canvas, nails, and paint in order that they may cut ribs from the willow and build themselves a canoe. Thus they will be able to make use of the rivers after the ice has broken up. Grub consists of a pail of dried meat and fat, which is enough to last the first few days; there-

[92]

after we shall have to rely upon wild game. The beaver-hunter must have as little as possible to drag with him, must be willing to go hungry often, and must be tireless on the trail.

We are restless and eager to be gone. But until the snow has become drained of surplus water and has packed down hard enough for the night crust to bear us up, it is out of the question to set out through the forest. For a week or more now we have been waiting for proper weather conditions.

It is some time after supper. The tent is filled with a cloud of tobacco smoke, and the light from a single tallow candle flickers across the faces of men who are sitting or lying about in every manner of position.

“We'll be pulling out of here tonight, or I'll eat my hat,” growls Jim, chewing away on a big piece of dried meat.

“That's what you say every night,” puts in Klondike Bill sarcastically, from where he sits on a caribou robe, with his feet drawn up under him, Buddha-like.

“Hey, Souzi! What do you think about it?” asks Dale, stretched out full length on his sleeping-bag, and staring up at the tent-poles.

We all turn to Souzi. He is a native son of this country and we all have great respect for his opinion on such a matter as this — that is, all save old Klondike Bill, naturally, for he has been living alone so long he has his own opinion about everything under the sun.

“Me see,” says Souzi, slipping out through the flap of the tent and going down to have a look at the lake. At every step, he sinks knee-deep in the snow. “*Nézōnilly* (No good),” he remarks laconically as he creeps back into the tent, sits down on a caribou robe, and immediately begins filling his pipe. He lights it with extreme deliberation, takes a few drags, then continues: " Soon little moon, good crust then, maybe so."

" To hell with him and his moon! " bellows Klondike Bill, contemptuously. " They've got moon on the brain, these here Indians. By golly, if a crust don't freeze with this new moon, it's sure to freeze with the next, and if they keep on predictin' that-a-way long enough, they're bound to hit it right some time, even if they gotta wait till next winter for it." To demonstrate his utter scorn for all Indian lore, Klondike Bill turned all the way over on his belly.

Along toward midnight the temperature suddenly drops; a mid-winter cold has set in. Snowdrift instantly comes to life. Dark shadows moving hither and yon, the cracking of whips, Indians shrieking out oaths at their moaning, wailing dogs. One by one the sleds glide out through the night, the sound of their bells growing more and more faint in the distance. Each driver sets his own course and soon I am mushing alone through the wilderness toward the east. . . .

It is spring in the forests of Canada. Like a sudden fermentation of nature, it first attacked the white peace of the North. Now it is seething and effervescing in all quarters. Day by day the ferment increases, until soon it is as a very storm of explosive forces and giddy resurrection. Brooks pummel their way through the snow-drifts, each singing its own triumphal song. The sparrow, the titmouse, the whisky-jack — all the birds which have not forsaken this land of snow — suddenly appear from God knows where and twitter their spring choruses from dawn until sunset. Sap begins to ooze up into the frozen branches of the birch, the dwarf spruce indignantly tosses to the ground its winter burden of snow, and the warmth of the sun eats its way through the thin ice in the coves and narrow channels.

Then the migratory birds arrive. The ducks are the first to appear, led by the stately green-winged teal, with an emerald-green speculum on each wing. At odd intervals all the others come streaming in: the black duck, the spoonbill, and the tiny gadwall, which is as quick as lightning and can escape a charge of shot by diving. On the dark streaks of open water they float in ranks and files, and when twilight falls, the whir of their rapid wing-beats may be heard all through the forest. Then huge flocks of geese and swans come plowing their way through the air. They are all on their way to the Arctic.

The rat-houses, which clutter the lakes, have all been split open on one side to admit the rays of the sun. About each hole in the ice small groups of muskrats are crouching.

On the southern slopes of the hills the snow is melting most rapidly. Patches of brown weeds and lichens have begun to appear. Here and there a cluster of frozen cranberries. This is where the hare romps blithely.

For some time now the bear has been sensing the arrival of spring. It has become so swelteringly hot in his den that he can no longer stand it indoors. He shuffles about near the door, claws away the pile of moss and branches with that flabby paw of his, and soon is standing outside, blinking into the sun.

Throughout a long winter the beaver has seen no daylight. He has been loafing on his warm bed of moss inside the lodge, with only an occasional short swim down under the ice to his cellar, whence he fetches a birch stick to gnaw. He has grown fat from idleness. But at length the light begins to grow stronger down there beneath the ice, and the walls of his house have commenced to steam. The beaver can no longer restrain his curiosity. He must go up and have a look round. Swimming close up against the ice, he turns over on his back and begins to gnaw. Now and then he must make a hurried trip back into the house to let out his breath, but he immediately draws in a fresh one and returns to his gnawing. He gnaws and he gnaws. At last he suddenly breaks through, and there is the world all sunshine and cooling breezes. Cautiously he cranes his neck, turns and twists his head in all directions, tests the air with his nose. Then he crawls out on top of the ice, where he squats for a time, taking everything in. A quick splash, and he is back under the ice; then his family knows that spring is here again.

Suddenly great activity is noticeable amongst the caribou. They must be thinking of getting back into the north, for the road is a long one and there is no longer any ice to rely upon.

The smaller lakes are already open. Close in against the banks hover schools of pike, their noses buried in the reeds. Hearing the slightest noise, they turn and scoot out into deep water, leaving a foamy wake behind them. The ice is beginning to recede from the shore in all the larger lakes, and all the rivers are swollen. The waters surge beneath the river ice, which now and then makes a mighty sucking sound. Then the ice-floes come crashing downstream, leaving, where they have passed, a river boiling with yellow mud. . . .

Thus I find the birth of spring as I fare through the forest on my beaver-hunt. The lakes are still frozen over when I bag my first game. I chop a hole in the ice, drive a spruce pole slantwise into the bottom, set a trap baited with a few birch twigs, and fasten it to the pole just beneath the surface of the water. The trap yields me two beavers, and both the dogs and I are soon well fed. I stretch the skins over an oval frame of willow and leave them to dry in the sun. At the next beaver-lodge I observe that the inmates have already been up for a peep at the sky. There, at sunset, I lie down with my gun and keep watch of the hole and am successful in shooting one beaver, just as it is crawling up onto the ice.

Every day it becomes more and more difficult to proceed by sled. In some places it scrapes along over stones, in others it keeps breaking through the ice. So I leave it behind, put packs on all the dogs, sling my bag over my shoulder, and splash along through slush and across rivers where the water swirls about my hips. Toward morning, when I roll myself up in my woolen blanket, there is hardly a dry stitch left on my back.

Occasionally I follow along an extensive bottom land where the birches stand thick beside river and lake. In one place I tie up the dogs and wander off to reconnoiter, for this region appears to be rich in beaver.

It is not long before my eye lights upon a dome of earth which rises some six feet above the surface of the river, close in against the bank. There are no beavers anywhere about, however. The lodge has been broken into by the Indians quite some time ago. These fellows usually go out pillaging before the ice has begun to break up. First they find the beaver's burrow in the river-bank, the animal's place of refuge in times of danger; then they chop a hole in the ice and plug up the entrance to the burrow. The beavers are thus forced to enter their house in order to breathe and, as a consequence, are extremely easy game.

Through the aperture in the roof I gain an excellent impression of the beaver's method of building. His material

consists of small birch logs and sticks, which he twists together and putties up with mud. The dome-like roof is so
thick and so compact that even a bear would have difficulty
in clawing his way through. Under the roof and well above
the high-water mark is a central chamber. The entrance to
this room is well under water, where remnants of the winter stores are still visible — a pile of birch and aspen stalks
and the roots of aquatic plants. In a wide semicircle adja-
cent to the house the woods have been gnawed off close to
the ground, so a fairly large family must have resided here.
But everything is abandoned and desolate-looking now. No
ruined beaver-lodge is ever rebuilt.

Farther up the river, just before it broadens out to form
a small lake, I come across a dam. It is of recent construction. Therefore the beavers cannot be far away, as the
purpose of the dam is to produce deep water and prevent
the bottom from freezing, for here it is that the winter
stores are kept. The dam is a masterpiece of engineering,
ingeniously accomplished by twisting sticks and long poles
together, plastering up the cracks with mud, and weighting
the whole thing down with rocks and earth. How the beavers
were ever able to anchor their original foundation here in
this swift-rushing current is more than I can comprehend.
The dam does not even seem to have thickness and solidity
sufficient to withstand all possible conditions. As a matter
of fact, it has not actually withstood the recent spring
freshet, which has broken through a channel close up
against one bank. There is evidence that the beavers have
already been at work repairing the damage.

In a little cove just above the dam I discover the lodge,
which is so constructed that one side immediately adjoins
the river-bank. The roof is marked with beaver tracks indicating that the animals have been busy with spring repairs.

Mud is dug up from the bottom of the pond and evenly plastered over the entire top of the house. In a birch thicket a short way back from the river, they have been busy cutting wood. A number of felled trees — some from four to eight inches in diameter at the base — lie in a tangle on the ground, which is white with stumps and bits of gnawed wood. Hard-trodden paths lead through the trees from the river to this lumber-yard of theirs. The wood is first rolled down the slope to the river, then floated downstream to the winter store-room under the lodge, or farther on down to the dam. The beaver is forever endeavoring to simplify as greatly as possible his transportation problems. In the river he takes advantage of the current and in the lake he will wait patiently for a tail wind before starting out with a heavy piece of timber.

Both lodge and cuttings indicate a family of more than average size. I estimate that there are about six animals living together here. Of course, I am not as certain of my estimate as an Indian would be, and shall have to wait until after I have shot the female before I shall know the exact number — the rings of her womb will tell how many young she has had. . . .

I have prepared a couch of spruce boughs behind a large tree-root. There I lie motionless, my gun ready, as I keep close watch of the river. Directly across from me on the other side of a cove and silhouetted against the thicket of birches stands the beaver-lodge. Like a moving sheet of dark glass the river flows between it and me. The sun sets behind the ridge, and the leaves of the trees flame with a golden fire. A pale twilight filters in through the woods, and all signs of life die away.

Now is the time for the beavers to come out. I must use my eyes and ears and endeavor to breathe as quietly as I can. Suddenly I hear a splash and I crouch forward — but no, that was anything but the mighty slap of a beaver's tail. Only a humble muskrat which turned up his rump and dove. There he is, swimming alongside the bank, twisting himself this way and that. It is the beaver's house-rat. He has his own private apartment in the beaver-lodge, with the full permission of the owners. Co-operation is the best thing for both parties. The muskrat has a grand time here where grass and reeds are always floating about on the water, and the beavers probably reckon themselves much better off with an extra sentry to keep watch.

Life rustles in the leaves about me. Small field-mice, in large numbers, are scuttling back and forth. Some of them crawl over my body, others hide themselves under me and apparently imagine that they have discovered the best hiding-place in the world. Across the river at the edge of the woods I see a dark form moving. A fox. Slowly he jogs along, his bushy tail waving behind him. Now and then he pauses, sniffs in the direction of the river, finally disappears in the brush. . . . A rushing sound in the air as of an approaching wind, and low over the trees a flock of wild ducks whir by. They swerve sharply, soar out over the river, plant themselves in the water with a confused splash, and rock there now like a fleet of small ships, only a few yards away. I keep staring out over the river; all is still, nothing happens. . . .

Then the water begins to eddy in one place, disturbing the mirror-calm surface of the pond as it continues to swirl round and round. . . . Noiselessly a head bobs up directly in front of the beaver-lodge. It turns and twists in all directions, then quickly ducks under the water. In a few moments it bobs up again, this time farther away from me. It stares intently up and down the river-bank, meanwhile sniffing the air with upturned nose. Again that head melts out of sight, this time coming up again on the other side of the house, whence it proceeds through the reeds to the bank at the point where the river broadens out. The same extreme caution, the same noiseless motion. Again it is gone, only to reappear in front of the lodge, as suddenly as ever. There it silently raises itself above the surface, remains thus for a time, then slowly glides under again, until only the black tip of its nose is visible. Then for the fourth time it disappears.

This is the beaver's look-out and is always one of the young. Its duty is to investigate conditions and to determine whether it is safe to proceed with the work. The welfare of the entire family depends upon the soundness of this youngster's judgment, for the otter, the wolverine, the lynx, and even the bear are all crafty hunters, and it is no simple matter to discover their presence. Finding no danger imminent, the look-out communicates this information to the others in the house. If, on the other hand, some harm befalls their sentry, few beavers will appear during the remainder of that night.

About five minutes pass, and then beavers bob up in several places — four in all. Indications are that they are all young animals, the elder generation remaining indoors as long as possible, in the interests of personal safety.

After a time one beaver comes swimming back to the house with a stick in its mouth. Another cautiously creeps up over the hill to the cutting-ground. At no time does it cease to maintain a sharp look-out for danger. Beside a stout birch-tree it pauses, settles itself on its haunches with its fore-paws resting against the trunk of the tree, and begins gnawing. It proceeds with extreme energy, all the time circling the tree. Suddenly it scoots away. The tree sways, and from another beaver out in the water comes the danger signal — two or three powerful slaps of the tail. Then the tree falls downhill in the direction of the river. In a flash the beaver is back at the tree, stripping it of limbs and gnawing the trunk up into six-foot lengths. One by one, it rolls these poles down into the river, grips them in its teeth, and floats them downstream. The beaver does not pause at the lodge; he makes straight for the place where the dam has been burst by the spring freshet. There he proceeds to wrestle with his pole, first with his fore-paws, then with his teeth, until it has been fitted snugly into place and fastened with straws and twigs; then he goes back for another.

I now catch sight of a second beaver, already at work on the break in the dam. From a quiet pool in the river, he digs up mud and stones and swims back with a load, which he hugs tightly against his throat and breast with his fore-paws. No beaver can carry much at a time, and many thousands of trips are necessary in order to build a new house or a new dam. Tirelessly they keep at it, now and then chinking up holes and stuffing up cracks and leveling out their covering of mud with their fore-paws. Contrary to popular belief, the tail is not used as a trowel.

For the first time now the old beaver puts in his appearance. He swims straight toward me, sniffing as though he guesses my presence. It is impossible for him to catch my scent, for the wind is blowing in my face and the eyesight of beavers is never very keen. Perhaps it is a subtle intuition that warns him that all is not as it should be. I decide to cease being a mere spectator, take aim, and fire. Klask! Klask! Klask! The danger signal sounds out over the water, as terrified beavers slap the surface with their tails. I catch a fleeting glimpse of the " lumber-jack " as he scoots down the slope on his belly and dives into the river with a huge splash. . . .

Luck is with me. I discover a number of other lodges along the same watercourse, and from one of them I succeed in bagging two black beavers, whose pelts are more valuable than those of the brown. White beavers are also to be found, just as there are white muskrats, but they are so rare that very few hunters have ever seen one.

I now get to work and make myself a permanent camp where I can tie up the dogs, so that at sundown and sunrise I can lie at my post near the beaver-lodges. When I return to camp, the dogs leap to their feet and stand there with ears erect and eyes blazing with expectancy, wondering for all they are worth how much meat I have brought home this time in that bag of mine.

It is not long before I have taken all the beavers there are to be had in this locality. No doubt there are a fair number of them left inside the lodges, but these have become so timid that it is not worth while spending any further time on them. Once again I sling my bag over my shoulder and continue my tramp through the woods, ever on the watch for new hunting-fields.

It is well that we have eaten well of beaver meat and have put some flesh on our bones, for we suddenly fall upon lean days. The ducks have scattered out over the country, and those that we find are exceedingly wary. It is only on rare occasions that I am able to bring one down with my rifle. Night after night I tramp along without coming across a single sign of beaver.

Then, at last, I discover a *mammoth beaver-lodge.* It is almost seven feet high and I am convinced that a large family, numbering at least ten beavers, are living here. Evening after evening I lie in wait, but, to my utter amaze-

ment, one beaver is all I ever see. As a compensation, however, he is a thumping big fellow.

How this beaver ever came to live a hermit's life in such
an enormous house, only the members of his own race will
ever know. Indians and old fur-hunters claim that such
solitary animals are really social outcasts. A parallel is
found amongst wolves. But even this does not throw much
light on the subject. Certain authorities hold that it is the
slothful animals that are exiled by their fellows. Others
claim that, in the case of the beaver, when one creature has
lost its mate, it is forbidden to take another. Animal society is built upon laws we have not always been successful
in unraveling.

My stalking of this hermit of mine begins to run into
time. No matter how crafty I am in choosing a hiding-place,
the beaver always seems to have a pretty exact notion of my
whereabouts. Sometimes I see the black tip of his nose protruding from the water, sometimes I catch a glimpse of his
powerful tail just as it whacks the surface and disappears.
By this time it is a dubious pleasure I experience as I lie
there in wait hour after hour without so much as moving
a limb. The mosquitoes have come to life again after their
long winter's hibernation. No slight amount of self-control
is necessary to watch them sit there and suck one's blood
until, drunk with it, they laboriously fly away.

At last, on the fourth evening, the beaver comes out into
the open. I am in the very act of sneaking through the .
birch thicket to my hiding-place when he breaks surface a
short way out and begins peering in all directions. I immediately dodge behind a tree. But the animal has either
seen or heard me — Klask! Klask! Klask! — The danger
signal cracks out like three pistol-shots. I am furious with
myself. Again the hunt has been ruined!

But the old beaver must be in a peculiarly fanciful state of mind this evening. He bobs up and disappears, after drumming a few times with his tail. It would seem that he now desires once and for all to find out what kind of thing I am, for he comes nearer and nearer to me, eagerly craning his neck and sniffing the air. At this point I fire. The beaver topples over backward, begins flopping about in the water and wildly thrashing his tail, finally sinking out of sight. I am confident that I have finished him. Pretty soon he will come floating up to the surface as slain beavers ordinarily do, and we shall be having rich meat and a succulent beaver tail for dinner tonight. Firmly convinced of this, I seat myself on a stump, light my pipe, and keep close watch of the water.

Five minutes pass, then another ten. No sign of a beaver floating to the top. I become uneasy and begin trotting up and down the bank, my eyes peeled for some sight of my game. The water lies there disagreeably calm, with not even a speck to mar its dark surface. What the dickens is the meaning of this? After a half-hour of helpless waiting, the awful truth begins to dawn on me. " *He sank!* " I hear myself saying. Now, it is rare indeed that a slain beaver fails to rise to the surface, but what luck that such should happen in this particular case!

I sit down on top of the beaver-lodge, fill my pipe, and try as hard as I can to work up sufficient courage to face the facts and take my blow complacently. As I sit there staring fatuously and unhappily at nowhere in particular, I become suddenly aware of something black far off near the edge of the ice. I gape, wide-eyed. Using a little imagination, I can make it seem like a beaver's belly. Yes, the belly of a floating beaver must look something like that. But — why — by Heaven, it *is* a beaver's belly!

My first impulse is to tear off my clothes and start swim-ming out after it, but I curb my desire, for the mosquitoes are too thick. I grab my ax instead and get busy making a raft. I work furiously, now and then taking a brief trip down to the bank to make sure that the beaver is still float-ing out there in the darkness.

No more wretched raft ever floated upon water. A few tag-ends of rope are all that hold it together, and no sooner do I set foot upon it than it sinks beneath the surface. I snatch off my clothes down to my shirt, sit astride the raft, and begin poling my way along.

It *is* a beaver! But the animal is so heavy that when, at last, I succeed in hauling him aboard, my craft imme-diately goes under altogether. This raft was none too sea-worthy before, but now it is a total wreck. I sit in water up to my navel and convulsively hold the logs together with my legs, in order to prevent complete disintegration. Half-way to shore, the raft and I part company, but I have a good grip on the beaver's tail and, fortified by the determina-tion never to let it go, even were it to prove my last beaver in all the world, I succeed in getting both it and myself back on dry land. . . . It is a drenched but happy fur-hunter who stands there with his prize on the bank of that beaver pond, his shirt-tails flying in the wind!

This was the largest beaver I had ever seen, and must have weighed somewhere about seventy-five pounds. An explanation of the animal's odd behavior was apparent when I discovered the mark of my bullet. The shot had broken off both upper incisors and had made the animal's head reel, so that it had flopped about as though drunk. It was an ideal killing, as it spared the valuable pelt any damaging rent or tear. Later on I reported this fact to a number of trappers, but I have yet to hear that this method of killing has come into general use.

I now turned back in the direction of one of my old beaver-lodges, where I knew there were three or four animals still left alive. After three nights of steady tramping I arrived at a stream the Indians call the Hare River. I had previously camped on the opposite bank and had left there some ammunition, a number of trifles, two beaver tails, and half a beaver carcass, all tied up together in a bag which I had hung from the limb of a spruce. The food would come in handy now, for the large beaver was already gone and I was as hungry as a wolf.

The stream had become swollen during my absence and had carried away my bridge. It was out of the question to attempt constructing a new one, as the river was now too wide and too swift. But I had to get across some way if I was to have anything at all to eat. So I took a grip on my ax and began felling one tall spruce after another, causing them to fall athwart the stream. But all were too short and were dragged downstream by the current. It is bitter indeed to be so near and yet so far from a hearty meal when one is hungry. Just then I spy a giant spruce somewhat higher up on the slope. Hungry and boiling with rage, I cut loose upon it. Even this falls short. All right, then! I lay down my ax and gun, balance my way along the log as far as I can, catch hold of the branches of an overhanging birch, and swing myself ashore.

Deep in thought, I shuffle up the bank. I am carefully planning out the menu for my coming meal and am on the point of deciding which would go better — boiled beaver tail or beaver shanks roasted on a spit — when suddenly I halt in my tracks. Standing directly under the tree from which I have hung my bag, is a black bear together with her two cubs, each one no larger than a cat. The old bear has her mouth full, and from the pleasurable manner in which she is working her jaws, it is evident that it is some great delicacy she is in the act of devouring. The cubs are rooting about with their noses in the undergrowth.

Dashed if they aren't standing there eating up that beaver of mine! Now, this is going altogether too far! I am in a fighting mood at once and rush up the bank, waving my arms in the air. A mad rout ensues. The old bear almost breaks her back fleeing into the woods, and the two cubs pile up the tree as fast as ever they can, making straight for the topmost branches, where they sit, looking down at me in utter amazement.

Off in the brush I find my sack ripped open, tea-pot and matches scattered about on the ground. A gnawed bone or two and a few scraps of gristle are all that is left of my beaver. In a bitter frame of mind I gather up what remnants I can find.

The possibility of beaver cooked in any style is now entirely out of the question, but a roasted bear cub or two may prove a fair substitute, I console myself, as I tie up the hole in the bag with a piece of rope, throw the sack over my back, and start scrambling aloft after those two little sinners up in the top of the tree. They appear to have anything but guilty consciences, those two, and stare from their respective perches with no more than ordinary curiosity at my approaching form. As I clutch them by the nape of their necks and put them into the sack, they utter a little squeak, and that is all. Descending from the tree, I take the rascals out of the bag and tie them with ropes, each to a separate tree. They immediately fall to playing, just as though nothing is about to happen, and when I pick them up in my arms, they cuddle up together, like two balls of cotton, as confidently as can be.

Here in my possession I have the makings of a splendid dinner, and that is not to be denied. Furthermore I am extremely hungry, so — I take the two bear cubs each by the nape of the neck and carry them over to the place where their mother's tracks disappear into the forest. Two little bear rumps bounding off through the brush are the last I ever see of them. — Those trustful little eyes, devil take them!

All right, but I am determined to have a drop of tea, in any event. The fire blazes up. I sit there lost in thought, waiting for the water to boil, when the shooting begins. It comes from the center of the flames, shot after shot, like the fire from a machine-gun. I dance off into the brush, busily feeling of myself to see if I have been wounded anywhere. I escape with the scare of my life, but that is bad enough. The loose bullets I had left in the sack with the beaver carcass had completely escaped my mind. They had quite naturally been strewn about on the ground when the bear was rummaging through the sack. And so a poor tired fellow couldn't even get a hot cup of tea into his stomach, just on account of those good-for-nothing bears. . . .

. .

One evening along toward the end of May, I am sitting in front of my fire and am busily at work skinning a beaver when I hear the clamor of dogs. I look about in surprise and whom should I see in the distance but Dale tramping along the shore of the lake, a procession of dogs waddling along behind him. Trofast is the first to catch sight of me. With a total disregard for the pack on his back, he comes racing through thicket and underbrush, jumps all over me, and almost knocks me down, so glad to see me he seems.

Dale greets me as casually as though we had parted but yesterday. Up until recently he had been out beaver-hunting with the Indian, Souzi, in the territory around Wolf Lake. They had fared well, tramping and trotting from one end of their country to the other, and, for the most part, had had plenty of food to eat. In addition to beaver they had taken bear and a half-dozen caribou. Dale has every reason in the world to feel contented. They had followed the old Indian custom governing two hunters when in partnership, of allowing each man ownership of every other beaver-skin which is taken, regardless of which man shoots the game, and it just so happened that Dale had all the larger skins in his bag.

For all practical purposes, they had exhausted the possibilities of the beaver country in which they were operating and had therefore parted company. Souzi had returned to his people on Great Slave Lake, Dale heading for my part of the country. The merest chance would be all that might guide his footsteps to a place from where he could see the smoke from my camp, but Dale always did have luck on his side. Our thought now was to make one last grand excursion together, during these last few weeks before the beaver season should be over.

There is a story which is told about a group of Indians belonging to the Caribou-Eater tribe. Late one autumn they were making a long journey and had reached the shores of a lake famous amongst the natives for the wealth of fishing it provided. They pitched their camp there and cast out their nets, but their luck was such that they did not catch even a single fish. Their hunters went out seeking caribou, but came upon no game. Soon they became so weakened by hunger that they were unable to leave their tepees. Each morning the nets were put out, but never a fish was caught. One by one the Indians all starved to death. At length none were left save one old squaw. The first time she paddled out to haul in the nets, she found them so chock-full of fish that she could hardly pull them ashore. This situation repeated itself day after day. The squaw's life was saved, and it is said that this very day she is alive and living in Fitzgerald.

All who have depended upon the Far North for their living have at one time or another stood face to face with the country's malevolent aspect. And when such a condition presents itself, the hunter can do no more than fight a hopeless battle. No matter how experienced he may be, no matter where he may turn his hand, the result is the same. Everything is doomed to failure. A curse rests upon his gun. Then suddenly and quite inexplicably the curse may lift and the country literally heap its bounties upon the erstwhile unfortunate hunter.

Ill luck dogs our footsteps from the very day that Dale and I set out together. We tramp westward through the forest for days and days before we stumble at length upon a beaver-lodge. At twilight we begin our watch, each in his own hiding-place. As I lie there staring out over the water, I suddenly hear Dale shout from behind his screen: " Kill that otter! " In a few moments the bullet-shaped head of an otter bobs up from the water a short way out. I fire and miss. Then, just before dark, the old beaver puts in his appearance. Dale wounds him sorely, but he dives and gets away. Evening after evening we lie at our posts, but the animals are wary and keep out of sight.

So we move on. We have come to the end of our grub, but we do not take this condition too seriously, believing that even should we fail to bag a beaver in short order, we should at least be able to shoot a duck or a muskrat or some other kind of game with flesh on its bones. But all living things seem to shun us. At length we come upon a tiny lake where some young pike are hovering with their heads in the reeds. We shoot two. The impact of the bullet striking the surface of the water stuns them and they float belly upward to the top. Some days later we bag a muskrat, which we carefully divide by cutting down the middle of its spine, each roasting his half on a spit before the fire.

The dogs give us no end of trouble. As usual when they are hungry, they become imbued with hunting-fever. Each time we cross the trail of either bear or moose, they do their best to break away. That means a good stiff run in order to capture them before their packs are swept from their backs. In those packs are our woolen blankets, our ammunition, and our beaver-skins!

One evening all the dogs suddenly go piling into a thicket, where they kick up a terrific rumpus. Soon Nigger returns in a most deplorable condition. He has been trying another fall with Porky, naturally. So it falls to our lot to hog-tie the dog and spend the better part of the night operating upon him with the pliers to remove the quills, in spite of his painful howling. Still, we couldn't complain, for the porcupine gave up its life for our subsistence. As a matter of fact, it provided us with more meat than we had seen in quite some time.

After a long hunt we at last find another beaver-house. But it is too late; the animals have left home, to go off on their usual long spring journey. In the meantime I succeed one evening in bringing down a loon. It tastes of oil and is as tough as wolf meat. And now the last straw: our tobacco supply gives out! Then the thought of a good smoke seems doubly alluring. We help ourselves out of this dilemma as best we can, Indian-fashion. First we try the leaves of a small plant with red berries, very likely the same weed which farther west goes under the name of *cannicannick*. The Slave Indians make from it a tea which has a fairly pleasant taste. As tobacco it gives us but slight pleasure, and we shift to a better brand: the inner bark of the willow.

There is little to be gained from continuing any farther into the wilds. It is so late in the spring that the beaver season is well over and neither of us feels any further urge to explore the unknown. Our only thought now is of food. The possibilities of running into game lie farther south in the valley through which we have come, and we both agree to go back. We are both rather ill and weak in the knees. And the mosquito, now giving vent to the full music in his soul, does little to improve our humor.

After two nights of forced marching we arrive early in the morning on the banks of the Hare River. It is now three days since we have eaten and the amount of food we had put under our belts before that was nothing to put fat on our bones. Instead of creeping into our sleeping-bags, we decide to use up our last energy in an intensive hunt for game. We make ourselves a pot of tea, tie up the dogs, and set out, each in a different direction. Dale takes the west side of the river, I the east. We are now concerned with one thing, and one thing only: to bring in something to eat — duck, muskrat, porcupine, field-mouse, sparrow, whatever we can find to shoot.

With my finger on the trigger I stealthily creep through the underbrush. From the crest of a hill I catch sight of a pair of ducks swimming in a tarn. I take no chances, but lie down flat on my belly and crawl noiselessly forward inch by inch, through brambles and over muskegs. When at length I view the pool again, the ducks have flown.

Then I proceed into a beautiful stretch of country, rounded birch-clad hills alternating with tiny lakes fringed with luxuriant green tapestries of rat-grass. Surely there must be at least *one* muskrat in all this country which, it would seem, was created simply as a paradise for his kind. Ah, there comes one, swimming! I attempt to call it in my direction, but it declines to evidence the slightest interest in the sounds I make, and I am obliged to try a shot at long range. I must so aim the bullet that it will strike the animal right on the tip of the nose, thus glancing off without tearing a single rift in the pelt! Three times I blaze away. The rat swims unconcernedly on its way toward a little stream, where I can expect at any moment to see it lift up its rump and dive down into its hole. Mad clear through, I let it have a shot right in the small of the back. The result of this is more or less complete disintegration. Carefully I pick up a fore-leg, a hind-leg, and a few scraps of flesh and fur. A most disheartening conclusion to the hunt, but, after all, a mouthful to chew on for dinner, I think to myself, as I stuff my game into the bag.

It appears as though, on the other side of a birch-clad hill, there might be another lake. Sure enough; I can already glimpse it shining through the trees and am just on the point of emerging from the woods when — the unbelievable takes place! A moose heaves in sight across the lake, runs out across a stretch of muskeg, and halts to sniff the air. What a mountain of edible flesh!

At such long range I aim too low and succeed only in wounding the moose in one of its front legs. With that, it swings round and begins limping back toward the woods. It is just at this point that a fuzzy white shape darts from

[114]

the woods and, before my very eyes, hurls itself upon the beast. I stare in utter amazement, until I suddenly recognize the familiar yelping of Trofast. Heavens, what a dog! He had probably thought to himself that we couldn't hope to do much hunting without him! So he had slipped his collar, a trick he can accomplish whenever he has a fit of hunting-fever, regardless of how tightly it fits. And here he is now, successful in running down his game and driving the moose straight in my direction.

Many a time have I seen moose and dog come to blows, but never before a battle so desperately waged as this one. Trofast is everywhere. Like a wolf, he lunges in at his adversary, first from the front, then from the rear. Now he is crouching on his fore-paws right in front of the moose, barking and doing his best to tantalize it; he escapes the hoofs and antlers of the other by a mere fraction of a second. The moose sees red, feels the pain in its leg, and is out for murder. With head bent low and stiff staring eyes it stands waiting for an opening, then limps in the direction of the dog. Like a sledge-hammer whizzing through the air, that wounded leg flies out at the dog. Mud from the marsh splashes up where it lands. Round and round they go.

I approach to within a short distance, neither of the combatants paying the slightest heed to me. At this point I deliver the *coup de grâce*. At the very moment the moose topples over, Trofast pounces upon its rump with a snarl and begins wrestling to make it lie still. He is more eager than cautious, however, for the moose is still kicking, and it is not long before Trofast is sailing high and far through the air. He crawls to his feet again and returns, limping stiffly. This time, to be on the safe side, Trofast stations himself high up on the belly of the moose. Ah, there is a dog who can well feel proud of himself!

Now I must make some effort to get hold of Dale. I set off in the direction of the river, shouting at the top of my lungs. All at once he breaks from the woods and comes running as fast as he can in my direction, his finger on the trigger. " What's up? " he calls from a distance. " Just shot a moose," I reply. " Oh, well," he says dryly. " I thought the bear had got you."

The fact of the matter was that Dale had just been look-ing for some bear cubs he had heard squeaking up in a spruce-tree when he heard my wild shouts. There had been no doubt in his mind whatever but that the she-bear had got her dander up and was venting her spite upon me. . . .

We remained at the place where I brought down the moose, for four days, simply gorging ourselves with meat. Meanwhile we fleshed and dried the moose hide and laid in a large store of dried meat. When we struck camp and set our course back in the direction of Slave Lake, both we and our dogs had tremendous burdens to carry. But moose meat makes one *nat-seri* (strong), as the Indians say, and when a man has a full belly, he has a different outlook upon life. . . .

Summer on Great Slave Lake

THE LARGE LAKES ARE STILL FROZEN OVER, BUT EVEN THE Barrens have lost their covering of snow. South in the forests the brooks are murmuring gentle summery songs as they wind through the woodland grasses, where only an occasional patch of snow gleams white. The spring thaw is over and the first swarms of mosquitoes are humming at the edge of each wood.

Busy indeed is Snowdrift, the easternmost trading post on Great Slave Lake. Every day new people arrive. One by one the sleds appear like black specks far out on the ice. They say they have come great distances; some from Artillery Lake, others from the head waters of the Coppermine River, a few all the way from the Great Fish River in the heart of the Arctic region. And there are those who came south earlier in the spring and are now returning from the beaver-hunt. Throughout a long winter most of these people have seen nothing of each other. Distances have been too great. Now and then one or another of them might have chanced to cross the trail of a sled up there on the Arctic plain and paused to wonder who had passed there before them. Occasionally, too, a pair of hunters might have actually met in the wilderness. But the chances of this are as remote as the chances of two ships far off in unfrequented seas crossing each other's bows.

[117]

However, everything will be otherwise now. The great loneliness and the bitter struggle for existence in lands of snow and ice are over. The light summer months are at hand, the days when man meets man and time passes with feverish gladness there on the shores of Great Slave Lake. A life of hearty good-fellowship prevails amongst these travelers from distant parts. Those who have already arrived at the post assemble in groups to stare out over the ice whenever a dog-train appears in the distance. And those who splash along behind their sleds out there feel a tingle of expectancy, for there is nothing like returning from the winter's hunt.

The Indian sleds frequently arrive with whole families. The long squaw-boats left behind at the upper end of the lake last autumn are now on runners, held in place by a kind of chassis. The boats are filled to capacity with tepees, pelts, bundles of dried meat, and large balls of melted deer-fat tied up in stiff, partially tanned caribou hides. Directly behind the sled comes the hunter himself. He is walking along on snowshoes, keeps cracking his whip and screeching at his dogs. After him marches his squaw, stout and self-reliant, and in her wake a queue of youngsters of all editions. The only redskin allowed to ride on the load is the youngest member of the family, who is just one winter old.and has not yet learned the use of snowshoes. Quite contentedly he sits there tied up in a caribou-skin in the stern of the canoe, experiencing his first long journey by sled.

All are clad in gala attire. The hunter has donned his one white shirt and his red neckerchief, which he has been saving all winter long for this very occasion. His caribou coat has been newly edged with wolverine fur, and he is wearing a brand-new pair of deerskin moccasins and a pair of finger mitts embroidered with red and blue flowers. The women, on their side, are wearing their best dresses, dark skirts heavily decorated at the hem, and over their heads dark shawls with long fringes. All the dogs are wearing bells; over their backs are embroidered leather blankets and from their collars wave the bushy tails of wolf and Arctic fox.

When the sled swings in round the point to the trading post, where a curious crowd has assembled, the great moment has arrived. Then the whips crack out like pistol-shots to excite the dogs, and with a jingling of bells and a waving of wolf plumes the party pulls in at a merry trot. Many questions are asked of the traveler who arrives from distant parts.

The white trappers are the last to appear. They remain out until the very end of the hunting season. For the most part they arrive in pairs, but there are some lone hands as well, who for a whole year have maintained themselves out on the Barrens with their dogs as their sole companions. All proceed as fast as they can and keep going for long hours at a stretch. The trappers who are slack on furs carry their canoes back with them bottom up on the load in order to have them next autumn when the time comes for them again to fare forth into the north. The lucky ones who have white-fox- and wolf-skins piled up so high that the sled itself is hardly visible can afford to leave their craft behind in the wilderness. Beside river and lake all through the wilds lies many a canoe bottom up, bearing mute witness to the fact that thus far have white men penetrated.

Altogether there are only about eight or ten white trappers who find their way to the post at Snowdrift. First, as usual, comes " Lone Wolf " Claeson. He has earned his nickname because he always goes out alone and because he is more eager to vanquish the wolf than any other man up north. This year he brings in some two hundred skins. Last year it was a hundred and sixty. No one knows where he goes to get hold of so many of these animals, for this is Lone Wolf's secret. He is a square-shouldered, sinewy chap, a perfect Northland type, a powerful friend and a dangerous enemy.

A little later the other white trappers arrive: "Mac," who is fifty-four years old, hilarious Bablet, and Klondike Bill, who has passed the sixty-five-year mark and is the only one upon whom the years have begun to tell, though he flatly refuses to admit it. Then comes the Swedish-Canadian, Joe Nelson, whizzing along behind his dashing dog-team. He is one of the most energetic hunters in these parts and this year has penetrated farther north beyond the timber-line than any other. He is grimy and as thin as a rail, but he smiles contentedly, for with the skins of wolf and white fox piled high on his sled, all is well with the world.

Open water has appeared off to the south and the ice of Great Slave Lake rocks and sways beneath their sleds when Price and Clark find their way in. Price is the strongest man in these parts. He can pick up a twenty-foot canoe and carry it on his shoulders as he would a toy. Clark is a small, wiry fellow, hot-headed and unafraid. It is in the middle of the night, as I lie sleeping in my tent, that I am awakened by a terrible commotion out on the ice. I run down to the lake, and there I see two dog-teams swimming in across the open water inshore as fast as they can paddle their legs. Two men are hanging fast to their sleds. They scramble ashore, shake the water from their clothes, calmly turn to me, and say: "How are you?" just as though it were the most natural thing in the world for them to come swimming in to the trading post from an ice-floe in the middle of the night. It is Price and Clark.

The white trappers are not dressed up in their choicest finery, as are the Indians. The stamp of the wilderness is still upon them. Their faces are covered with a heavy growth of beard, and their trousers are adorned in the rear with many a canvas patch. Arrival at the trading post means that a year of toil is over and the time for pleasure at hand. Then the razors come out, the blue trousers and the white shirts, for there is no feeling quite so grand as to loaf about in the sunshine, like a new man.

Happy days are now at hand for the white men's dogs, as well. And truly have they earned their reward. Early and late they have strained in the traces and, were one to reckon it out later, they have hauled their sleds many thousands of miles during the course of a long winter. There have been short rations for them on many occasions, there have been times when they were obliged to struggle onward until they had the taste of blood in their mouths, but, regardless, they have hopped up in the morning and stood there shivering with the cold as ice-caked harnesses were strapped on, ever ready to continue their labors. Then, when warm weather returned, they suffered from the other extreme: their winter pelage made the heat of their own bodies almost intolerable to them. And the glittering reflection of the sun on the snow stabbed at their eyes like sharp needles, and some of the poor beasts became snow-blind. But their days of toil are over now, and the dogs all know it. Now they may gorge themselves on fish, sleep, and absorb the summer sunshine. . . . But for the dogs of the Indians it is otherwise: their bitter months of starvation have set in.

The peace of early summer dwells over Snowdrift. On

the slope of a hill facing Slave Lake stands the Hudson's Bay Company's trading store. Its brown log walls are steaming with warmth. On the steps in front sit a group of men, smoking and gaping at the sun. The factors are running in and out, each doing enough work for ten men and a boy. Farther up the slope, behind the store, gleams a white cluster of tepees in amongst the spruces. The tent-flaps are drawn to one side in order to admit the sun. On the floor sits the squaw, at work, surrounded by a tangle of untidy brats, whilst the master of the house lies smoking or sleeping, on a caribou robe off in one corner. Outside their lodges the Indians have erected tall scaffolds of poles where great slabs of caribou meat hang in rows, drying in the sun. Dogs are everywhere. One stumbles over ravenous, emaciated dogs wherever one attempts to walk. Some lie baking themselves in the sun, their legs stiffly extended; others skulk about amongst the lodges in search of something they can steal. When the opportunity presents itself, they dart like lightning into some tepee and do their utmost to dig out something to eat. Then the squaw is after them with a snowshoe, dishes, or whatever she can lay her hands on, and with much yelping and howling they beat a rapid retreat.

Smoke rises in lusty billows from countless crooked chimneys and from the open smoke-holes of the tepees. But far off into the distance Great Slave Lake stretches like a dazzling white tapestry studded with spruce-clad islands. . . .

. .

To see white faces and to hear the speech of white men again is a grand experience for all of us trappers whom

fate has assembled here in this outermost trading post on
Great Slave Lake. Not only for them who have lived alone
with their dogs, but to an equal extent for those who have
been out in partnership. The latter have sat alone together
so many evenings that they know all about each other. But
here are other men with other thoughts, men whose words
are pleasant to hear when they deal with all the various experiences they have been through in their lives. They tend
to broaden one's outlook.

We are a little fraternity of nine white men of five separate nationalities. Not one of us knows much about the
other eight. Once in a great while when men meet in a tent
or beside a camp-fire on a long winter's evening and the
sighing of the wilderness gets into their blood, giving rise
to a spirit of confidence, it may happen that a man may
open up. At such times it is a relief to talk oneself out. But
on all other occasions a man's past is as a sealed book, respected by one and all. In the Northland a man begins a
brand-new life. He is taken for exactly what he is worth,
and not one of his personal affairs concerns anyone else in
the world.

But during the course of conversation it cannot be denied that now and then an ever-so-little opening may occur
in a man's speech through which one catches a fleeting
glimpse of his past. Thus do I know that Mac, during the
glamorous Wild West days, made his living as a cowboy
down in the States. That he spent most of his life in the
saddle is self-apparent, for he is so bow-legged that it is
quite amusing to see him waddle along on snowshoes behind his sled. Klondike Bill is an old-timer from the
Yukon. He was in the gold-rush of '98, made his bonanza,
and squandered the whole of it. Since then he has combined fur-hunting with gold-digging. He has been every-

where. He has tramped behind dog-trains over the Lord
knows how many miles, and the Northland has engraved a
map of itself in the furrows and wrinkles of his face. For
forty years he has been roaming the North and he is still
as poor as ever, and just as happy-go-lucky — as certain
as can be that somewhere deep in the wilderness a new
bonanza awaits him.

But there is one chap about whom I know absolutely
nothing, for he is taciturn and careful of every word that
he utters. Well, if he has something he wishes to conceal,
that is his affair, not mine.

In spite of the fact that we differ in many respects, the
country seems to bind us together. The first matter to engage our joint attention is the preparation of a banquet. It
shall be the feast of all the feasts we have longed for during the entire year past. We assemble in a little cabin
which has been standing here for many a year. It is built
of heavy timbers and has withstood many a blow. And so
we hold a proper banquet, the merry-making and story-
telling continuing well on into the night.

These people are not so much interested in hunting for
its own sake as for the sake of the free and rugged life in
the wilds it entails. The words falling from their lips are
possibly dull and commonplace, but behind them echoes
a deeper note, the note of adventure. It sounds a tonality all
its own in the speech of these men of the Northland.

We relate of the things we have seen whilst roaming our
own part of the country. One has discovered a new river,
another a new lake which takes a man a whole day to
cross. A third has stumbled upon a little hollow in which
small stunted spruces are growing, far north in the Barren
Lands. But he is shrewd enough to refrain from mentioning its exact location, for wood is worth its weight in gold

out there on the Arctic prairie where a man must haul fuel long distances north by sled. But we take rivers, lakes, and mountain chains and patch them together into a map. A day's journey by dog-sled — about thirty-five miles — is our unit of distance, and that is good enough.

There are many things which happen during the course of a year when one lives face to face with the wilderness and must rely entirely upon his dogs and his gun. The first matter of interest is the caribou, for they represent food. We have all encountered them, have seen the herds streaming out across the country, beneath a forest of ant-lers; we have all gorged ourselves on their flesh, haunted by the possibility of a day when the country would be empty of them, and the cold press in upon us and squeeze the life from our wretched bodies. We piece our recollections together and build for ourselves a picture of the caribou and its migrations, but we never succeed in discovering the first clue to the solution of the riddle of this mysterious animal.

Klondike Bill tells us about the time he was almost trampled underfoot by a herd of many thousand caribou. He had to crouch behind his sled, he said, whilst the herd, terrified by wolves, rushed by on every side. Joe had a hand-to-hand encounter with wolves up in the vicinity of the Coppermine River and escaped by the skin of his teeth. Bablet relates how once he was on the point of losing his dogs up on the Barrens — the very worst situation which could have confronted him. They were just making off with the sled in chase of a band of caribou, and Bablet had had no other choice but to shoot his train-leader. "The best dog that ever worked in the traces," he concludes. We others are not so willing to take his word on the latter point, however, for what trapper will ever admit that any but his own are the best dogs in the land? And woe be unto the man who, by innuendo or otherwise, dares to belittle them! Such is even worse than to mention to a man his wife's imperfections! A trapper may curse at his dogs and flog them unmercifully, but he always stands ready to do battle for them.

Price has had a tough time of it during the latter part of the winter. He was on a long journey east when the caribou vanished completely. The dogs starved and one of them — one of the most powerful beasts I have ever seen — began to get nasty. A primitive struggle for supremacy developed between dog and man. The dog was harnessed at the time, but it had become so wild and violent that it dragged the rest of the team with it when it decided to launch a lunging, snapping attack. At length, hopping up on the sled, it continued to give battle from there. Price conquered after a time, but it was a victory dearly won, and he would rather have fought with a grizzly bear, he says. Later, on that same journey, he became snow-blind, was taken so whilst he was off looking to one of his traps and had to feel his way back over his own tracks in the snow in order to find his dogs. "Wasn't much fun," he adds dryly.

But, just the same, the one who had had the toughest time of all was certainly old Klondike Bill. Last autumn he had set off into the country with five big strapping dogs, and this spring he returned with but two. The other three he had eaten about Christmas time when he was starving on the shores of Kasba Lake. We all know of the affair, but it is a matter which no one ever mentions.

" Have you seen Blacky or Hornby? " That is the question whenever several trappers get together. Two years ago they had set out for the Barren Lands, each in a different direction, Hornby [1] in the company of two young Englishmen. That was the last that had ever been heard from them.

From Bablet we learned the fate of the former. Never again will the hearty, intrepid Blacky swing up in front of the trading post behind his dog-team. He starved to death. . . . At first he was in the company of two other white trappers. They became lost, ran out of provisions, and were about done for when a party of Indians discovered them and helped them down to Snowdrift. The others took it easy for the remainder of the winter, but not so with Blacky. On his way out he had come across a region infested with martens. He wanted to return to that district, even though he was no more than skin and bones, and had been badly frozen into the bargain. The Indians found him, and Bablet, upon hearing of this, set out at once to look for him. On the bank of a little stream he came across a tent. Outside on the ground lay a skeleton and a few bones gnawed by dogs. . . . It was said that Blacky wished it thus, because of a woman. Possibly. But according to his own diary, he had waged a tough battle against cold and starvation, had struggled until he dropped; and it is this fact that brings him to mind.

But of Hornby and his two companions, there is still no news. " He's probably done for, too," one declares. " If he was alive, you can bet your boots the Indians would have got wind of it, after all this time. Can't say as there's any reason to feel sorry for him, though; he sure knew what he was doing. Besides, he was figgerin' on dying up here in the North, and wasn't scared to, either. The real shame is about those English greenhorns that was with him."

[1] John Hornby, one of the most colorful adventurers of modern history. *Snow Man*, by Malcolm Waldron (Boston: Houghton Mifflin Company; 1931), is a story of his last two expeditions into the Barren Lands of northern Canada. — TRANSLATOR.

" It was bound to be like that. The country sooner or later does away with all these fellers that try to act tough," says Klondike Bill. " Hornby was a regular dare-devil. I've seen him set off down the meanest rapids in the Taltson River in a little birch-bark canoe. A feller that figgers on staying alive don't act like that. And there he goes, starting out on the Barrens like the devil was after him, without a proper equipment. Just think of that! Oh no, don't do to take any fool chances with this here country," old Klondike Bill concludes.

This calls forth a discussion of other events of a similar nature. There is mention of the man who died of scurvy in his cabin, with a whole pile of *The Saturday Evening Post* beside the bunk where he lay. " Read to forget his troubles and got just what he deserved, for he didn't even know enough to boil himself some spruce needles to put himself back on his feet," one of our group remarks.

Then there is the story of the man who had been found frozen to death in the forest. He was found kneeling in front of a pile of kindling-wood, with the matches right in his hand. He had been in the act of making a fire.

" How about that Finn and his partner that started down the Mackenzie some years ago? " I ask.

" They got good and tired of each other and began to scrap," answers Mac. " Then one of them took sick. He lay there in bed day in and day out and had a good chance to think his partner over. One night he shot him. Sent a bullet up through the bottom of the top bunk. Swell shot, right in the head. Later he made away with himself, but first he wrote a few lines in his diary."

" Saw McGraw awhile ago," says Clark. " I don't think he'll last long. He's been hanging out along up Wolf River way for years, and now he won't even talk to folks. Shuts himself up in his cabin whenever anyone comes his way."

" It'll turn out for him like it did for Bugs Christy," says Klondike Bill. " There was a crazy bat, all right. For years he used to go wandering around through the woods all by his lonesome, and you can't name a place he hadn't been to. He was batty enough to begin with, but he got battier all the time. Once he came paddling down the Slave River in a canoe he had made himself. It was built in three sections with partitions in between. What was that for? Oh, if one section got stove in, he could keep afloat with the other two! He sure thought that was a peach of an idea. Another time he put up a cabin on an island somewheres around Fort Resolution. But he left out the doors and windows. Instead, he left a hole in the roof and used to crawl up and down a ladder whenever he wanted to come in or go out. That was so's bears couldn't get inside! "

" Where is Greathouse this year? " asks Price.

" No one can keep track of that fellow," says Lone Wolf Claeson. " The older he gets, the faster he can travel on snowshoes. Now he's up near the Barrens, and, the next thing you know, he's hundreds of miles farther south in the woods. He's seventy years old now; by the time he's a hundred, he'll be downright dangerous. He's right gruff in his manner, but as good-natured as a bear at heart. You ought to see him when a band of Indians blow in and stop at his cabin! Then you'd see a circus for fair! 'What in hell do you fellows want? ' he says to greet them. ' Do you think I'm slaving and sweating around here just to feed lazy swine like you? Get out, you can't get a thing to eat here! ' The Indians calmly walk into the cabin and sit down on the floor. They know him! Greathouse scowls around at them, throws some wood on the fire in his stove, and gets ready to boil and fry up some food. He digs up some meat, storms around, rattling his pots and pans, and all the time muttering a line of mean talk. ' What the devil's got into you? ' he growls. ' Can't you leave a man in peace? Hard enough work hunting food for myself and the dogs. Then a lot of good-for-nothing sponges like you come around! No sir-ee! There's the door, now get out! That's all I've got to say. Go on and shoot your own caribou, for you can't get a bite to eat here, not so you'll notice it — heathens! ' Around on the floor the Indians continue to sit, smiling. Naturally, they don't comprehend a single word he says. ' You deserve to starve to death, the whole gang of you! ' Greathouse winds up, and then he dishes out the best that he's got in the house! "

" Montro wasn't down in Mackenzie last year, at his old place up the Nahanni River," puts in Price.

" Reckon not," says Claeson. " Slim Bein was there in his place. And he got about a hundred lynx, too. . . . Nahanni, yeah, that's some place! " he continues, and then he is off with a yarn of his own. " Spent a year there my-self, right near Dead Man's Valley. Rocky Mountains stick-ing straight up in the air, deep valleys, full of marten, lynx, gold, and hot springs. Saw deep layers of coal there, too. Once I found a hole carved right out of the face of a cliff. Steps cut into the rock led up to it, and there was a smoke-hole which went right up through to the top and from the inside looked just like a telescope. The floor was covered with mountain-goat dung. I should have looked around for flint and suchlike, but I was too busy. Could have made myself a fortune in Nahanni, as sure as you're alive. Fur-hunting — pfut! But gold! There wasn't a river where you couldn't see gold on the bottom, and it wouldn't have been any trick at all to wash out ten dollars a day. But there must be some place where there are *heaps* of it — a regular Klondike, somewhere there in the Rockies. If it only wan't for the Indians! They're worse in Nahanni than any place else; they think the white man will take their land away from them and make it harder than ever for them. You have to keep your finger on your trigger all the time you're up there, for you can never tell what may happen. Once three trappers were found shot dead in the woods. It was clear that the redskins were the ones who had pulled the trick, but what could be done about that? A heap of human bones found in the wilderness. Report it to the Mounties, who start investigating. They examine the bullet-hole in the skull, fold what's left of the hands over what's left of the breast, pat some dirt over the whole business — no evidence; finished! "

" No matter how you look at it, life up here in the North means a hell of a lot of work, and that business about gold, it's just like the rest of it," says Klondike Bill. " No, we ought to have it like other folks — regular chairs, good food, and cigars. Can't see how anybody can make it pay up here. . . . But there's nothing you can do about it. I've been out here in the country twenty years now, and I reckon I'll be mushin' dogs in these parts for the rest of my born days. And when the time comes for me to cash in my chips, it'll probably be somewheres near Slave Lake. Funny about that. . . . But, death and tarnation, if it wouldn't be slick to take a trip up to Edmonton before I forget the taste of whisky and what an honest-to-goodness skirt looks like! Eight years since the last time. — Yep, if I can stake a claim this winter, you bet that's what I'll take and do! "

" A regular skirt is all right compared with these brown old gypsy women; but you'd better not think of bringing one of them back up here with you, without first thinking something about a midwife. That's my advice to you. You know these woods have been right shy of midwives since Harry lit out for the Yukon." This is Mac's sage advice.

I ask what Harry had to do with it, and Mac relates the story:

" That was some years ago now. Harry and Dan and a Russian were traveling somewhere east of here. Dan had been foolish enough to take his wife along with him — a pretty little thing, too — not a day over nineteen. The three of them each built a cabin some distance apart from the others and started in trapping. Later on, during the winter, Dan's wife showed she was going to have a baby. That was as clear as could be. What the devil was he going to do? There was his wife in the very midst of the primeval forest. Well, he let things drag along and didn't know how badly he was off until one day it got right bad with his wife. With that, he jumps into his canoe and paddles over to Harry's place. He talked a lot of wild talk, which wasn't to be wondered at. But Harry simply says: ' All right,' slings some food to his dogs, and goes back with Dan. And then, without batting an eye, he ups and delivers her kid. It was a boy. It wasn't so easy for the mother, as you can imagine, but later on she was so crazy with gratitude that she was ready to fall on Harry's neck every time she saw him. . . . Now, it isn't everyone who, on a moment's notice, can throw down his gun and go on duty as a midwife. But, you see, Harry always was a mighty handy fellow with his mitts. . . ."

Thus the gossip of the country is spread. Some bits we learn first-hand, others have passed through many mouths. Whether an event takes place in the vicinity of Lake Athabaska or north near the Mackenzie delta, a thousand miles away, it is no time at all before the news of it has spread through the length and breadth of the land.

After discussing one thing after another, we turn to the one serious problem which confronts each one of us: into which part of the wilderness shall we venture next? We figure this out for one or perhaps for several years in advance. Time has no value up north. The days flow past in a steady stream and one sails along with them, unheeding. A winter passes before one fully realizes it, and, before one knows it, one is busy preparing for the next.

We all have our plans. " To the far end "; that is the motto for most of us. We dream of fields unknown, where it is possible to drift in a canoe into the very heart of some vague fairyland where the caribou graze and where the plains are swarming with wolves and white foxes. . . . We know what the hard bitter reality is like, and appreciate the danger of dreaming. But even old Klondike Bill, who is surely the sagest man amongst us, cannot refrain from letting his fancy roam now and then as he sits there puffing on his pipe, a far-away look in his eyes. — " Damn funny how we're always anxious to get to lands *beyond,* even though there are other places just as good," we hear him mutter. He hits the nail on the head.

As the hours pass by, the mood of the party changes. Mac walks to the center of the floor and, in spite of his bow-legs, begins dancing a jig which would do credit to a youth of twenty. Then Bablet bursts into song. He knows hundreds of ballads which he has picked up in the four corners of the globe. And when it comes to yodeling, it is hard to find his equal.

Our spirits mount with each song and are at their highest pitch when we all join in singing the favorite song of the North:

There's a Husky,[1] dusky maiden in the Arctic,
In her igloo she waits for me in vain.
Some day I'll put my mukluks [2] on and ask her
If she'll wed me when the ice-worms nest again.

Refrain. In the land of pale-blue snow,
When it's ninety-nine below,
And the polar bear is roaming o'er the plain,
In the shadow of the Pole,
I'll clasp her to my soul,
Then we'll be happy when the ice-worms nest again.

And our wedding feast will be of oil and blubber,
In our kayaks we'll roam the bounding main;
When the walrus turn their heads to rubber,
We'll be happy when the ice-worms nest again.

Refrain. In the land of pale-blue snow, *etc.*

Other verses are unprintable.

Any other things which may happen when a handful of fur-trappers get together for a party in the wilderness of northern Canada are not for the knowledge of others. The Indians make excellent neighbors, for whatever may leak out during the light summer night is a secret safe with them. . . .

The caribou bucks are making for the north. In bands, both large and small, they are strolling soberly along over the lakes and in through the forests.

All the tents are so pitched that they command a splendid view of the whole broad expanse of the lake. To the south there is a narrow sound, separating an island from the mainland. Through this passage lies the route of the migration, and when the wind is behind them, the animals

[1] Eskimo. [2] Sealskin boots.

make straight in the direction of the trading post, whence hosts of sleds go speeding out to meet them. It is always a race to see which hunter will be first to reach the herd. The Indians stand in the stern of their toboggans, screeching and shouting at their dogs and shooting off their guns in the air in order to excite them further. The bucks whirl about in their tracks, and the chase is on; far out over the lake it continues, until sleds and fleeing beasts are no more than tiny dots on the horizon.

We whites have but a slim chance at the game, for all day long the old squaws sit in their tepees and keep a hawk-like watch. As soon as the caribou are in sight, a sign is given to the hunters, whose dogs lie, for the most part, fully harnessed. It is also a dubious pleasure to go hunting in close community with twenty other toboggans, with the Indians firing from all sides.

This is the season when the natives feast themselves on the newly sprouting horns of the deer. In velvet, they are but a few inches long and are covered with a pale green hairy skin. Lodged in the throat of each animal is a handful of insect larvæ. In olden times these constituted a great delicacy for the Indians, but today, as soon as the animal is slain, these grubs are dug out and thrown aside. Nor are the hides worth tanning at this season of the year. They are full of holes caused by bots or warbles.[1]

The last of the herd has passed. The sun is eating through the ice. Soon it is a carpet of sharp-pointed needles which bring blood to the paws of the dogs. All the dogs must then be shod with moccasins. Along shore there are wide lagoons of open water, and out near the solid ice there floats a thick slush of pulverized crystals. The floes

---

[1] The larvæ of the gad-fly, inch-long grubs which hatch in the flesh beneath the skin and eventually eat their way through and fall out on the ground. — TRANSLATOR.

begin to shift with the wind. Soon they are gliding off toward the west and we can see them like a white strip across the horizon. Then we hastily set our nets. But the wind soon changes, and that white expanse comes creeping back in our direction. Now we must shove off in our canoes and rescue the nets as quickly as possible, for the ice-blocks are piling up; they sweep everything before them as they crash with tremendous force against the shore. There the vast sheets of ice break up, and from that moving rampart, down its entire length, loose ice is precipitated in glittering cataracts with a sound as of jingling bells.

This year there are two fur-traders in Snowdrift. From the very first, their stores are packed to the doors with Indians. Some are leaning over the counters, others are lying down on the floor, with sacks under their heads. Otter-, fox-, beaver-, marten-, mink-, and muskrat-skins find their way over the counter until there is a mighty mound of pelts. In front of each Indian there collects an ever-mounting pile of conglomerate trash and fripperies, until the last skin has been handed over. Whatever they may chance to desire *must* be theirs; otherwise they will tear up the store and make away with its entire contents. Autumn is still far distant, but no red hunter ever stops for an instant to think that he may be flat broke when the time comes for him to buy his winter gear. It is summer now, and a checkered shirt he must have, and red silk handkerchiefs he must have, and candied fruits and a huge pile of sugar he must have, as well. Later on he will somehow find a way.

Privately there exists a perfect understanding between the two factors, but when it comes to business, they sing a different tune. Then each must do his best to attract the best of the hunters to his store, and indeed this is a difficult game of poker to play. They are forever watching each other out of the corners of their eyes. They are as jealous as small-town blacksmiths.

One evening I am helping one of the factors to press and pack up the skins he has taken in. Pelts of all varieties are laid one on top of the other in a kind of grill-work packing-case, covered at the top with a few boards. I crawl up on top, dance and hop around up there, as the factor binds it together with ropes. We have in all eight huge bales of pelts, weighing some 135 pounds apiece. We must now carry them down from the warehouse to the store, the only place where it is dry enough to keep them.

Before we start moving them, we pause to wipe the sweat from our brows and to have a little smoke. " You've certainly got enough skins," I say. But the factor shakes his head sadly. " Two bales less than the other fellow over there," he says, mournfully pointing in the direction of his competitor's cabin. " All next winter he'll never let up talking about how he had two bales more than I did, and what a clever business man he is." I object that it isn't necessary for our competitor to know how many bales we have, but the factor answers despondently: " He's been told that already. He knows that at this very moment we are working with the skins and that we are all ready to lug them over to the store. He'll keep an eye on us, his wife will keep an eye on us, even his kids will keep an eye on us. There won't be any mistake about the count. Just look there now! "

I peep out the door in the direction of our competitor's place. There I catch sight of a cluster of faces, their noses flattened against the window pane. A whole family of fur-traders, neatly framed behind the glass.

A feeling of compassion for the broken-hearted factor comes over me at once. With him I have undertaken a piece of work and I must see it through to an honorable finish. But how? Then I have a grand idea, the same which, in his day, gained for Tordenskiold [1] both honor and acclaim. " Listen," I say. " What if we were to carry some of these bales out across the yard *twice,* first over to the store, then out the back way, over here again, and back over to the store? There's nobody outside and our trick can't be observed from the window where they all are."

The trader's face lights up. So we put on the most innocent expressions our faces can command, and lug bales till our shoulders ache.

Never before had so many bundles of skins found their way into a trading store in Snowdrift. There were at least fifteen before we had finished. I insisted that we keep at it until the count stood at thirty, but when the factor asserted that there weren't that many skins to be found throughout the Slave Lake territory, I was obliged to give in.

After this coup on our part, it was remarkable how meek our competitor appeared when the number of pelts for the year later came under discussion. Yes, he was even downright retiring, and that was not at all like him. . . .

. .

Drum-beats in the air. Day and night their monotonous rhythm sounds out over the lake.

" Might as well take a trip over and have a look at that foxtrot of theirs," says Price, " for, with that racket going on in our ears, we won't be able to get a wink of sleep anyhow." We hop into a canoe and paddle over to the In-

[1] Peder Tordenskiold (1690–1720), Norwegian-Danish naval hero of the Great Northern War. In 1716, by a clever ruse, he defeated a Swedish fleet outnumbering his own ships six to one. — TRANSLATOR.

dians' camp, which has recently been moved some distance
farther away from the trading post.

Quietly we glide along through the light summer night
and arrive in a little cove where, at the edge of the woods,
tepees are pitched in serried ranks. Bordering the water is
a chalky white beach, strewn with upturned canoes. A
mighty fire is roaring on the beach, and clouds of sparks
blow out across the water.

Two of the largest tepees have been turned into one and
are literally packed with Indians in gala attire. It is here
that the dance is in progress. The elders bid us welcome
and seem to be highly flattered by our visit. We are shown
to a place at the door. Inside, crowds are packed against the
walls of the tent. The center of the floor is deserted, for
a dance is just about to begin.

Two Indian boys cut loose upon the tomtom, a caribou-
skin stretched tightly over a frame of bent willow; to this
accompaniment they begin singing a wild and plaintive
song. The crowd becomes animated at once as the rhythm
takes effect. One hunter leaps to the center of the floor and
begins the dance with short staccato steps, round and
round, with bended knee and arching foot. Others of the
men join in until there are four dancers in all, circling
around the tent.

Then each catches hold of a lady, and, with that, all
burst forth into song, forming a close ring and moving
about in a slow rhythm. Each dance calls forth an exchange
of presents, which most of the dancers hold between them
as they move around. It may be a muskrat-skin, or a ragged
woolen coat, or a pair of moccasins, or a pipe which fat
old women, weather-beaten hunters, young boys, or young
girls — whoever the dancers may be — clutch tightly between them as they go tramping around with the most

serious expression in the world upon their faces. At various intervals the chain is broken and the men swing up to their partners with rapid sliding steps. Meanwhile the song continues mechanically, monotonously over the steady beating of the drum, until the refrain — "*Hi-hi-he, hi-hi-he-ho, hi-yi!*" — is reached, when it is roared forth in a shrill discord.

Round and round, almost endlessly, it seems, the circle moves. It is suffocating there in the tent, the dancers puff and snort, and an odor of damp clothes permeates the air. But the Indians never seem to grow weary. Rhythm seems to be a part of them, and the sound of the tomtom awakens their more primitive instincts. Off in the corner sit the aged who are too weak to join in, but they slap their thighs in time with the drum-beats and nod their heads approvingly. Between dances the young drummers race down to the fire, where they squat, warming up the tomtom. Returning, they cut loose again.

Marlo, the chief, comes over to us. "*Téotenny dol-thli hata sentilly* (It will be all right for the white man to dance)," he says. So each of us in turn makes an attempt at it, to the intense amusement of those who remain to look on. But it is no laughing matter for the one who is in the heat of it; he tries to appear unconcerned as he prances about with his Indian girl, but he makes a poor job of it, as the sweat streams from his face. In short, our primitive pleasure in this dance of nature soon wears off, and it is not long before we have all had enough of it — that is, all save old Klondike Bill.

He has been through thick and thin in his day, but this is the first time he has ever taken an active part in a native tepee-dance as it is performed by these eastern tribes, though, judging by appearances, it will not be the last. He

has entered it heart and soul. At one moment he is swinging up with a girl of fifteen, the next he is shuffling along
with her grandmother.

It is a side-splitting farce to see that big awkward fellow
stumbling about the floor, his face beaming with pleasure,
in his hand a muskrat-skin and an ancient worn-out shirt
which he holds between himself and two old squaws. Time
and rhythm mean nothing to him. Where the others take
three or four steps, Klondike Bill takes one enormous
stride. When the time comes for the man to swing lightly
up on his toes to meet his partner, Bill drifts aimlessly
about on those long legs of his. Where the dance is supposed to proceed noiselessly to the simple beating of the
tomtom, he blurts out with the refrain — " *Hi-hi-he, hi-hi-
he-ho* " — and when the others join in the chorus, he
bursts out with the old Indian war-song in a manner terrible enough to cause a genuine scalp-hunter to turn in his
grave. Sometimes the words fail him, but this does not
faze him in the least; in place of the original text he
supplies a strident " *tra-la, tra-la-la-la!* " The worst part of
it all is that he imagines himself to be putting up a most
remarkable performance.

After having thus taken part in some half-dozen dances
in succession, he comes puffing and sweating over to us
and asks what we think of him. " Never saw anything so
disgusting in all my life," answers Joe, mercilessly. " Why
don't you take a couple of redskins and go join some circus? " is all he gets from Price, whilst Clark assures him
that, before seeing Bill in action, he had never known what
real dancing was like.

As though this might have any effect upon Bill! He
simply smiles indulgently, digs down into his pocket, and
fishes out a most curious assortment of rubbish. Rat-skins,

neckerchiefs, odds and ends of plug tobacco — some bearing the marks of teeth — a pipe, a knife, and God knows what all!

" Where in the world did you get all that? " we ask him.

" From the young girls," answers Klondike Bill, with a knowing wink.

" What did you give them in return? " we keep at him.

" Return! What kind of talk is that! " snorts Bill, contemptuously.

We explain to him that the custom is to *exchange* presents during the dance.

Bill looks us up and down. As though we could tell him what was what! Exchange presents, pooh! We ought to stick round these parts a mite longer! Jealous, that's what we were, just downright jealous because he had made a hit with the women! Oh no, we couldn't fool him!

The next time Bill comes over to us, his pockets are stuffed tighter than ever with rubbish, and his conceit knows no bounds. We gather round him then and try to get it through his head that he cannot go on robbing the Indians in a friendly gathering like this without making bad blood. Either he must abide by the custom of the dance and give presents in return, or he must get out while the getting is good. Arguments prove of no avail. Then there is no other way out of it but to leave before hard feelings are aroused amongst the natives. We have but one canoe, so Klondike Bill is obliged to come with us, much as he hates to do so.

On the way home we are none too pleasant with him. Without beating about the bush, we make it clear to Klondike Bill what we think of him and his tepee-dance. But we might just as well have spared our breath. He ignores us and disdains to reply. With a smile on his lips, he sits

there staring dreamily back in the direction of the Indians'
camp, where the fire is flaming up against the sky and the
sound of the tomtom keeps rising and falling. . . .

. .
. .

" Twenty eggs fried in butter! " says Mac, emphasizing
each word, and, with that, the old discussion is under way.
Joe insists that the eggs must be boiled, and demands furthermore a pot full of baked potatoes. Price wants the potatoes cut up and fried in the pan until they are brown and
crisp, whilst Klondike Bill merely goes off into contemplation of what it would be like to swallow down a dozen
oranges, one right after the other.

This is before the arrival of the spring steamer. Weeks
ago the two Indians Souzi and La Loche set out for Fort
Resolution with their canoes bound fast to their toboggans. They are expected back at almost any time now with
their precious cargo of eggs, potatoes, and oranges. But
they have almost two hundred miles to paddle back and
a most uncertain passage at this season of the year. Their
canoe must find its way through the open lagoons inshore
and must often be carried over broad stretches of ice.

A wind from the lake has sprung up during the night,
and the ice-floes come drifting in toward shore. We manage
to rescue our nets just in the nick of time. It is a light summer night, and none of us are eager to creep back into our
sleeping-bags. Instead, we light a fire down on the beach
and put a kettle of whitefish on to boil. As we are sitting
there, several of the dogs suddenly scramble to their feet
and prick up their ears. We hear an odd, scraping noise in
the distance. Then the bow of a canoe appears from round
a jut of land. There stands Souzi with a long pole, pushing

[143]

ice-cakes aside. Foot by foot the boat threads its way in through the floes. At length it reaches the trading post, where willing hands have soon hauled it ashore.

A short time afterwards one fire after another flames up along the beach. It is amazing how much a trapper can put under his belt, even when potatoes cost fifteen cents apiece. . . .

The last of the ice disappears in time, and Great Slave Lake stretches off into the distance, like a great blue hand in which lie emerald islands. The fish seek shallow water, and all evening long the lake trout skims the surface with its fins. The nets are filled with silver every single day. With expressions of the utmost indolence on their faces, the dogs doze all day long, surrounded by fish which even *they* have been unable to crowd into their stomachs — and that is a great deal! Mosquitoes appear in dark humming swarms and we take refuge on the beach whenever we want to rest. In the evening we all gather down there for a quiet smoke, as we watch the setting sun change Great Slave Lake into a sea of rosy flame.

Red Neighbors

ONE DAY, ALONG TOWARD THE END OF JUNE, THE FUR-traders set off south down the lake for Fort Resolution; early next autumn they will return with a fresh supply of merchandise. A short time afterwards the trappers follow them south. The Indians move out onto the islands, and I am left alone in Snowdrift.

Here is my canoe, here my nets, my guns, and my dogs. Forest and lake are at my disposal. I sit in my shirt-sleeves in front of my tent and feel like a millionaire.

At sunrise I push off in my canoe and paddle out in the lake to my nets. The dogs follow me eagerly along the beach. When the fish are hauled ashore, the dogs pitch in and eat as many as their stomachs will hold. The fish that are left I split in half and hang up to dry on a scaffold I have erected in front of my tent. Then the gulls come sailing in from the distance, the limbs of the spruces are black with ravens, and the whisky-jacks sit a few feet away pecking at the rich cleanings of whitefish.

When the sun beats down too fiercely, I sling an ax over my shoulder and make for the forest. I have a contract with "Hudson Bay" to chop them three hundred full-length logs and thirty cords of firewood. Where the spruces stand thickly together, the work proceeds with a steady rhythm. The edge of my ax bites into the wood, making the sap ooze out, and one tree after another majestically falls to earth.

After a day of toil I hop into the canoe and make my usual evening pilgrimage over to the river mouth to try my luck at trolling. There are plenty of trout to be had. They are continually pulling and jerking on the line, and in no time I have a boatful. With that, I call to the dogs and paddle homeward. The canoe glides gently forward over the silken water, whilst the light from the setting sun sparkles with a ruby phosphorescence in the ripples of our wake. . . .

The Indians have settled with their families on the islands off Snowdrift. Occasionally I take a trip out to see them and am always received with the utmost hospitality. Now and then they offer me a bit of dried meat which a few of the more economical housewives have managed to save from the winter's hunt, but otherwise their diet is the same as mine: fish.

The majority of the Indians are troubled with coughing. They catch cold every year with the coming of spring. The remarkably sound health they enjoy all winter long forsakes them as soon as warm weather sets in. Of those who are suffering with tuberculosis, it is invariably predicted that spring will see the last of them. But in so far as possible they pay very little attention to themselves. Cheerfully they enjoy the bright summer days, and when the hunters paddle off in their canoes, they sing so that their voices echo far out over the water. . . .

Chief Marlo has not cut his hair like the others, for he is a member of the old school. Black and straight, it falls down over his shoulders. How old he is, not even he himself knows. " When I little, big battle, Dead Men's Island," he says. Now he is too feeble to join in the hunt. He remains indoors most of the time, smoking his pipe and giving advice. In a face of wrinkled parchment shine a pair of fun-loving eyes, and it may well be, as it is said, that he can still draw as fine a bead on a fleeing caribou as anyone.

Each evening when the sun is setting over Great Slave Lake, Marlo emerges from his tent and totters down to the beach. There he sits for a long time.

On one occasion I sit down beside him. Not a word has passed between us when he nods toward the sun, just as it is slowly slipping down into the water in an orgy of red, and " Who you think make sun? " he asks.

" Who do *you* think? " I parry.

" Jesus — mebbe so," he says hesitantly. Just how sincerely he believes this to be true is pretty hard to know, for he immediately begins talking about how the sun, from the very first, has been the all-powerful god of the Indians. He flings out his arms to it and says: " First all water, then sun."

But when Marlo begins to talk about his people, he is bitter and terse: " My rich country. Caribou, musk-ox, fish, much food. Before, Indians all over. Great hunters. White man come, Indians die, all-a time die." He points off toward the north where the woods melt like a bluish mist into the distance behind which lie the Barren Lands, and then he quietly adds: " When caribou come from *Land without Trees*, Indians choose new chief." I object by saying that he certainly has a number of years left to live. But Marlo shakes his head conclusively, as though he is positive of his statement. " When caribou come," he repeats, knocks the ashes from his pipe, and totters back up to his tepee.

It so happens that I spend the night in the Indians' camp. I notice that most of them leave their tallow candles burning whilst they sleep, a thing I have seldom seen them do during the winter. I inquire as to the meaning of this custom, but they shrug their shoulders and ignore the question. Later on I receive the following explanation: In winter the Evil Spirit cannot walk abroad without leaving his footprints in the snow. Thus one knows where it is keeping itself, and can be on one's guard. But in summer no tracks are visible, and then the Indians leave their lights burning in order to keep the Evil Spirit away, in case it is hovering about in the vicinity of their camp.

One day Pierre La Loche pulled from the lake a stalwart beast of a trout. It must surely have weighed in the neighborhood of forty pounds. He drags it into camp, lays it on a pile of dry spruce branches, and covers it over with fresh leaves. Meanwhile all the young boys in the camp gather about him in a laughing, noisy circle. Each of them has a hunting-knife tightly clasped in his fist. I ask what is about to take place, but La Loche replies secretively: " You see." Then he touches a match to the pile of spruce branches, which immediately flare up in a sheet of flame. This is a signal for the youngsters to crowd in close to the fire, their knives held high in the air. Some minutes pass. Then La Loche grasps the trout by the tail and hurls it off in the brush as far as he can. As he does so, the whole band of youngsters are after it and, with yells and shouts of jubilation, begin slashing into it with their knives. The first to reach it cut off good-sized chunks of the flesh and race triumphantly off with them. It is a point of honor for each to eat as much as each has cut off, and down goes that half-raw fish, no matter how large the piece, and soon there is nothing left of the trout save bones and scraps of the skin.

The youngsters also have another pastime. Once in the

woods I discover them eagerly circling about one of their number who is wearing a birch-bark mask. But no one will explain to me the mysterious point of this game.

One day, as I am prowling about the island, I come upon two boys bathing in a sheltered cove. This is an unheard-of situation! The only explanation I can think of is that they have observed me in swimming and, out of sheer curiosity, are desirous of finding out what it is like to get water on their bodies. This is something which the Indian conscientiously tries to avoid throughout his entire life. He may wash his hands, he may even go so far as to squirt a little water in his face, but the latter is positively as far as he will go. None of the Indians are able to swim. But, in spite of this fact, they intrepidly set out in their small canoes down the most turbulent river rapids or in the toughest kind of weather on the lakes. And seldom do they come to grief, so dexterous are they in the use of their paddles.

After the Indians have remained upon one island for a week or so, they move on to the next. This constant shifting of their summer camp is characteristic of most of the northern tribes. It is their own odd form of cleanliness. About their tepees piles of garbage and offal soon collect. Therefore, instead of sweeping up and keeping their premises clean, they simply move on to a new place. There is at the same time a tendency on the part of these Indians to keep moving ever eastward in the direction of caribou country. With constant regularity thus they shift their camps, and on many occasions I find it extremely difficult to discover their whereabouts. The distance out to them is constantly increasing, and my visits grow less and less frequent.

It is over a week since my last visit when one morning I

set out for the islands. As I come gliding into a cove where a number of tepees are pitched near the beach, I am met by a singular stillness. No children are playing about the camp, no men come running down to the lake to give me a hand with the canoe. No living thing is in sight, save the dogs, skulking about amongst the tepees.

As I step ashore, I notice some canoes, half-loaded with all kinds of gear, as though their owners were in the act of moving. Up at the edge of the woods I come upon a man sitting on a stump. He rocks from side to side, his face buried in his hands. It is Drybone. " Hallo! " I call. " What's up? "

He looks up at me with red, streaming eyes and says: " White man's sickness. All Indian sick. Some die, me pretty soon, too." And, with that, he buries his face back in his hands and moans softly.

I go from tepee to tepee, and a most sorrowful spectacle meets my gaze. On the bare earth strewn with spruce twigs lie the huddled forms of the sick — men, women, and children, wrapped up in skins and filthy rags. They are shivering although the air is stifling inside, and they cough up blood and stare at me with strange eyes.

Off in the woods I find three corpses, covered over with aspen leaves.

An old woman is the only one who has escaped the ravages of the disease. She is sitting in front of one of the tepees and is staring vacantly off into space. The epidemic struck suddenly, she tells me, shortly after several of the hunters returned from a journey south. Of late the people of the camp have been unable to procure food, for no one was strong enough to haul in the nets. She begs me to help her bury the dead before the ravens can get at them. And then the camp must be moved over to the nearest island, for

[150]

to remain here where the Evil Spirit reigns will mean that death will surely claim them all.

With the aid of a hunting-knife and a crude spade carved from wood, I manage to dig a groove in the earth deep enough, with some crowding, to accommodate the three corpses. Over a covering of moss and turf I plant a cross made from two sticks lashed together, and then, according to ancient Indian custom, I surround the grave with a fence of tall pointed poles.

In the meantime the old woman has made a fire down on the beach and is burning up all the personal possessions belonging to the dead. Then we get busy breaking up the camp. We take down the tepees and roll them up into small compact bundles, and, one by one, I carry the sick down to the canoes. Room is found for the dogs and we shove off, I in one canoe, the old Indian woman in another.

Seldom have I experienced such a weirdly melancholy feeling as I did on this particular voyage. In front of me in the bottom of the boat lie the sick, one on top of the other, all of them covered over with a layer of tepees, caribou-skins, and rags. In the bow, a dozen Indian dogs tightly squeezed together. Some of them sit motionless, their heads on the gunwale; others attempt to crowd back on top of the sick. In a twinkling, I must use the paddle to drive them back where they belong.

Abreast of me glides the other canoe. In it sits the old squaw, paddling. She is bare-headed, the wind rustling and clawing at her hair. But she pays no heed to this condition, merely keeps on paddling. Her face appears carved in stone, and there is a far-away look in her eyes. Round about us, and bathed in sunshine, lies the heaving expanse of Great Slave Lake; off to the west there is a faint haze through which the dim outlines of islands may be seen.

Behind me stretches the mainland with its tiers of forest and bluish hills — the Indians' country. . . .

When, after a time, we reach the nearest island, I set to work cutting poles and branches of spruce. Then I raise the tepees. It is midnight before I have finished pitching the camp and have comfortably installed the sick. About time to be getting home! Just as I am about to hop into the canoe, the old squaw approaches me with a dog she is holding on leash. It is no more than a mass of shaggy hair and nothing much to look at, save for the eyes. " You take," she says.

I explain to her that I want no pay for what I have done. "*Kli nézōn* (Good dog)," she says, pointing to the animal.

It had belonged to her husband, whom I had but recently buried, and it would have been an insult to her had I refused, so I stowed the dog away on board and started off.

If I managed to reach home without swimming half the distance, it was not the dog's fault. Never shall I forget ·the tussle we had there in that frail canoe, when my passenger decided that he would accompany me no farther. Along toward morning I arrived back at Snowdrift. I was met at the beach by all my dogs, their tails standing pugnaciously erect on their backs, ready to give this new member of the family a baptism of fire.

Thus it was that Skøieren[1] came to me. I gave him this name because he was so shaggy and whimsical that it put one in a good humor simply to look at him. I had him for two years, and never have I seen a more dependable slave in the traces.

A week passed, and then I learned from experience that

---

[1] *Skøieren* — Jester, Fun-maker, or, possibly, Mischief. — TRANSLATOR.

the disease which had afflicted the Indians could attack the white man as well. It must have been some kind of influenza, for it began with chills and fever and a splitting headache. It came at a time when I was living from hand to mouth. Fish was my sole diet, and this I had to procure by hauling in the nets. So far as I was concerned, it might just as well have stayed there till it rotted, for I was unable to swallow a mouthful of food, in any event. But there were nine dogs I had to provide with good board. So there was nothing else for me to do but to struggle out to the nets each morning. Then the autumn storms set in, and if I had felt groggy before, my health was at least not improved by my flopping about in those stormy seas. The remainder of the time I spent inside my tent, with my sleeping-bag drawn tightly up to my nose.

It was at this time that my hatred for bitches flared up anew. A little corn-yellow Indian bitch had strayed in from the woods and had settled herself in our camp. She wreaked perfect havoc there in the ranks of my splendid dogs. Old friendships were promptly broken asunder. A state of warfare sprang up, each dog against all the rest, the devil take the hindmost. Even Trofast and Spike, who were brothers and had seldom had a serious quarrel with each other, came together with bloody results. In the end Spike was obliged to flee into the lake, where Trofast kept him in swimming longer than was good for him. Meanwhile that little yellow bitch scampered coquettishly about, pretending not the slightest interest in such silly goings-on, and helping herself to the fish which was intended for the other dogs. Under such circumstances it sometimes happens that even a sick man will show some signs of action. One day I decided that I had had just about enough, so I crawled out of the tent and caught the beast. A stone round her neck and a grave in Slave Lake — these were just what that corn-yellow bitch had deserved.

Day in and day out I lay on my back in my tent. Perhaps it was ten, perhaps it was twenty days — I'm sure I don't know precisely. The ravens, which before had been confidence personified, became more and more bold. Through the open flap of my tent I could see dozens of them holding a grand banquet on the scaffold where I had hung my precious dried fish. Gradually they made themselves more and more at home and at length managed to do about as they pleased around my tent. Among them was a shiny black old male. He had a habit of hopping right up to the tent-flap, where he would squat with his head on one side as he bored into me with those glittering eyes of his. " The Black Devil " is what I called him, and I doubt not in the least that he was all of that.

One day the sound of voices reached my ears from out on the lake. I crawled over to the flap and peered out. Two men were sitting in a canoe, two geologists I had met earlier in the summer. My appearance could not have been very inviting, for they remained some distance out from shore. " Any people here? " they called out over the water.

I explained that I was the only person on the place, but that the Indians were in camp a day's journey off to the east.

" Have you any food? " they then asked.

I replied that I had fish-nets.

With that they threw ashore a sack of oatmeal and a slab of bacon.

" Has there been sickness around here? " was their next question.

" The Indians are dying like flies out on the islands and I haven't been so well myself," was the answer I gave them.

[154]

With that, they turned their canoe sharply round and made the foam fly as they paddled away to the south.

" Hold on! What's the date today? " I called after them. But they didn't even stop to turn their heads.

The Caribou

*" They are like ghosts; they
come from nowhere, fill up
all the land, then disappear."*
— OLD INDIAN SAYING

THE BRIGHT ARCTIC SUMMER DWELLS OVER THE SHINING
water and over the northern plains. On the brownish-gray
ranges which border the Polar Sea caribou are grazing,
strolling about in sparse flocks. These are the does and
their young.

As the month of August progresses, harsh autumn storms
boom in across the Barren Lands. The sea, before so art-
lessly blue as it played amongst its myriad islands, now
comes dashing ferociously in at the shore. And, with this,
the does become restless. They no longer graze at random,
they begin trekking. From east and from west and from
the islands in the north the droves set out for the same destination. It is as though a command has been passed about
amongst them, to the effect that the time has now arrived for
them to gather at the old meeting-places. Drove by drove,
the herd forms and the great migration up into the land
of trees is under way.

Farther south on the Barrens the bucks have held themselves aloof from the others. During the summer months,
singly or in pairs, they have gone chasing into the wind,

pursued by swarms of insects. Then a coolness creeps into the air and they begin grazing in earnest until their bodies are sleek and fat. Soon they, too, feel that same strange ferment seething in their blood. From near and far they gather together on the plains bordering the larger lakes, sniff each breeze from the north, and wonder how long it will be before the does will be coming along.

The herds meet, immediately join forces, and continue on south in one body. An experienced doe takes the lead, with a body-guard of powerful bucks tramping along on either side of her. Behind these follow the others in an endless procession. At one time they spread out over the plain; at another they mass so tightly together that it is impossible to distinguish one beast from another, their antlers clashing together with a singular rhythmical sound.

With unfaltering certainty the head doe leads the way. Through the familiar passes, over the habitual trails beside the large lakes, swimming across to the other side at the very spots where their kind have swum since forgotten ages, the herd moves on. A few drop behind with broken legs, hundreds of others are swept to their death over cataracts. Nothing halts the herd. Deer swimming across lake and river, sweeping across the Arctic prairie, a sea of antlers as far as the eye can reach.

But behind the caribou follow the wolves; and over the heads of the latter, the ubiquitous ravens. In the lead run the killers — the old experienced wolves who know how to segregate one deer from the herd and overpower it. As soon as they see an opening, they rush in and surround their victim, bowl it over, snatch a morsel or two from its quivering carcass, and hasten on their way. Then the main pack arrives. They gobble up the partially eaten carcasses strewn out over the plain and make short work of any wounded or straying caribou they may chance to run across.

Always, wherever there are wolves, there are ravens. Even before the caribou has been killed, they arrive on the scene, circling about over the heads of the struggling beasts. When the battle is over, wolf and raven gorge themselves, side by side.

At length the white fox comes tripping along in small bands, whilst an occasional wolverine slinks forward, shielding itself behind one stone after another. And far off to the south, canoes, one by one, come paddling north to meet the herd — the Barren Land Indians.

Southward, steadily southward, the army moves. Hundreds of miles lie behind it now. It is late October. The cold days have set in. Hoofs now strike against frozen moss. The smaller lakes are rimmed with ice. At last a thin green stripe appears across the horizon — the timber-line. As though obeying one command, the army halts on the plains bordering the large lakes. The rutting season is at hand.

The bucks present a magnificent appearance. With bulging necks, they stamp and storm about, seeking battle, their mighty crowns of antlers thrown proudly back. And battle they surely find, desperately waged and sometimes to the death. They come together with a shock that can be heard a long way off, after which the victors trot off by themselves, each with a little harem of does. The young bucks stand off to one side, occasionally sneaking in a bit of stolen romance whilst their elders are fighting. The does take the whole matter phlegmatically, graze along as though nothing were out of the way. They probably reckon one as good as another and don't care a snap which one it is.

The rutting season lasts three weeks, and then the herds move on into the woodland. Gradually the masses spread out. The bucks withdraw and continue even farther south.

Soon a long winter sets in, during which the deer drift about like ships lost at sea. At one time they fill every corner of the country for miles around, at another they seem to have been blown completely away. More often they trot along against the wind, but sometimes they march blindly, followed by the wolf packs. All fat has been drained from their bodies, save those of does without young. Their shiny brown summer coats have been exchanged for thick coverings of long, shaggy hair. Shortly after Christmas they begin dropping their antlers — discarded horns lie everywhere in the forest.

Then when spring comes and the first indication of warmth creeps into the air, the does become restless again and, in thin droves, begin threading their way back into the north. Irresistibly they are drawn toward the Polar Sea. At first they graze slowly along, with long halts here and there on their way; later, as drove joins drove, they proceed at a brisk trot. It is urgent that they reach the Arctic wastes before bringing their young into the world.

The bucks remain south for a time to loiter about in the woods. They let spring pass and wait for the coming of summer before they set out for the north. As long as the ice will bear their weight, they have no need for haste. They do not have so far to go as do the does, nor do they have that extra weight to carry. They make for the north in a leisurely march. But they have lost their majestic appearance; in place of their mighty crowns of antlers they now have no more than a pair of velvet green stubs, an inch or two long.

The migration back into the Arctic has begun. Wolf and raven and fox and wolverine assemble to follow on the heels of the deer. "*Atvamalise!* (Sleds under way!)" say the Indians, and stare off at the herds, disappearing into the north. Then they strike camp, harness up their dogs, and turn southward into the forest. Their great " meat time " is over. Without the caribou, there is no purpose in remaining on the Barrens, and no redskin dares to follow the herd into lands where the dreaded Husky lives.

. .
.

The Barren Ground caribou is somewhat larger than the Norwegian reindeer and has a heavier and broader sweep of antlers than the latter. The other deer of northern Canada is known as the woodland caribou and need not be mentioned further in this place. It is considerably larger than the Barren Ground caribou and is best represented by the Osborn caribou, which inhabits the regions in the vicinity of the Rocky Mountains.

How many caribou actually exist on the Canadian tundra is somewhat difficult to estimate. Ernest Thompson Seton, heading an expedition in 1907, estimated their number at thirty million, and both he and other naturalists before him have agreed that not even the herds of wild buffalo which in former years grazed on the southern prairies could possibly equal them in number. The Government expert W. H. B. Hoare told me in 1930 that he reckoned the number to be somewhere in the neighborhood of five million. Those who, perhaps better than any others, would be in a position to judge of their actual number are the experienced trappers who, year after year, have observed the caribou during their migrations. In tents and around camp-fires they have discussed the matter and compared notes from the four corners of the land. Even the Indians, who, for hundreds of years, have found in the caribou their staple food, fail to understand the laws which govern the migrations of these creatures. Nor can science give us any special enlightenment. The variability of the creature's instincts and the purpose of its eternal migrations still are riddles, unsolved.

Presumably, as in the case of the migratory birds, a combination of circumstances makes for the annual mass movements of the caribou. Certain of these circumstances turn on points of animal psychology and for this reason may never be made clear; others are fairly obvious.

Thus, it is certain that the question of nourishment is a factor of the utmost significance. In winter it is easier for the deer to scratch through the snow after food in the tracts farther south than it is in the ice-bound regions of the Polar Sea. But even these considerations are not conclusive. Caribou are to be found both in the vicinity of Great Bear Lake and on the islands of the Arctic.

Another view of the matter is that movement from one point to another is necessary in order to allow for the continued growth of vegetation on the grazing ranges. In spite of the enormous area of these tracts, it is astounding how much these millions of animals can devour. Since it takes years for the reindeer moss to grow again, it is easily understood that the caribou must have a vast territory to supply them with food.

There is one unmistakable reason why the does seek northern pastures with the coming of spring. The islands of the Arctic are their natural refuge when it comes time for them to calve. The insects are not so troublesome, and the wolves are less numerous. Furthermore, it must be admitted that the calves develop more rapidly there in the bright sunshine of the Arctic summer, a condition which proves of the greatest importance later when the herds seek the mainland, infested with beasts of prey.

It is unknown how many separate herd migrations take place over the ranges north and east of Great Slave Lake. Presumably there are three: first, from the stretches east of Great Bear Lake south to the northern shores of Great Slave Lake; second, from the plains north and northeast of Mackay, Aylmer, and Clinton-Colden lakes south to the eastern shores of Great Slave Lake; and, third, from the ranges north and east of Dubawnt Lake southwest in the direction of Lake Athabaska.

These migrations are, on the whole, separate and distinct. But it may happen at times that herds come together and intermingle. In the autumn of 1929, for example, a herd was discovered east of Lake Eileen trekking in a northeasterly direction — no doubt the Dubawnt migration, which had strayed from the Athabaska range. At the same time another was reported east of Aylmer, Clinton-Colden, and Artillery lakes moving south in the direction of the large lakes which form the source of the Thelon River, where the herds joined forces during the rutting season.

As a general rule, however, the herds follow, from year to year, the time-honored routes for their spring and fall migrations. Any variation from the rule is due to some special condition.

Of late years, for example, it has become particularly noticeable that the caribou have shunned wide stretches along the western extremity of the Arctic coast where before they were rich in number. It is a matter of record that, west of the Coppermine River, tame reindeer have been imported from Alaska in order to compensate this loss. The reason why the caribou have disappeared from these parts lies in the fact that the Eskimos have recently acquired the use of fire-arms. Then, when the does were moving north, seeking the islands of the Arctic in order to calve, they were met by armed natives who had posted themselves in the narrow passes. Thus the herds swung aside from their accustomed course, chose a more easterly route, and there-after abandoned their ancient ranges. Naturally, this was a most unfortunate occurrence, not only from the standpoint of the natives who were dependent upon the caribou for their subsistence, but also from the standpoint of the welfare of the caribou themselves, for the does were thus deprived of the islands, their securest refuge during the calving season.

The Canadian Government is alive to this circumstance and has already ordered the erection of a number of outposts, located in the districts affected. This will unquestionably cause a partial shifting of Eskimo tribes, which, to an ever-increasing degree, are going in for the hunting of pelts and are no longer able to get along without a trading post.

It is a well-known fact that the caribou, which, not so long ago, were numerous in the tracts farther south, are becoming more and more scarce in those sections. The use of modern fire-arms, no doubt, lies at the bottom of this fact, as well — not because the animals were slaughtered in greater numbers, but because the herds became frightened and uneasy. In some cases broad belts of burnt-over woodland, in others the increasing numbers of wolves have caused the herds to turn aside. Climatic conditions, during both spring and fall migrations, also play an important part, though perhaps most frequently during the winter months, when the herds spread out. It is a pretty general rule that the caribou always move into the wind. If the snowfall has been light, they seem to prefer to remain on the open plains, as was the case east of Slave Lake in the winter of 1929–30. If, on the other hand, the snow lies deep, the caribou follow south through the forests and may continue on into regions they have not visited in many years. This happened during the winter of 1930–1, when there was an unusually heavy fall of snow.

Of other factors determining each altered course we know little or nothing.

It is the enormous area of the country that makes it so difficult to learn anything definite about the habits and herd movements of this animal. They have been studied in divers places and at various times, but it is clear that little will be known until a combined survey is made. It will be necessary to make simultaneous observations throughout the entire country.

For one of the Government's men I initiated some such mass observation, with trappers, fur-traders, and police as the natural observers. If from these men, who see more of the caribou and know more about it than anyone else, we are able to assemble such information as concerns the size and course of the herds, the relationship between bucks, does, and calves, et cetera, a splendid beginning will have been made. On the basis of such material the wanderings of the caribou over wide areas could be charted. We should then know something definite about the species, and partially lift the veil of mystery from the life of these puzzling creatures of the plain.

At one time or another the alarm bell has been rung and the statement uttered that the species is in grave danger. There are hardly any grounds for such a supposition. It has been pointed out that these animals have disappeared from tracts where multitudes of them once roamed. But this fact signifies merely that the caribou have altered the course of their migrations, especially in favor of tracts farther to the east.

THE CARIBOU

If one accepts Hoare's estimate that there are five million caribou in all, and if one makes due allowance for the losses inflicted by wolf and wolverine, there would still be an appreciable surplus of calves every year. How many of these animals are annually shot by hunters can hardly be computed accurately. If, however, one makes a rough estimate of the human beings who are dependent upon the flesh of the caribou — a handful of white trappers and a few Indian and Eskimo tribes whose numbers are constantly diminishing — it would still seem that a steady increase of caribou is possible. This coincides with the view of the Indians who, influenced by the Canadian police, are, to an ever greater degree, abandoning their practices of purposeless mass slaughter. And now with the advent of the Thelon Game Sanctuary the caribou are assured of safe access to the western territories, provided this protected area is properly administered.

In this connection an additional fact of the utmost importance must be mentioned here. Trappers who live on the flesh of the caribou are simultaneously waging war upon its arch-enemy, the wolf. In order to gain some impression of the havoc wreaked by wolves, one would have to witness with his own eyes their wasteful slaughter. Often they slay for the sheer pleasure of killing and devour but a small portion of each carcass. Their murderous instincts affect, first of all, the calves. To throw some light on this situation, let me give some figures gleaned from the plainsmen east of Slave Lake: the dozen or so trappers who assemble there for the winter hunt, do away with some five hundred wolves annually. When one pauses to reckon that each wolf slays on the average of at least fifty caribou per year, the number of the latter whose lives are saved by men total twenty-five thousand. The deer in turn shot down by the hunters to provide themselves and their dogs with food constitute, in proportion to this, but a meager drain upon the herd.

If one looks a bit more closely at the other side of the question, with regard to the welfare of the people who live in the North, it is clear that their very existence would be threatened were the hunting of the caribou to be limited to any appreciable degree. It would then no longer be possible for men to fare forth into the mighty wilderness where the dog-sled is the only means of transportation and the caribou the staple food of dog and man.

And were we to deny the Caribou-Eaters their free nomad life on the trail of their daily bread, we should be robbing them of the very nerve-spring of their existence.

Autumn Journey to the Land
of the Caribou-Eaters

THE FACTORS HAD JUST RETURNED TO SNOWDRIFT WITH
a new stock of merchandise, and the Indians came paddling
in from the islands in order to purchase toboggans and
their winter supplies of ammunition, tobacco, and tea. Then
they set their course eastward to Fond du Lac, whence they
would start out for their hunting-grounds in the interior
of the Barren Lands.

Dale was bound for the land of the Hudson Bay Eskimos. I, too, had made up my mind to leave Indian country
behind, was thinking of going up north on my own, and
was in the very act of making last-minute preparations,
when I met Antoine.

Antoine was not a member of the Slave Lake tribe of
Indians; he was a Caribou-Eater. The hunting-grounds of
this tribe lie far off to the east and southeast of the lake.
There a mighty arm of the forest extends far into the
Barren Lands; it is crossed and recrossed by countless
rivers and chains of large lakes. It is richer in fish and
game than many another section and in olden times was the
scene of many a bitter conflict between the tribes.

From the caribou these Indians derive most of the food
they require. They live a more isolated life than the other
tribes and are renowned as an energetic, nomadic hunter-

folk, covering vast distances in the course of their travels. There exist many legends concerning their adventurous life, and their bitter struggles against hunger and cold when the caribou fail to appear. To be sure, the Indians who live in the neighborhood of Snowdrift are dependent upon the caribou during the greater part of each year, but the name " Caribou-Eater " has a natural association with the eastern plains, where the ancestors of this present folk chose emphatically to settle.

Originally there were large numbers of them, but sickness has claimed its toll, and today only a small group of them are left; these live on the banks of Nonacho Lake (the lake " with a string of islands "). It was from this district that Antoine had come.

I was sitting in front of my tent and struggling to repair a snowshoe when he suddenly appeared in front of me. Without uttering a word he picked up the snowshoe and with swift dexterity laced it with babiche; before I knew it, he smiled and returned the snowshoe to my hand. He then paused to admire my dogs and asked me whither I was bound. I motioned toward the north. Then he said: " *Si, nen, Thelon thési, white fox thlé, nézōn* (I, you, Thelon River go, many white fox, good)." I asked where we would be able to find fuel so far in the interior of the Barren Lands. He flung his arms out in the direction of the east and answered: " *Nacha tué, detchen thlé, sentilly* (Big lake, lot of trees, all right)."

This interested me, not so much because of the hunting possibilities, but because it would give me an opportunity to live with the Caribou-Eaters and, together with them, penetrate into the country which had haunted my mind ever since I had come north: the country lying at the source of the Thelon River. The lower reaches of the river had been traced out by Tyrell; it winds its way through endless expanses of treeless plain before, at length, it emp- ties as a mighty stream into Hudson Bay. But its head waters are unknown. They have forever been veiled in mys- tery. It is known, of course, that the Caribou-Eater Indians annually make long journeys by dog-sled to the upper Thelon, but they jealously guard the secrets surrounding this part of the country. Word had been spread abroad con- cerning a tract of forest growing about several large lakes in the very heart of the Barren Lands.

In the last analysis it is probable that this is the same freak of nature which Samuel Hearne heard mentioned when, in 1770–2, together with the Indians, he made his famous journey across the Barrens from Prince of Wales Fort on Hudson Bay to the mouth of the Coppermine River. In his travel notes, he writes: " For more than a generation past one family only, as it may be called . . . have taken up their Winter abode in those woods, which are situated so far on the barren ground as to be quite out of the track of any other Indians. . . . Few of the trading Northern Indians have visited this place; but those who have, give a pleasing description of it, all agreeing that it is situated on the banks of a river which has communication with sev- eral fine lakes. . . . The accounts given of this place, and the manner of life of its inhabitants, would, if related at full length, fill a volume. . . ." [1]

Antoine and I immediately came to an agreement. We decided that we would fish and hunt moose along the Snow- drift River until the caribou should appear from the north.

[1] Samuel Hearne: *A Journey from Prince of Wales's Fort in Hudson's Bay, to the Northern Ocean. Undertaken by Order of the Hudson's Bay Company, for the Discovery of Copper Mines, a North West Passage, &c. In the Years 1769, 1770, 1771, & 1772.* (London: A. Strahan and T. Cadell; 1795.) — TRANSLATOR.

On our first journey by sled we would follow the herd on their customary migration in a southeasterly direction as far as Otter Lake, where Antoine had arranged a meeting with other members of his tribe. Together with them, we would proceed to the main village of the Caribou-Eaters, on the shores of Nonacho Lake, from there making a rapid journey with a large following of Indians in the direction of the Thelon River.

Seven miles east, where the Snowdrift River empties into Stark Lake, was a well-known fishing-place. Thither we paddled, Antoine with his wife and children, and there, on the bank of the river, we raised our tents. We soon made the acquaintance of several other families belonging to the Slave Lake tribe. These, too, had planned to wait for good sledding before proceeding on into the Barrens. They were headed in a more northerly direction than we, in order that they might meet the Indians who, during the autumn, would be traveling through the country by canoe.

There would be another month before snowfall, and I thought it would be just as well to put this interim to some good use. " Hudson Bay " was in need of dog-feed to last them over the winter and I undertook to supply them with five thousand or more fish at eight cents apiece. During those years I had had a good bit to do with the Hudson's Bay Company: had felled, floated, and hauled hundreds of logs for the three new trading stores which Dale and I built, had chopped scores of cords of firewood, and had otherwise picked up odd jobs from them during the summer months when there was nothing else to do. Thus I was always able to earn a bit of loose money. But this fishing contract of mine stood in a class by itself. It was an economic triumph, for, as it turned out, there were no end of fish in the Snowdrift River that year.

With the bright, sparkling autumn days at hand, it was grand to be a fisherman. Each morning I would paddle up the river to see to my nets, and when, at noon-time, I turned back, I would be sitting to my knees in fish. With ears erect and eyes ablaze with expectancy, the dogs would be standing on the outermost stones in the river to meet me. Skøieren would wade right out in the water and peep over the side of the canoe in order to make sure for himself what prospects there were for lunch.

The Indians did not have many fish left over. They cast out their nets in the simplest manner possible, in the immediate vicinity of their tepees, and never did they make any notable catches. When at first I shifted my nets from place to place in order to discover, by experiment, where the fishing was best, they simply smiled superciliously. But after observing the excellent results I obtained, they began to study my movements. One morning I discovered Indian nets set on both sides and immediately in front of each of my own. I objected strenuously. The Indians took the whole affair as the most normal thing in the world, hauled in their lines right under my nose, sang and joked, boasted of their catch, and enjoyed themselves hugely whenever they peeped into my canoe, where only the very smallest variety of fish glittered in the bottom.

There was no law to prohibit the Indians from setting out their nets wherever they desired, and it did one no good to fume when met by smiles and a clear conscience. Therefore I chose other tactics, based upon my knowledge that all the fish were swimming downstream and that the Indians were somewhat lazy. I drew out all my nets and set them several miles farther upstream, right at the foot of the first rapid. No one cared to follow me that far, and once more the fishing was excellent.

This affair caused no rift whatever in our friendly relations. It was a hard and fast custom which took me, each evening, over to my neighbors to pay them a visit. In Antoine's tepee a place was always reserved for me on a huge caribou hide where I could stretch out and make myself at home. The hunters would assemble, and far into the night we would lie there, drawing on our pipes and chatting about hunting and distant lands. These people knew a minimum of English, their vocabulary being confined to such words as " white fox," " lots," " sticks," " far," " sleep," and a number of other words of this kind. I had, in the meantime, begun to acquire some insight into the Chipewyan language. My vocabulary was limited, my gutturals had a singular ring and caused an excusable stir, but I stammered away at it and made steady progress.

I surely found no lack of clothes for the winter, for I had the young girls of the camp to make them for me. They made me mittens edged with caribou-skin, duffels (socks), and deerskin parkas. But I had to work like a blacksmith in order to avoid getting Indian sizes. The young girls could never stop giggling whenever they made mention of the white man's moccasins which had to be so inconceivably *nacha* (large).

François, who lived in the tent next door to mine, was a Dogrib from the plains south of Great Bear Lake. He had just come east and, I dare say, felt himself somewhat outside the circle of the other Indians, who, for the most part, were Chipewyans and who had but slight respect for a *Klincha,* their word for " Dogrib." It would be difficult to find a more odd piece of work than was François. His moods were as changeable as the moon — they ranged from marvelous ecstasy to deep despair. His most conspicuous trait was his imagination, which he allowed to run wild. As a rule, it concerned itself chiefly with proving what a monstrous clever fellow he himself was. There was no hunter in the land quite so remarkable as he, his dogs stood in a class by themselves, and he was the champion musher! The fur-traders did whatever he wanted them to do, and the women wouldn't let him alone! But he always failed to mention that he was up to his ears in debt to " Hudson Bay "; nor did his declarations stand in the way of his begging one thing after another from me. He wound up by offering to exchange his four " marvelous " dogs (emaciated curs) for my five.

One day he was taken with a notion to move over into my tent and he belly-ached about it so long that I finally gave in. The Indian no more relishes living alone in a tent than he does setting out on a long journey through the woods alone. Furthermore, François was now deep in the throes of that emotion which will cause most men to do anything to gain a confidant. He was in love, as deeply as an Indian can be. The maiden's name was Tha (Marten) and she was the daughter of the only other Dogrib in the place; they lived down by the mouth of the river. People in love have their own peculiarities, and François proved no exception to the rule. For long periods of time he would lie in the tent without saying a word, merely smiling to himself. And with steady frequency he would come creeping into the tent late at night, after his clandestine meetings in the forest. But at times grave misgivings might sweep over him and he would ask me: " What you think of married man? " Usually I would answer that many fine people had embraced matrimony. Then he might inquire, for the twentieth time, my impressions of Tha. My customary observation would be that Tha was a fine girl who would surely keep him well fed on dried meat and well shod with moccasins. Then François's beaming face would indicate that mine had been a most satisfactory reply to his query.

One evening I heard an outburst of howling and screaming from the direction of the Indian camp. Tsall was beating his wife. Earlier than she had expected, he had returned from the hunt and had discovered a situation which is sure to arouse the ire of a husband, whether he be brown or white. In truth, Tsall found things pretty hard; he himself was well past fifty, whilst his wife was a passionate young thing, hardly twenty years of age. In a black mood he broke camp that very evening and moved his wife, children, and starving curs to a place some distance north up the lake. The others giggled long and loudly over poor Tsall, who could not control that wife of his.

With constant regularity the Indians went out after moose, and often indeed the camp could boast of fresh meat to eat. Moose-hunting, if performed on foot and without dogs, is a most exacting sport. When it is said of a man that he is a good moose-hunter, it means that he enjoys the highest esteem in which the Indians can hold a person.

Antoine was the champion moose-hunter of the village. He seldom returned from the forest without having felled at least one, sometimes several, of these game. Once he allowed me to accompany him. We were two days on the trail of one moose. How distinctly I remember little Antoine as he went weaving or walking alertly along in front of me! Now he would bend down quickly and feel of the lichens beneath his feet, now he would point off to one side where a wolf or a fox had crossed the trail. If a twig should happen to crack beneath my foot, he would send me a lightning-like glance. Nothing escaped his attention, and his step was as light and noiseless as that of a lynx. It was approaching midnight of the second day when he suddenly

[174]

halted, closely examined the trail, and pointed to a birch-covered slope ahead. We sneaked forward each by a different way and felled the moose, just as it came dashing past.

We flayed and quartered the carcass and spread the hide out over the pile of meat. According to Indian custom, we then took with us the most tasty portions of the meat: the tongue, liver, and back-fat. When, at midday, we came paddling back into camp, all were up and about, as is the tradition when hunters return from the field. It was also part of the custom that each person who met us was given a mouthful of the newly killed game to taste.

The following day all the men set out to transport the moose meat back to camp in preparation for the great autumn feast of the hunters. At these gatherings no women are permitted to be present.

We betake ourselves to one of the larger tepees and seat ourselves in a circle, our legs crossed beneath us. We wait. Suddenly, through the door of the tepee a little Indian boy appears carrying a pot of meat, so enormous that he is almost hidden behind it. Steam rises in billows from the pot, and the whole tepee is filled with the delicious aroma of moose venison. The Indian lad digs down into the pot with a forked stick and throws a huge chunk of fat in front of each hunter. He follows this first with one, then with another piece of lean meat, the result being an enormous portion for each one to feast upon. I squint out of the corners of my eyes at the others. There they sit, in silence and as stiff as pokers; no one would ever imagine that they have it in mind to partake of this food. Then Antoine gives the signal, and, in a flash, the entire assemblage pounce upon the food before them. They dig their teeth into gigantic pieces of meat and, with large knives, cut it off close to their lips, thus proceeding mouthful by mouthful. No sound is to be heard, save that of over-stuffed mouths chewing and the sound of cracking marrowbones. Everything is swallowed down; no more than a few slivers are left. A series of pleasurable belches are heard, whereupon, our pipes lit, we sink back on our caribou hides with a delightful sensation of having overeaten.

Then comes another evening early in October. In the largest of the tepees the hunters are seated, staring into the open fire. Now and then one of them pushes aside the tent-flap and glances out. Down on the beach the squaws are standing in groups, peering out into the darkness. The mood of the night is definitely autumnal, with a gurgling from the river and a soft murmur from the lake. We are awaiting the moose-hunters. Three days ago they departed into the east, and tonight they must surely return. The eldest of the squaws has predicted it so, and thus there can be no doubt in our minds, for she feels it in her bones, and her intuition has seldom proved false.

As we are sitting there, we hear a sudden cry from the beach. Like one man, we leap to our feet and race outside. My, but those squaws have sharp ears! Every now and then the wind ever so faintly brings us the sound of distant paddles. These sounds increase in intensity and duration and, at length, the canoe grounds on the beach. The women run over to it. Suddenly a stir runs through the crowd, immediately followed by a wild cry of jubilation: " *E-then! E-then!* (Caribou! Caribou!) " Then it seems as though the devil himself is let loose. " *E-then! E-then!* " they all cheer together, dancing round and round in each other's arms like crazy folk, slapping each other on the back, smiling and laughing. Antoine puts both arms around me and whirls me away, the end of it being that I tumble over

backwards down the sloping bank of the river. After re-
gaining my balance somewhat, I do not hold myself aloof
from these Indians. The last trace of civilization is blown
to the four winds. I clutch little Antoine in my arms, and
round and round we dance until our breath gives out, and
then we shout, " *E-then! E-then!* " until our throats are raw.

Yes, the caribou had arrived. East of the mountains the
hunters had encountered the herd streaming out of the
northwest.

Early next morning we drew in our nets and struck camp.
Hanging from a cache I had in the neighborhood of six
thousand fish, waiting to be called for.

We paddled all the way up Stark Lake to its inlet, and
there, on the beach, we pitched our tents. At that point a
series of hills rose steeply from the water's edge, and
it was behind this ridge that the caribou were trekking.
The canoes were hauled ashore and turned bottom up in
the bushes, their period of usefulness now past. The larger
lakes were rimmed with ice, and the ponds were already
frozen all the way across. But we would have to wait for
good sledding.

We rambled about by ourselves and shot enough game to
meet our needs. We tied the meat up in the hide of the
slain animal and slung it over our shoulders like knap-
sacks. Many times we found it quite a problem to make our
way down the hillsides in the darkness with these heavy
loads on our backs.

Late one evening I came shuffling home through the dark
woods with a heavy bundle of meat on my straining back,
when I became aware of a strange rustling in the bushes
ahead. To be on the safe side, I raised my gun. Suddenly
there was the sound as of a heavy weight tumbling down
the slope and bringing up short with a bump. Silence for

a moment; then from down there in the darkness I heard the juicy exclamation: "*Taislini!* (The devil!)"

"Hey!" I cried.

In answer I heard a grunt from the bushes, where the Indian Inzoé was struggling to get back on his feet with the weight of half a caribou carcass on his back.

Later, whenever I met Inzoé, I could never hear the end of that meeting. "Hey!" he would shout time and time again, laughing all over that wrinkled face of his.

Glorious were these bright autumn days when, with my gun slung over my shoulder, I would rustle along those wooded slopes on the look-out for caribou. With a chill brilliancy all its own, the sun would shine down through the tops of the trees, over muskeg and ice-locked pond.

I rambled about wherever I chose, and nothing required me to hurry. If my fancy prevailed upon me to sit down on some hillside for a rest and a quiet smoke, I did so; if it crossed my mind to climb a ridge far off in the distance for the sake of the vista which lay beyond, I did so. Should evening close in on me before I knew it, I would simply make a fire, roast some meat on a spit, and sleep right where I was. When it suited my mood, I would resume my hunting. Shots rang out among the hills, and many a fat caribou buck fell to the ground. But there were times when I would merely sit on a stump and allow the flocks to pass in front of me, for, when the autumn sun is flooding the forest with light, and the only sound to break the stillness is that of hoofs rustling through dry leaves or striking against frozen lichens, there are moments when even a hunter allows his mind to wander from the business at hand.

After living in the wilderness for a number of years, a man learns to sleep when and where he can. But even in slumber he retains a certain alertness. The howling of the wolves or the flapping of the tent in the wind does not disturb his rest in the least, for these are commonplace sounds. On the other hand, the very moment something *out of the ordinary* takes place within ear-shot, the hunter is awake with a start, ready for instant action, and on more than one cold winter night, bare-legged and in his shirt-tails, he must fly out into the snow. The dogs are the most frequent source of trouble. Many times they slip their chains and cause the fur to fly in the ensuing brawl. The hunter must go out and beat them until they separate. At other times it may be a wolf prowling about close by, and it is for protection against these that a loaded rifle stands ready outside the tent.

Thus it was that I awoke one night in my tent, sat up in my sleeping-bag, and listened. A soft squeaking sound reached my ears. What in the world could that be? It wasn't a fox, and it wasn't a beaver or a muskrat; more than anything else, it resembled the squeaking of a bear cub. I ran outdoors just as I was and peered round in the darkness. Well, if it wasn't Tøs, who had just given birth to puppies! Eight little crawling things lay beneath her in the snow, and Tøs was the proudest mother in the Northland. Somewhat touched over this happy addition to the family, I patted Tøs's head and called her a good girl. Yes, now I should have quite some dog-train next year!

I allowed her to keep five of her pups. But a few days later, upon returning home from the hunt, I discovered that she had devoured three of these.

Only Trofast, Jr., and Spike, Jr. — a pair of powerful youngsters I kept with me for two winters — were still alive. Carefully I wrapped them up in a caribou hide, laid them in the sled, and started off over the long stretch west to the trading post. There I arranged to have Tøs and her children boarded over the winter.

Tøs had mysteriously turned up in my camp one time and, since no one knew anything about her, I had kept her. Later on I met several Indians to whom she had belonged in turn, but none of these would take her back. She was no longer fit for the traces and had been cast aside. The story of Tøs is typical of the fate of a good many dogs up north. Born in Fitzgerald, she had once been known as one of the best train-leaders on the Slave River. Later she had been sold to an Indian for three white fox-skins. He had lost her in a poker game along with everything else that he owned. After that, Tøs had passed from one Indian to another, at one time sold for pelts, at another swapped for some other dog, and with each successive transaction she had dropped in price. At length she had found her way far up north amongst the Caribou-Eaters. No longer was she the leader of a hunting pack, however; she was only a contemptible " squaw-dog," used to draw wood and water inside the camp, a bitch anyone felt privileged to kick. She had finally been scarred for life — one eye was put out, and her ears torn ragged from a beating with a stick; there was no longer anything to remind one that Tøs had once been the ablest leader in Fitzgerald.

Originally her name had been Queen, but when I got her, I dubbed her Tøs.[1] And she surely lived up to her Norwegian name! Her frivolity I could, if need be, endure, but her thievishness and the systematic manner in which she went about picking fights were unforgivable. Perhaps she was not to be blamed for the vices she had picked up during the course of her hard life, but, even so, I had other things to do than to deal with vicious dogs. And, for

[1] *Tøs* — a girl of loose character. — TRANSLATOR.

a time, I also managed to overlook a number of other things, for, after all, Tøs had a right to existence: she was an unusually fine breed of dog. But when, with the years, the habit of eating her own progeny grew on her more and more, even this redeeming feature was lost, and there was no longer any excuse for keeping her.

• •
•

The snow had come to stay and the caribou bore off to the east. Therefore we struck camp, loaded up our toboggans with everything we possessed, and followed on their heels through the woods. The other Indians soon turned north and we parted company with them all, with the exception of Weeso and his family. They had decided to accompany Antoine and myself to the camp of the Caribou-Eaters. Weeso's squaw was nearing the final stages of pregnancy and I asked Antoine if it was his thought that she should undertake such a long journey in her condition. Antoine merely smiled and answered that it was *sentilly* (all right), so there was nothing more to be said about that.

After several days of travel we again caught up with the caribou, which were grazing slowly along through the woodland. We pitched camp and hunted for a time, until the game thinned out. Then we proceeded in a straight line to Otter Lake and settled down there to await the arrival of the Caribou-Eaters. According to their understanding with Antoine, they were to come hither for the purpose of hunting marten, but his explanation as to the exact time was so complicated that I was unable to comprehend it at all.

The wolves were late in arriving, but now they appeared

in droves. Every single night the woods rang with their mournful howling, and the ground was covered with their sign. As a rule, they would run in single file in a long line. Here and there one could see, from the tracks in the snow, where one of their number had stepped out of line, presumably to allow another to pass and take a turn at breaking trail. But, coming up on the game, their lines would spread out. The wolves must certainly have been out of touch with the caribou for some time, as they were emaciated and terrifically hungry. On many occasions they would come right up to the tents during the night, and we were obliged to keep constantly on our guard against them. One night they carried off one of Weeso's dogs. The tail and a patch of blood in the snow were all that was left of it. They also made quick work of the caribou carcasses we had left in several places out in the woods. They had tossed to one side a heavy covering of spruce-trees as easily as though they had been matches. These wolves were all gray, though of varying shades; I did not observe a single white wolf, such as are found in the Barren Lands.

. .
.

Phresi was indeed a heavyweight. Standing beside her, Antoine, her husband, seemed hardly to exist at all. But they made a good team, none the less. Phresi was possibly not so virtuous as she might be, but she was an energetic worker — was cutting up dried meat, sewing, and tanning from morning till night. Antoine, for his part, attended to the hunting, and there was always a rich cache of venison beside the tepee. There were three children, of whom Kachesy (Little Hare), a girl of seventeen, was the eldest. Yes, here was as proper a marriage as could be found out there in the forest. The only thing which bothered Antoine was that, unlike the other hunters, he could not beat his wife when he thought she needed it.

One of Phresi's many duties was to keep track of the calendar. On a strip of bark she would make a scratch with her knife for each day that passed. One day she and Antoine were busy counting scratches. When they had finished, Antoine said: " Short time, my people come."

And it was not long before, one evening, the sound of bells was heard through the forest. Six steaming dog-trains pulled up in front of the tepees, tall men clad in heavy caribou parkas hopped out of the sleds, pushed their hoods back from their heads, and looked smilingly around. These were the Caribou-Eaters.

We greeted each other and betook ourselves to Antoine's tent, which was soon packed. A pot of meat was brought forth and emptied in silence. Not until our pipes were lighted did the conversation begin. Tijōn, the eldest of the Caribou-Eaters, and Antoine talked in hushed tones about all the different things that had happened during the year. Misfortune seemed to interest them most. When at last they were finished, Tijōn turned to me. " Ségué — oh, brother-in-law!" he began. " You Antoine's friend. You follow Indians to Thelon River. That is all right. I show way. First many sleeps without fire. Always cold wind, maybe empty stomach. If brother-in-law not afraid, white man and Indian make big journey. Many caribou and white fox die."

I replied as best I could and did not fail to emphasize the fact that the Caribou-Eaters were renowned as huntsmen. With that, we came to a mutual understanding.

The next morning we struck camp, but this did not take long. In a trice the tepees were down, trussed, and tied to

the sleds, the dogs were harnessed, and we were off. The
new arrivals started on ahead, for they had little or no
dunnage to carry. Furthermore, they had to visit the trap-
lines they had established on the way down. Antoine,
Weeso, their respective families, and I formed the rear-
guard. We had packed all we owned into our sleds, and the
dogs had a hard time of it, for the snow was loosely packed
and the hills steep.

Antoine's load was the heaviest and the oddest of all.
On his sled towered an omnium-gatherum of tepees, stoves,
snowshoes, pots, traps, skin rugs, and a pair of caribou
heads. Back in one corner of the cariole was a squeaking
litter of week-old puppies, all cuddled up in a ball. In the
midst of all this his squaw was enthroned, the mighty
Phresi, in all her ponderous glory. In front of the sled
struggled four little black Indian dogs, their tongues hanging out of their mouths, their backs straining as they tugged
for all they were worth. On snowshoe behind the sled
walked little Antoine, swinging a cudgel and every now and
then bursting forth with a wrathful: " *Taislini!* " The dogs
would cringe beneath his blows, steal a furtive glance back
at him, and strain harder than ever in the traces. Occasionally he would dash up ahead and cut loose upon the whole
train at once, causing them to emit the most heart-rending
howls and screams. But they would move on again, Antoine returning to his place behind the sled, where he would
tramp along with swinging arms, his snowshoes trailing
through the loose snow. His curved pipe hung from the
corner of his mouth, and the smoke from it would trail
out behind him like a bluish streamer floating on the clear
frosty air.

At noon we made tea and ate a bit of dried meat soaked
in fat. After lunch we continued on at the same even pace

[184]

until long after dark. It was a grueling task for us, hauling those heavy sleds, particularly when climbing hills,
and more than once we had to stop and help each other pull
and tug the sleds over a tough spot. Down grade we slung
the dog-chains about the sleds to act as brakes, but, even
so, we had a devil of a time guiding them through dense
woods and round sharp curves in the pitch-dark. The little
Indian boys, who had trudged faithfully along on snowshoe behind the sleds, began to grow tired. Every now and
then they would have to make a gallant little spurt in order
to catch up with the procession, and this was really quite
a strain on the youngest of their number. Even I was immensely tired and had just begun to wonder whether these
crazy Indians had it in mind to keep on all night, when I
suddenly swung out upon the surface of a lake and saw a
camp-fire flaming in a clump of spruces. The dogs also
saw it and hastened their pace; tired as they were, they
made the last stretch at a brisk trot.

The first to arrive were busy, putting the camp in order.
Amidst a confusion of dogs and sleds, men were rushing
hither and yon in the firelight. Some were carrying huge
logs and throwing them into the fire, already piled as high
as a man's head. Others were dragging in spruce brush,
which they then scattered over the camp-site and tramped
down in a large semicircle about the flames. A thick covering of spruce twigs completed the floor of the camp. Back
from the fire a way, the sleds were arranged end to end
so as to form a circular barricade.

When we arrived, we unhitched our dogs, chained them
up, and gave them beds of spruce branches to lie upon;
then we pitched in and helped with the general work. In the
course of an hour the camp was fully settled and it was
time to be thinking of ourselves. We took our seats facing

[185]

the fire, each with his back to his own sled, the eldest in the middle. Heavy pots were stuffed with snow and, by means of long poles, lifted into the flames. Tea and meat were produced. About the flames there appeared a whole row of spits on which caribou heads, knuckles, ribs, and kidneys were roasting. One leg of meat after another was buried in the snow with the flat side to the heat; this was the food for the dogs, which first had to be thawed out.

First we took out the large pot of meat, for in this we each had a share. The eldest helped themselves first. With their fingers they reached down into the pot and pawed around until they had located the choicest pieces of meat. Fat and marrow were usually their portion. Then came our turn, and we others did likewise and reached down into the pot. One learned very quickly to discard all semblance of modesty. The meat was cooked on one side only; the other side was raw, but it slid down one's gullet easily enough, for all that.

When the pot was empty, we each put to good use the titbit roasting on our respective spits. Here, too, only the meat nearest the bone is eaten, the coarser cuts, such as would be used as a " roast " by civilized people, being eliminated and thrown to the dogs. The true delicacies consist of liver, heart, kidney, fat, marrow, breast, and head of caribou. The marrow is eaten raw, all else half-cooked. The head, placed in the flames without removing the skin or even the hair, is the best part of the entire beast and provides a whole menu in itself. From it one has the brains, the fat behind the eyes, the nerves of the teeth, the tongue, and, most delicious of all, the nose and lips of caribou, with their own peculiar taste of chestnuts. In addition to this, the gourmands amongst the older Indians have their own special dishes, such as blood and the contents of the stomach boiled together into a kind of soup, the tissues of the larynx, et cetera.

Such was the Caribou-Eaters' diet, which was also to be mine during that and subsequent years. Moreover, it is the only diet which is effective, day in and day out, during the course of a long, cold winter when one is obliged to nourish oneself on meat *exclusively*.

These people are past masters in the art of butchering a carcass and of preparing food. With firm sure hands they turn and twist the meat on a spit, until a delicate brown color appears. They use a heavy broad knife, and hack as frequently as they slice. They know where every muscle and every joint of the carcass lies, and seldom do they cut in the wrong place.

Our meal finished, out came our pipes. We chatted and joked as the flames licked up the dry wood and sent a shower of sparks up through the trees. Beyond the circular glow from the fire, the land lay blue-white beneath the stars. Some time before, the dogs had already curled themselves up, their noses buried beneath their tails, and now our own bedtime had arrived. One by one, we rolled ourselves up in our sleeping-bags and, like a row of mummies, we lay there side by side, our feet to the smoldering fire. The winter night crept over the camp. . . .

Next morning I found the Indians busy putting up a tepee. When I asked Antoine what the meaning of this was, he replied: "Little Indian coming." Weeso's wife was about to give birth to her child.

Along toward noon we heard the small cries of a baby coming from the tepee, in which the women had remained the whole morning. That meant that there was now one more Indian in the forest. The father, who all this time had behaved in an unconcerned, almost indifferent manner, now began to show signs of interest. When he learned that it was a young hunter that had come into the world, it may be that he was proud. He behaved as though full honor for the birth was due him, though he did most graciously propose that, out of deference to the mother, the journey be delayed two days. The day was bitterly cold, at least 40° below zero.

Two days later, at five o'clock in the morning, I heard someone at work building up the fire. He was bustling about, chopping up wood and lugging it into camp, things no Indian would ever dream of doing the night before. After a time I felt a kick in the middle of my back, as a warning to climb into my clothes before my sleeping-bag should catch fire. One by one we crept out into the cold and stood shivering for a moment, our backs to the fire. But there was no time to think of our own comfort. Morning is a busy period. In a flash we gulped down our breakfast, made fast the coverings over the sleds, and harnessed up the dogs. With that, we were off into the darkness.

We now drove for several days through dense spruce forests and over chains of lakes. The cold was so sharp that even the Indians were occasionally obliged to get out of their sleds and walk briskly along beside them in order to keep warm. Weeso's wife, the young mother, had been given a place in one of the Caribou-Eaters' empty sleds, and there she sat wrapped up in a blanket. As she sat there, busy with her child, whilst the sled bumped and skidded along, it was hard for one to believe that she had been through the pangs of child-birth only a couple of days before. Occasionally the sled might happen to capsize in the deep snow, whereupon she would merely hug her child tightly to her breast and wait patiently for someone to come to her assistance.

Food for ourselves and the dogs we picked up along the way. Each morning one of the hunters would start out a half-hour ahead of the main party. As a rule, he would shoot enough caribou for everyone. It also fell to his lot to prepare the midday camp-fire. When, from a long distance, we would catch sight of that column of smoke, rising straight and white through the tops of the trees, we would feel our spirits rise.

One evening, when we were searching about for a camp-site, we discovered a splendid place where plenty of dry evergreens were growing on the shore of a lake. The finest place one could wish for to spend the night. Just as we were about to pull up, however, someone spied a small island some distance out from shore. It was as clear as day that that was the place for us. The matter was not even discussed, for a redskin is enchanted by the possibility of camping on an island, even when it lends itself most wretchedly to this use. From there he can spot the caribou from afar. Furthermore, in ages past, his ancestors had sought refuge on islands when there was danger of being harassed by the enemy.

Nothing was said, but I do believe that even the Indians were convinced that there are times when it is wiser to remain on the mainland! Seldom have I seen a more forbidding place than that island. A strong biting wind blew in across it from the lake. We couldn't get a fire to burn, which wasn't to be wondered at, since our only fuel consisted of green birchwood. The smoke from it caused the tears to run down our cheeks. . . .

Not many words were spoken that evening. With our backs to that wretched blaze, we threw some dried meat into our stomachs, swallowed down some tea, and disappeared into our sleeping-bags. When we departed from the island next morning, it was plucked absolutely clean. We had not left standing so much as a birch-rod one could use as a dog-whip.

At length we found ourselves crossing Nonacho Lake. We drove for several hours in between numberless islands, at length arriving at the mouth of a narrow valley where smoke was rising in billows through the tops of the trees. In a few moments we saw a village of tents ahead of us. The camp of the Caribou-Eaters.

CARIBOU

MUSK OX LINED UP FOR DEFENCE

INDIAN WOMAN WITH PUPPY

ANTOINE

INDIAN CHILD WITH A
CLUSTER OF WHITE FOX SKINS

ON THE TRAIL WITH THE INDIANS

THE SNOWDRIFT RIVER

INDIAN CAMPS

THE INDIANS RETURN FROM THE WINTER HUNTING,
CANOES TIED TO THEIR SLEDS

THE GRAVES OF HORNBY AND HIS TWO COMRADES
ON THE BANKS OF UPPER THELON
THE HERDS OF CARIBOU DISAPPEARED AND THEY STARVED
TO DEATH
(*Taken by R.A. Williams of the Royal Mounted Police*)

THE FIRST AIRCRAFT TO CALL AT SNOWDRIFT

FAREWELL

To the Upper Thelon

Before setting out for the Thelon, we would have to bring in enough venison to last the women during our absence. This took longer than we expected, for a period of intense cold set in and the caribou became shy. Day after day we hunted in and out amongst the countless islands of Nonacho Lake, and there was many a rousing chase, when the game stormed off across the ice, the dogs galloping at their heels.

In time we succeeded in caching an ample stock of meat, but still there were no signs of our departure. I grew impatient and began to prod the Indians. They replied: " To-morrow, maybe day after tomorrow," and the days passed as before. It was difficult indeed to detect the reason for the delay.

But after a little I made a discovery: I had brought with me from the trading post a small quantity of bacon, sugar, and a number of other trifles I imagined might come in handy if ever I found myself in a tight place. Now the Indians were not thieves, but they were beggars. Every once in a while I would give them a little something, but I always held back as much as I could. As time passed, it became more and more apparent that my companions were deliberately delaying our departure until they could consume all the eatables I possessed. Certain of this fact, I lavishly doled out to them everything I had. In the end I experienced what all other white men experience when they try to live with the redskins: I became exactly as poor as they. My dog-team, toboggan, sleeping-bag, gun, ammunition, ax, a little tea, and a handful of matches were all that I had left.

No sooner had the last of my reserve stores found their way into their bellies than the Indians began to talk of departure. The women set to work sewing moccasins and repairing the outer garments of their menfolk. The men, in turn, busied themselves hunting for birchwood, preparatory to making snowshoes of an especially small design for use on the Barrens. In the course of a day they had cut the material and fitted the parts together; then the women did their share of the work by lacing the frames with babiche. The sleds and harnesses were inspected and a new backboard was fitted to each toboggan. This was made especially wide in order that the cariole might be as comfortable as possible.

The evening before we were to depart, all the hunters assembled for a powwow. The proposed journey to the Thelon was discussed with great seriousness from every possible angle. In spite of the fact that these families, as long as their history records, have roamed across the wastes on the trail of caribou and musk-ox, they never seem to feel at home there. They have the forest in their blood. From the woodlands they fare forth, and to the woodlands they return; only there are they in their element. The Barren Land is to them *a foreign land,* where fuel must be transported long distances, where there is material for neither snowshoe, canoe, nor sled, where many an Indian has starved and frozen to death, the land where the dreaded Husky reigns.

TO THE UPPER THELON

During the powwow it was Tijōn and Antoine who, for the most part, held the floor. Experiences from former expeditions were recalled and refreshed in their memories. Tijōn knew of a little hollow in the interior of the Barrens where trees grew — enough fuel to last one day. This was of the utmost importance, for otherwise we should be obliged to cart wood over long stretches by sled. The danger of losing one's dogs in the heart of the Barren Land was minutely discussed. We were advised to make our sled-ropes double length. Finally the route was discussed and, during the course of the conversation, illustrated with many jerky movements of the hands. From what I could understand, we were to proceed eastward from a place north of the Taltson valley.

Throughout the discussion there was one matter which the Indians never even brought up: the question of food. It was, as a matter of fact, taken for granted that we should hunt our food along the way, aside from the little dried meat and deer-fat which were reckoned to see us through the first few days. Our party consisted of eight men and thirty-two dogs to feed. . . .

One clear starry morning eight dog-trains turn out across Nonacho Lake and proceed single file, in the sleds the huddled figures of men wrapped up in their sleeping-bags. At the head of the expedition a little fellow is running along on snowshoe. He moves forward with a swaying rhythm, his arms swinging briskly at his sides. There is a faint jingle of bells which keeps time with the even trotting of the dogs. Hour after hour passes. At length the sky above the eastern ridge pales, and soon the sun is shining brightly over the white expanse of the lake. The huddled forms in the sleds begin to shake themselves. Men sit up, blink their eyes in the light, call back and forth to each other, and begin lighting their pipes. The dogs wave their plume-like tails in the air and quicken their pace, whilst their steaming breaths trail back on either side of them.

Thus began the expedition of the Caribou-Eaters to the land of the upper Thelon. First we crossed over the northern arm of Nonacho Lake. From there we proceeded until we came to another large lake, thence to a little cove which led us up through hilly country, thickly wooded with spruce, to another chain of lakes and streams.

As soon as we had left Nonacho Lake behind us, our toil began. Early and late it was hurry, hurry, hurry. Everything was taken at a furious tempo. In the twinkling of an eye the Indians would size up every situation, whether it was a question of dangerous river ice or difficult terrain. Without hesitating for a moment they would choose their course as though they could see right through the landscape. Their haste was perpetual, for, though they never knew where the caribou would be next day, they did know that the winter has its own way with those who waste time.

We spent the night in a common tepee, where each man had his regular space. Mine was nearest the flap, and a narrow space at that. The lower half of my sleeping-bag stuck outside in the open; my head was pillowed on Isep's legs.

At five o'clock in the morning Antoine would begin to grunt. One of the younger members of the party, whose turn it was to make a fire in the stove and put the pot of meat on to boil, would crawl shiveringly forward amongst the huddled forms of the sleepers. Then it was one-two-three with breakfast, breaking camp, and harnessing up the dogs, and long before daylight the sleds would be moving off through the woods.

We all took turns breaking trail at the head of the procession. The snow was three feet deep, and after one had been tramping along on snowshoe for some hours, the strain began to tell on one. Where the woods were dense, trees must be felled to make passage-way. The man up ahead had to be quick with his ax if he hoped to avoid halting the entire procession. Save when absolutely necessary, the Indians did not bother to lead the way on snowshoe. They preferred to leave the breaking of the trail to the dogs, urged them on through deep snow and dense woods, where they floundered along with whip blows raining on their backs. No mercy was shown the dogs. No Indian ever stops to realize that it is to his own advantage to keep his dogs in perfect condition and to refrain from beating all strength out of them. The dog is, to him, a contemptible creature he may safely abuse, merely taking proper care not to beat it to death, a situation which always augurs misfortune. And abuse their dogs they did, early and late. Were one dog to shirk in the harness, the Indian would cut loose upon his entire train. If all were performing their labors satisfactorily, he would bombard them with a constant rain of sticks and branches, which he would break off along the way and throw at his team. But the greatest crime of all would take place when an Indian happened to single out one particular dog as the object of his spite. Then the lash would fall with unflagging precision upon the poor brute's nose and eyes. The animal would scream and cry, bend and twist itself, until finally it would close its eyes and lie quite still, digging its nose deep in the snow. Each time the whip would crack, a paroxysm of trembling would run through its body and it would utter a gasping moan. But by this time the Indian would himself be so worn out that he would be incapable of inflicting further punishment.

Christmas was drawing near and the air was terrifically

cold. But on the lakes there were still broad belts of surface water beneath the snow, which had formed no crust as yet. The Indians were clever at locating these belts of water, and we maintained a steady zigzag course in order to avoid them. Even so, we were obliged at times to pass over them. Then we would grasp the trace, run along beside the dogs, and urge them forward in a splash of slush. After each one of these episodes we would have to turn the sled over on its side and scrape off the ice with our axes.

The Indians, who are reluctant to chop a few cords of wood when they are paid money for it, did not consider this kind of life laborious. They enjoyed it. Many a time when we were proceeding across some lake with the sun shining brightly, Moose might take a sudden fancy to make a flying leap from his sled far out into the deep snow. There he would land flat on his back with his arms outstretched and remain in this position for some time without moving, simply staring up at the sun. Then he would take a head-spring and bound to his feet without disturbing the impression of his body in the snow.

It was Moose, too, who was leading the party one moonlight night when we were threading our way along beside a river which, in this spot, was a turbulent rapid racing close to the face of a cliff. There was only a narrow ledge to drive on, and all of a sudden the sled ahead skidded so that its stern slid into the water with a splash. I had all I could do to keep my dogs and sled on dry land, but there went that dark-skinned heathen up ahead — singing!

How Jonas ever managed to pull through every type of situation was a puzzle to me. He used crutches. His left foot was bent at an angle. But as though that could stop him! Now he would wriggle along like a worm through the deep snow, now he would limp along on one foot, now he would let himself be towed along behind by the sled, acting as a brake when the way led steeply downhill. If anything went wrong with the dogs, he would take a flying leap from the sled into their very midst, would set things to rights with the one in trouble, at the same time lashing out at the others with his whip. Then he would limp to one side and throw himself into the sled as the dogs fled forward in a panic.

Whilst crossing the lakes, we were constantly on the look-out for caribou. Glimpsing a herd, we would spread out and give chase to them at once. In a twinkling we had flayed our prey, quartered them, and divided the meat equally amongst our entire party, with the exception of the head and back-fat, which belonged to the actual slayer. Then we would stow the meat away in our sleds and proceed on our way with hardly any delay to speak of. As a rule, we drove on far into the moonlight evening. At such times it seemed as though we were journeying through a strange world of blurred light and dark shadows. There was no use trying to avoid the puddles of surface water. The sleds were constantly passing through them, and there was no point to our stopping to scrape off the ice. The dogs had a tough time of it, but they strove willingly, for moonlight was something they enjoyed.

The work of pitching camp went like clock-work. Each of us had his specific job to perform. Some would chop wood and spruce branches, others would set up the tent and install the stove. Only Tijōn and Antoine were able to take things easy, for they both enjoyed the elder hunters' right to leave the harder tasks to the young fellows.

Within the walls of the tent it seemed homelike after a day of toil in snow and cold. With the winter night enfolding us, we were drawn closely together, and differences in race were soon lost sight of. An oddly cosy feeling came over

our little band, and many a matter came out which otherwise would never have been mentioned in the presence of a
white man.

We sit in a semicircle about the stove, bending forward,
our legs crossed beneath us. It always takes the stove a short
time to warm up, but now it is red-hot and crackling away
like a little machine. We have just partaken of a dinner of
venison, and the pot is sending up clouds of steam from the
door, where we have stood it aside. The voluptuous aroma
of venison, mingled with the odor of damp clothes, permeates the air. One by one the pipes are lit, and soon a
cloud of smoke hangs over our heads. The tallow candle
which stands on a post in the center of the tent shines dimly
as through a mist. Suddenly a gust of wind bellies in the
tent, and the flame flutters round and round in a circle. We
remain sitting in the semi-gloom, where, in the glow from
the red-hot stove, I can dimly discern the outlines of stooping bodies and sharp-featured Indian faces.

" *Detchen* (Wood) ! " grunts Antoine.

In a flash, Isep jumps into his parka and throws his
mitten-strings over his shoulders. Then he disappears out
the door. We hear the sound of chopping through the still
night, and in a short time he returns with a mighty armful
of wood, which he throws down beside the stove. A gust of
wind follows him into the tent and we catch a fleeting
glimpse of stars and snow.

The conversation turns to hunting, and Tijōn tells about
the caribou. He was a little boy when he shot his first game,
with a bow and arrow; since then he has shot many. He talks
at length of the Caribou-Eaters who starved to death a
good many years ago and advises me to eat reindeer moss
whenever there is danger of going with an empty belly.
Then he goes back to " the old days " when the Caribou-

Eaters were a powerful people who made long expeditions up into the land of the Eskimo after musk-oxen. " There were many many sleds in those days," he says. " And when musk-ox die and the hunters hold a feast, you see many tepees, like big forest, in the *Land without Trees*. But now — ! " He makes a disparaging gesture in the direction of his fellow-Indians. The Eskimos he wants nothing at all to do with. In the past he has occasionally come across one of their ancient camps and found there the skin of an animal he has never seen alive (the seal). It also happened, that he has seen the tracks of " big snowshoe " in the snow and strange men far off in the distance. Aside from this, he has but one thing to say about his northern neighbor: " *Husky nézōnilly* (Eskimo bad man)! "

Johnny begins to discuss dogs. He prefaces his remarks by reporting how excellent his own dogs are, then mysteriously hints about what happens to certain kinds of dogs when they get up into *foreign country* — the Barren Land. I sound him out, and he replies that such dogs never return to the woodland. He cites the example of a certain white trapper's dogs, nearly all of which were consumed. I cautiously suggest that perhaps they ran off after the caribou and got lost, or that they had had thin coats of fur and had frozen to death. But Johnny shakes his head in the negative; there is but one explanation: the *foreign land* gobbled them up!

The Indian's ability to orient himself in the wilderness has always been a source of amazement to me, and, in order to keep the conversation going, I begin speaking about the compass. I have lost mine long ago, but I take out my watch and illustrate as well as I can. The Indians look on with smiles on their faces and conclude that I am talking nonsense. Just when I am all wound up and stumped for words to explain the action of the needle's magnetic attraction for north and south, Tijōn takes me by the arm and says: "Come, you see!" Together we leave the tent. The sky is bespangled with stars, and beneath them, over the woods, flame the Northern Lights. Tijōn points to the Great Bear, the North Star, and the Pleiades. I cannot follow him through all the figures he draws, with strange descriptions, in the heavens, but I understand very well that he is explaining *his* compass to me. Then he directs my attention to the aurora and says: "Good clock." He points at the northern wall of the tent and describes an arc over to the east. "Morning early, you see," he says.

"But," I ask, "what do you do when there are no stars, no Northern Lights?"

Then he points to the tall snow-drifts and makes it clear to me that those who have eyes in their heads after a storm can guide themselves along by these, and he explains how one can tell north from south from the bark and the limbs of the trees. At length he adds: "Maybe big wind in *Land without Trees*, maybe nothing see, but Indian always know way, *here!*" Smilingly he touches the tip of his finger to his forehead.

Then it is my turn to tell about the land of the white man. They want to know all about the great canoes on the water which no one can drink. I explain that I come from a land on the other side of this great water, a land where there are trees and snow just as there are here. They want to know if one must keep mushing many weeks in order to get there. Isep asks if it is true that the white men have engaged in a huge war with each other. He wants to know exactly how many hunters were killed. When I tell him that as many hunters as there are caribou in the land of the Indian were killed in this war, it becomes silent there in our tent.

But the drollest question of all comes from Antoine, who wishes to know whether anywhere in the land of the white man there live in the water women who are just like fish.

As the hour grows late, the conversation gradually lags. We lean back on our sleeping-bags to indulge in personal rumination. Suddenly Moose pipes up with the song about the hunter who lay out in the forest longing for his sweetheart. " *Setzōniazé* (My Beloved)," it begins, and the weird sadness of its tones sounds out through the winter night where the forest is a great hall, illuminated by stars and the Northern Lights. . . . Then we creep into our sleeping-bags and listen drowsily to the howling of the wolves, which, in its never-ending mournfulness, is the true heart-song of the great wilderness. . . .

We kept making steady progress eastward. The spruce forest became more stunted in nature, and the landscape leveled out. We ran across more and more tracks of the marten, and the Indians were busy setting their trap-lines. It is always their custom to return to the forest by the same route. All were eager to set their traps in the most favorable spots, and sometimes a lively quarrel broke out. Once Moose had set a mink-trap in a hollow close beside a hole in the river ice. Johnny asserted that he had discovered the mink tracks before anyone else and flung the trap far out into the snow.

" Damned lie! " retorted Moose, and insulted Johnny by calling him a *nogwieh* (wolverine), which meant that he was a thieving rascal. With that, they came together in the snow, kicked and clawed at each other, pulled each other's hair. It was not long before Johnny gave up, for he was as weak as he was treacherous. Grumbling, he brushed the snow from his clothes, came over to me, and immediately began to hold forth upon the subject of Moose, his baseness of character and his doubtful past. He just better look out, that Moose! There were many stories about him, having to do with both women and other things. And if he thought that Johnny was afraid of him, he was making a terrible mistake. Johnny was *natsehré* (strong), and once he *made up his mind* to fight, he was not to be fooled with. Moreover, he could not quite decide whether to beat Moose to death or not, though he rather imagined that things might end thus.

This affair rankled Johnny all day long. Suddenly, with a black expression on his face, he came over to me and started to tell me all over again about Moose. He also said something about parting company with the others, for, as a matter of fact, he was worth more than all the rest of the outfit, he said. As usual when in a vile mood, he took it out on his dogs. When we were on the point of pitching camp that evening, one of them showed signs of having received a terrific blow over one eye. A sturdy dog, chalk-white, and a hard worker in harness. When it came down to the fine point, Johnny asserted that the trouble with this eye was due, not to his own abuse, but to the fact that he had a spoiled dog in his team, which, even so, was the jauntiest team of all! He would undertake to cure it. He took a mouthful of plug tobacco, chewed it for a while, then held the sore eye open and squirted a stream of tobacco juice into that raw place. " Good medicine! " he said, whilst the dog howled piteously. Next day the eye was white and glassy, the optic nerve dead, a condition which Johnny considered most unfair, considering the excellent treatment he had administered.

One day, whilst we were crossing a lake, we caught sight of two otters. Isep shot one; the other disappeared into a hole in the ice. The journey was at once interrupted, and all took part in a hunt for the escaped quarry. Indefatigably the Indians wandered about on the ice and drove long, pointed poles down through the snow in order to discover, if they could, the otter's breathing-hole. At each hole they stationed themselves with raised guns. There they stood like posts hour after hour in the biting cold and refused to give up until nightfall. Seldom in my life have I witnessed such patience. And the otter — yes, it was in all probability plunging down the rapids in the river a short distance downstream.

Up until this time we had been pursuing the same course as the caribou and had regularly been able to butcher all the meat we required. Each time we shot something, we held a banquet and lived a life of gluttony. We would fell three or four caribou at a time, for it is astounding how much eight hungry men and thirty-two greedy dogs can stow away inside them when they set about it. Whenever we had enough to meet our requirements for the day, we never even thought of laying in a stock of meat for the next. The Indians were opposed to breaking camp with heavy loads for the sleds — quick light driving was to them of the utmost importance.

And if ever I were to mention the future, they would answer light-heartedly that, if there were caribou today, there would be caribou tomorrow.

But it was becoming more and more evident that we were in danger of losing contact with the caribou, which seemed to have swerved off on a more southerly course. This thought highly amused the Indians, for the previous year they had followed the herd all the way over to the Thelon; they shot all they needed, and never once did they have to stop and break trail, for there were hard-trodden paths all the way.

This was an error in calculation. But, for the time being, there was nothing else to do but to keep moving eastward with the hope that sooner or later we would again fall in with the herd.

Our meals were now all upset. At one time we were able to shoot some game, at another we couldn't find so much as a single track. Our bellies began to cave in and our spirits drooped. One evening we were particularly hungry as we sat about the stove and dreamed about food. I came out with the hopeful thought that on the morrow we would have meat in the pot. Immediately the Indians were on top of me, asking me how many caribou I thought we would fell. " Oh, two or three, I believe," I replied, jestingly. Then, when they all wanted to know how I knew, I realized that my statement had been taken seriously and that they imagined I was gifted with powers of divination. I felt somewhat ill at ease and did my best to change the subject. But I was unsuccessful, at best.

Next morning Isep started out on snowshoe a half-hour in advance of the main party. We could take no chances. Even if we were to drive in silence, the sound of our bells would frighten the game. We had been driving only a short time when we heard several shots ring out in rapid succession. We were approaching a lake, and there we saw a number of caribou dashing back and forth in confusion. Altogether we felled three deer. One had been merely wounded by the first shot and was running away with its tripes dragging along in the snow behind it. I stood ready to deliver the *coup de grâce* when Johnny crowded in ahead of me, let go his sled, and permitted his dogs to dash off on their own initiative. Like wolves they raced straight for the caribou, which halted and pointed its antlers in the direction of the approaching storm. Down it went in a confusion of barking dogs, harness, and sled. " Dogs fine caribou-hunters," came dryly from Johnny.

After the head had been severed from each carcass, we dealt out the leg bones amongst ourselves, split them, and ate the marrow right there on the spot. We first removed the stomachs and filled them half-full of blood, then carefully cut out the hearts, kidneys, and all visceral fat, and these we stuffed into fragments of the intestines, which were first washed in snow. Our days without food had given us a new view of what may be eaten. Nothing went to waste.

After having divided the carcasses, we made ourselves a fire and held a grand feast. All during the meal I was the center of attraction. Three caribou had, in truth, been slain and thus my prediction had come true. All were eager to know if I could divine the presence of caribou at any time I wished. I did not make much of a reply; instead, I cloaked myself in mystic shadows like any soothsayer and thanked my lucky stars. It may just as well be mentioned in this place that when on later occasions of food shortage I was called upon to prophesy the future, I was foolish enough to yield to flattery. On one day I predicted two caribou, on another I predicted four. On both days we went with empty stomachs. My authority was undermined, and I never again indulged in prophecy.

The forest began to thin out as we neared the Barren Lands. A river we had been following for several days led us eventually to a lake which the Indians called *Satin-tué*. It extended off to the northeast and was about twenty miles long and two and a half miles wide. Off to the east we could see the snow-covered plains rolling away into the distance.

On the shores of Satin-tué we made our camp, though it was in the middle of the day, and each set out in a different direction to hunt. Again no food in sight. We hunted until far into the evening and, one by one, returned to camp empty-handed. This was not very encouraging on the very eve of our departure into the Barren Lands. The dogs had put in long hours of heavy work on extremely scant fare of late; nor had we ourselves exactly overeaten. At any rate, it was entirely out of the question to think of turning back. The country lay empty behind us. Onward, steadily onward until they crossed trails with the caribou, that was what the Indians were used to doing.

. .

So we start out over the barren plains, a boundless sea of snow beneath a glittering sun. The eye loses all sense of proportion, everything flattens out into a deceptive white-ness. Before me rises a tall mountain. I drive and I drive, and it isn't a mountain after all, only a gently sloping plain. Giant trees seem to rise from the blanket of snow far off in the distance. But, as I draw near them, I discover them to be merely the tops of an osier bed rising some few inches above the surface of the snow. Is this land or ice which lies beneath my feet? Suddenly dogs and sled avalanche down an invisible precipice and we are buried deep in snow. I crawl excitedly about, look in all directions, and catch sight of Antoine. He is standing up on the brink, slapping his thighs and laughing boisterously.

The Barrens beneath the sun — ah yes, but the Barrens when storms from the Arctic come sweeping in across the plain — God help the man then who does not know how to help himself!

From Antoine came the order that henceforth all the sleds were to remain close together, for, as he said: " Big wind, nothing see." We halted to get our bearings. Antoine

[206]

was our compass. In a flash he would make up his mind as to the point we should steer for, and, with a quick wave of his arm, he would point out our course. We held strictly to this course and did not turn aside even for snow-drift or wind-swept rock. We were now carrying fuel in our sleds. We were obliged to go sparingly with our wood and to cut it carefully up into small pieces. Thus we sacrificed much of our comfort indoors in the tent.

Animal life had undergone a complete change. We had left the woodland creatures behind us and had now arrived in the domain of the white fox and polar wolf. Everywhere we found evidences of the depredations wreaked by the wolves — caribou skeletons scattered far and wide out over the snow.

In a few days now it would be Christmas, and we had only a few hours of daylight at a time. The sky was often overcast, and at such times we were careful not to keep going after dark. Thus we made but slight progress, though we pressed forward as energetically as we could during the day. Our journey was frequently interrupted by halts for the purpose of trying our luck at hunting.

And then there were blizzards. We ran into one on the evening of December 23. Everywhere the air was filled with blinding sheets of snow lashed by the Arctic wind. Shielding our faces behind our raised hands, we plowed along in search of a somewhat sheltered camp-site. But it was not long before the dogs lay flat down in their traces. They could no longer endure the beating of the snow in their faces, and the wind had otherwise so thoroughly penetrated their coats that lumps of ice were clinging to their very skin beneath the fur. Somehow we managed to raise our tent in the lee of a huge snow-drift and, as one man, we all crept into our sleeping-bags.

[207]

On Christmas Eve the weather improved and we were able to proceed as far as the eastern shore of *Natel-a-tué* (Lake Eileen) before another blizzard roared in upon us. This storm was not quite so severe as the one on the previous day, but it was bad enough. Inasmuch as we ought to be somewhere in the vicinity of the wooded hollow of which Tijōn knew, we decided to camp where we were for the night, even though there were still a few hours of daylight left. From Lake Eileen great eskers [1] roll away to the east, and behind one of these we found a camp-site — as splendid a place as we could wish for, since we soon found enough sticks of wood to provide us with warmth for our tent.

But no Christmas Eve is complete without a feast, and this we had yet to procure. All of us, with the exception of Jonas, who was having great pain in his bad knee, immediately set out hunting. Unlike the others, Antoine and I left our dogs behind and proceeded on snowshoe. Since there were no caribou tracks in sight, Antoine thought it best to seek other kinds of game. We would hunt for hare, he decided.

It was but a short distance to the large esker rising directly from the edge of the lake. It was overgrown with wind-stunted spruce which lay flattened out over the snow. These were the haunts of the polar hare. We found many fresh tracks in the snow and we immediately set to work scaring up some game. I have had considerable experience with many kinds of animals, but I soon learned that even a bear-hunt is a delightfully mild pastime compared with pitting oneself against the polar hare in the heart of the Barren Lands, especially when one is without dogs and entirely dependent upon one's rifle. Mournfully I recalled the

[1] Huge ridges of glacial gravel. — TRANSLATOR.

pleasant rabbit-hunts back home in the forests of Norway, where one strolls out with one's dog and one's shot-gun, sits down on a stump, lights up a pipe of tobacco, and calmly waits for the game to come tripping past. No, here it was quite a different matter: with a sharp northwest wind penetrating our very bones, Antoine and I went prowling about, lifting each bush and kicking in each hole, our freezing fingers cramped and blue about the triggers of our rifles, ready to blaze away at the very moment our quarry should scoot out into the open. To make matters worse, our quarry did not scoot out into the open. Like a dog, Antoine followed the tracks in the snow, whisked up and down, back and forth. For my part, I could swear that I had examined every square inch of that desolate landscape. There were plenty of tracks, to be sure, but dashed if there were any signs of the hares themselves.

Suddenly I heard a shot and at the same moment I saw Antoine fly like the wind over to something in the snow and madly pounce upon it. Now what under Heaven! Up on top of the esker, whom should I see but Jonas, standing there, his crutch in one hand, his gun in the other. With a long and difficult shot he had felled the hare at the very moment Antoine had chased it from cover. How Jonas had ever managed to come out to this place of ours was a puzzle to me, until I saw his tracks in the snow. From the tent to the top of the esker I discovered a deep furrow carved through the yard-deep snow. That plucky little devil, he had dragged himself along on his belly!

Twilight had begun to fall and we turned back to the tent, where we prepared the hare and waited for the caribou-hunters to return. Later in the evening they appeared. The result of their hunt was one ptarmigan. So, after all, we had a Christmas Eve spread and this fact gave us much pleasure. With painful care we divided the food equally amongst ourselves and swallowed, as it were, all but the skin and the feathers. But Christmas Eve was no grand affair for the dogs.

Next morning, when we were ready to strike camp, Johnny found that he had lost all but one of his dogs. He had been careless enough to allow them to run loose during the night, and now they were unquestionably roaming the wastes in search of some game of their own. The chances that they would find their way back to the tent were certainly not great, but we decided to wait over a day, in any event, to see if they might not turn up. Johnny scraped up sticks of wood from near and far and made a little fire up on a hilltop so that the dogs might catch scent of the smoke. There he sat, half-frozen, all day long and half the night, in his endeavor to keep his fire burning. Along toward morning the dogs, tired and footsore, came trotting into camp.

Before we again broke camp, Antoine had a surprise for us. He dragged out a caribou stomach half-filled with blood and inner organs, which he had hidden away during an earlier hunt. He could not have given us a handsomer Christmas present. It was frozen as hard as a rock, but we chopped it up into fine bits with the ax and threw these into the large pot, which we then filled half-full of snow-water. The result was a greenish mess, but we drank it down greedily. Scraps of the skin of the stomach were dealt out equally and these we chewed carefully and swallowed bite by bite.

This proved to be our last meal for some time. We continued east for three days without food. A couple of times we experimented with some black lichens thoroughly boiled in water. They didn't taste at all bad, but they were not in the least degree filling. Aside from this it was tea, morning, noon, and night. We made enormous quantities of it and drank it scalding hot.

None of us were particularly spry as we tramped along on our snowshoes. It was a question of sparing the dogs as much as possible, so it was a rare occasion indeed when we could hop onto the load and ride. Gradually our gnawing hunger gave way to a feeling of general flaccidity. We felt the cold keenly at night, and in the daytime it was just as bad, for the icy snow of the Barrens would find its way in through the minutest rift in our clothing. The cold remained constant day after day and I am sure the temperature never rose above 40° below zero.

Nevertheless, the hardships which we ourselves endured were nothing compared with those which afflicted the dogs. It was a week now since they had eaten anything resembling a square meal, though they worked faithfully in the traces from morning till night, none the less. Their tails drooped and there was no longer the old pulling-power in their gait, but they moved along somehow. It is unbelievable what these dogs of the Northland can endure in the way of toil and deprivation, and inspiring is their patient willingness to work until their last ounce of strength is gone and they drop in the traces.

We crossed the divide, a conspicuous elevation in the terrain off to the northwest, and thereafter all the streams flowed east towards Hudson Bay. The third day after our meal of frozen caribou stomach we sighted some stunted spruces along a river course in a small valley. There we pitched our tent and held a general council to decide on the best course for us to pursue. Even the Indians could see that it would be dangerous to continue on our present course. Not a fresh caribou trail to be seen, and the wastes to the east of us gave promise of nothing. Hence we agreed

[211]

to turn due south on the following morning. Everything considered, that must be the direction in which the caribou were holding themselves; hunting was the one matter which concerned us now. Along the way, too, we might cross the sled-trail of some white trapper who had a cabin somewhere along the edge of the forest. The Indians had heard about this cabin, but none knew its exact location.

I should like to mention in this place that not once, either then or on later occasions when we were suffering from hunger, did I ever hear the Indians mention the possibility of eating the dogs. This was due to an old superstition to the effect that dogs are cannibalistic and therefore unclean, a belief I shall treat later. It has happened on occasion that white trappers have eaten their dogs, but amongst Indians I have never heard of such an occurence.

After concluding our conference, there was not much daylight left to us, hence we drove off with our dog-teams, each in a different direction in order to try our luck at hunting. Antoine and I, as usual, struck out together and set our course farther east. We had been driving steadily for some time without observing the slightest sign of life when suddenly, amongst all that white, we became aware of something green. We swung out of the river basin, and there, ahead of us, stood one tree after another, a forest of tall luxuriant conifers. At the foot of an elevation, they followed the slope down in the direction of a lake which stretched off into the white distance as far as the eye could reach. We halted our dogs.

" *Chizi-ta-tué, detchen thlé* (Lynx Lake, many trees)," said Antoine, pointing across the lake to a range of hills off to the north. From there he described the arc of a circle from the lake to a point northwest and added: "*Thelon Thesi!* "

TO THE UPPER THELON

So we had reached the Thelon at last! . . .

Here lay the woodland bordering the great unknown lakes from which the Thelon sets out on its long journey through the wilderness. Far, far away where the river pours its mighty waters into Hudson Bay, train-oil lamps were flickering in igloos and slant-eyed men were hunting the seal with harpoons; here on the banks of its upper reaches stood the sons of the forest, the Indians, scanning the horizon for caribou. . . .

But there was no time to be lost in contemplation. We were sorely in need of food. It seemed hopeless to consider the caribou, but we might possibly have some luck with small game. There were tracks of the polar hare, ptarmigan, and white fox. The latter must have discovered an El Dorado in this region, for they had cut regular pathways through the snow. It was bitter indeed to have attained our goal and to have discovered a veritable gold-mine in white fox alone, only to be without an ounce of meat with which to bait our traps.

We first gave our attention to the tracks of the ptarmigan. We circled round and round as we followed them, until Antoine finally pointed up at the sky. This was to indicate that the bird had probably taken wing at this point. Thereupon he turned the ptarmigan-hunt over to me, whilst he himself climbed up a slope to snoop around after hare. I left my sled down by the lake and loosened up the harnesses of the dogs in order to allow them more comfort when they lay down. Then I set off afoot to discover, if I could, further signs of ptarmigan. A short distance from the sled I came across some tracks. Bursting with eagerness, I went ranging around, already seeing in my mind's eye the bird roasting on the spit. Then something caused me to look up — I assure you, I received a shock! Out on the lake stood a wolf. It was glaring straight in the direction of the dogs, curled up each in his own little nest in the snow in front of the sled a short distance away from me. I raised my gun and fired. The wolf went head over heels, but was up in a flash, threw his head round, and began biting himself in the haunch where the bullet had struck, then limped off across the lake at an incredibly rapid pace.

The report from my gun had awakened the dogs with a start; they caught sight of the wolf, pranced high in the air from sheer eagerness, and, as one, leaped forward in the traces. There went my sled! I sprang over to it, hurled myself upon the long steering rope, which was trailing along behind in the snow, and caught hold of it. At that moment my wild journey began, the galloping dogs dragging me swiftly along through the snow. I simply had to hang on, for if ever I let go of that rope, it was farewell to my dogs. What a situation! Sometimes I was sailing along on my back, sometimes on my belly, my eyes blinded by the snow that was hurled in my face. It was worse when we got out on the lake, where furrow after furrow of drift snow frozen as hard as a rock dealt me one smart blow after another. Whenever I could momentarily catch my breath, I would yell to the dogs: " Whoa! Whoa! " until I thought my throat would burst. I begged and I implored and I swore and I cursed. But the dogs heeded nothing. Blind and deaf, they continued to race along after that fleeing animal — food! I ached all over and it seemed as though I should be unable to hold on a moment longer. Then, thank God, the sled capsized on a snow-drift. It dug into the snow as it dragged along on its side, and, since I was acting as an additional brake, the dogs soon slackened their pace and halted.

There was no profit in continuing the chase. The wolf

is a sturdy beast, and it is impossible to bring him down unless one strikes him directly in the heart or brain. I drove back to Antoine and found him pacing beside a fire. He had started one hare, but it had been too quick for him and had escaped before he could fire his gun. This he explained, and mumbled words to the effect that there must be something wrong with the country.

So all we could do was to return to the tent.

It was late afternoon and the mood of the Barrens was expressive of both good and evil. Directly ahead of us stood an enormous drift of snow from which a perfect blizzard of loose flakes was blowing. Overhead the cloudless heavens were glittering with stars, and a gentle moonlight streamed down and reflected itself in the myriad dancing snowflakes. The tent was almost snowed under, but we were finally able to find it. None of the others had returned as yet from the hunt. We made a fire in the stove, sat down on our sleeping-bags, lighted up our pipes, and settled ourselves to wait. Not a word was exchanged. But the same question was probably haunting us both: " Wonder if the others shot anything."

The hours crept by. At my side I caught a glimpse of Antoine's sharp profile. Motionless he sat there, stooping slightly forward, his legs drawn up beneath him. As I sat brooding over my own thoughts, the whole affair suddenly seemed unreal to me — the Indians, the flickering semi-gloom inside the tent, the snow-covered wastes. . . . My mind began to wander. A memory took form . . . Marseilles, once when I was there looking for a job . . . along the quays huge piles of sacks and boxes filled with meat and fruit . . . incredible that there could be so much fruit in the world, that there were folks who could eat all the fruit they wanted . . . and the meat . . . it must have

been pork, for it had thick rinds of fat. . . . Just think
of that — Marseilles! . . .

Damn those Indians, were they never coming? The wind
was increasing. The tent walls bellied and bulged.

Then we heard the faint sound of bells in the distance.
We listened tensely for a moment, and then we knew the
answer to our queries. The tone of the bells, in a clear language all its own, bespoke the tired trot of hungry dogs.
With rimy faces and with their clothes covered with snow,
the men staggered into the tent and took their places
in front of the stove. They said nothing, we asked no
questions. . . .

Only Johnny was missing. We waited up for him until
late that night, but he did not come. So we had lost one
man. I urged that we remain over one day and search for
Johnny, but the others wouldn't hear of this. When I stated
that he would in all likelihood perish, they simply laughed
at me and answered that he would get along all right. Next
morning the Indians struck camp to move due south as decided. There was nothing else for me to do but follow
along.

We had been driving quite some time when suddenly
the procession of sleds up ahead came to a halt. " *E-then!* "
I heard someone shout excitedly. And indeed it was true!
Ahead on the plain a wandering band of caribou! They
had already got wind of us and were running in a long line
up the slope of an esker and soon disappeared down the
other side. A powerful buck which was running in the wake
of the others paused momentarily on the summit of the
esker to stare in our direction, his mighty crown of antlers
held high, his shaggy mane gleaming snow-white in the
sunlight.

Forgotten was our hunger, forgotten the white trappers'

cabin. The primitive instincts of the Indians flamed up.
Here were caribou; chase them, kill them! They were willing to stake all on the turn of one card; they would risk a
senseless intoxicating chase for the chance of seeing the
game drop in the snow, remote though that chance might
be. They were like wolves with the scent of blood in their
nostrils. We could now see the deer storming across the
wastes far away in a cloud of snow. The chase seemed so
hopeless. . . .

The sleds swung round; all jumped aboard, stood up,
and began brandishing their arms, yelling and whipping
up their dogs. The commotion seemed quite unnecessary;
the exhausted animals were at once transformed, for they,
too, were hunters by instinct. Like wild things they threw
their last ounce of strength into the harness and started off
in a mad reckless charge across the frozen prairie.

Then began a chase I shall remember all my days; over
the broad flats we went, up and down the wave-like swells
of the tundric plain. At one moment I would glimpse an
Indian sled ahead of me, at the next it had disappeared
over the crest of an esker, and at the next I would catch
sight of the caribou like pin-pricks on the horizon, then
these too would disappear. We traveled north, we traveled
south, we traveled in all directions, according to the tracks
of our game. I had no idea where I was; I merely held
tight to the sled and let the dogs go. On and on we flew into
this world of endless white where the sunlight met the distant horizon in a blinding glare.

The hours passed and the dogs began to slacken their
pace; they had reached the end of their strength. Then the
meaninglessness of it all came over me: to wear out our
dogs completely merely to pursue a luckless chase, instead
of continuing south where some way out of our difficulty

would somehow present itself and where we might perhaps locate the white trappers' cabin. The more I thought about it, the more roiled I became with these feather-brained Indians whose lack of common sense had led them to waste a perfectly good day.

Then I caught sight of Moose's sled in a hollow some distance ahead. In a flash he halted his dogs, jumped out, tied the leader to the tail of the sled, put on his snowshoes, and began dashing across the snow. On the crest of an esker stood a caribou buck. It wheeled about in terror and began zigzagging away at a trot, Moose after it.

Good lord, how that fellow could run! Tired and worn out as the rest of us, he nevertheless went like the wind. With swift, gaining strides he glided along over the snow and would spurt as though his life depended upon it whenever he cut an angle from the trail of the buck. Tirelessly he kept on, all the time growing smaller and smaller in the distance as I watched him.

Here was a typical Barren Land Indian to the uttermost depths of his being, with the ability to put everything he had into the last crucial moment. Here was the hard cold struggle for existence as it has developed amongst these Indians for thousands of years. To wrest nourishment from the country, cold and hunger notwithstanding, is for them a question of life or death.

A shot rang out. When I drove up, I found the caribou kicking up the snow as he lay there in his death agony. Soon we had all gathered about the slain beast. Seldom have I seen an animal skinned and quartered with such solicitude. The marrow and the fat we ate right there on the spot, washing it down with a cupful or two of blood. What remained of the blood we immediately drained off into the stomach pouch. After giving the dogs a taste, we threw the remainder of the meat into the sleds and drove off. A stain on the snow was all that was left of the buck.

We traveled cross-country back to our original tracks in the snow in order to head south from there in search of a likely camp-site. After we had been driving for a time, we caught sight of some black specks against the snow in the distance. At first we anticipated either caribou or wolves, but soon we saw that it was a dog-train dragging a sled. It was Johnny. He was jabbing along on snowshoes behind his sled, a loose dog trailing in his wake. He and his dogs seemed barely able to crawl along.

Then we heard his story. While out hunting the evening before, a fog of blowing snow had closed in on him and he thought it better judgment to spend the night where he was. On the following morning, when he returned to camp, he found the tent gone and had started out to follow our tracks in the snow. He had been on the go since early morning, but had made little progress, for, as he said: " *Ber-basthi* (I'm hungry)." When we told him about the caribou we had shot, his spirits rose at once.

We had an entirely new feeling that evening as we sat together in the tent and listened to the kettle of meat simmering on the stove. Every particle of the caribou found its way under our belts. The dogs received their share, which might have been larger had not all the Indians carefully gathered up all the gnawed bones and thrown them into the fire. To have given them to the dogs would have betokened ill luck.

Once again we resumed our journey southward. It was extremely difficult going, no less because of the cold, which was so intense that one could not remain still an instant without beginning to grow stiff. We floundered along for quite some time, ever on the look-out for the caribou herd and the white trappers' cabin. About us lay the snow-fields devoid of any sign of life, and we encountered one disappointment after another. We did manage to shoot a pair of lone caribou, but their meat did not go far with our hungry band. At length we were snowed in tight for two days during a blizzard; then it was that our spirits reached their lowest ebb.

But at last one evening, just as we were on the point of pitching camp, Isep discovered the faint trail of a toboggan in the snow. We did not dare risk the possibility that drift snow might obliterate the trail, so, after a brief halt, we loaded all our stuff back on the sleds and continued on our way throughout a long moonlight night, with frequent rests out of deference to the dogs, which every now and then would drop in the traces. Countless times we lost the trail. Then we would spread in formation out over the plain and would search high and low, now and then creeping about on all fours as we felt in the snow for signs of the trail. Thus we proceeded until sunrise, when we glimpsed the forest's first outposts — rows of dwarf spruce growing in the lee of each elevation. In a snug hollow we built ourselves a mighty fire, poured scalding tea into ourselves, and continued to follow the sled-trail down the length of a long, narrow lake. Just as we were rounding a jut of land, we spied smoke curling up from a clump of spruce, and a log cabin cosily situated in amongst the trees.

Jonas was the first to pull up in front of the door. Two dumfounded trappers came forward, wondering for all they were worth who in blazes had managed to find his way out into this part of the country. Their amazement hardly diminished when they saw a tattered Indian limp out of the sled with his crutch, lay his hand on his belly and say: " *Long time, misu dowté* (Long time, no food)." This mixture of English, Cree, and his own Chipewyan language was the very best that Jonas could do in the way of speaking a foreign language.

Hospitality is the law of the land, but to provide for a starving band like ourselves was a problem in itself. Old McKay and Clark didn't know what they could find to offer us, for they had barely enough to scrape through the rest of the winter themselves. Mac presented me with a large slab of dried back-fat left over from the autumn hunt; this slab was two inches thick. I shall never forget him for that. I was tempted sorely to swallow the whole thing down just as fast as ever I could, but luckily I had common sense enough to refrain from doing that. I cut it up into small bits and stuffed my pockets with these, went about like a living warehouse and nibbled fat for over a week. The dogs also received their share, and it was amazing how this braced them up. To get along on little and to recuperate quickly are second nature to these animals.

We learned that the caribou had gone on strike in this part of the country as well. After the autumn trek had passed in October, the herds had become sparse and few in number. McKay and Clark had been forced to use all their time hunting food for themselves and their dogs. Trapping had had to go by the board. Thus they had wasted a year, and no combination of toil and saving had amounted to anything. To begin with, there had been their autumn journey through the wilderness from Fitzgerald, following a canoe route of nearly four hundred and fifty miles, with fifty portages; then there had been their daily struggle for food through a long winter of cold and storm in the Barren Lands. After all this they would find themselves poorer than they were the day they had set out through the wilderness and would have to go in debt to " Hudson Bay " in order to buy their next year's equipment. But, even so, Clark and old Mac had nothing but good humor to express. Good luck or bad — why, great Heaven, it is the gamble that makes the life of a trapper such an interesting adventure! One must always take the bitter with the sweet.

We remained with our hosts for three days, then set out in a northwesterly direction and kept going until we crossed the trail we had made on the way out. Thereafter we made for the camp of the Caribou-Eaters at the rapid pace always chosen by Indian hunters when they are returning home to their wives and children. We drove as often at night as during the day and, in the darkness, took many rash chances as we traveled over steep rough country or over river rapids where the ice gave way beneath us and the water splashed about our carioles. Crossing the larger lakes, we would lie in our sleds and sleep. We did not once pitch our tent; instead, we slept beside an open camp-fire wherever possible and then only long enough to allow the dogs to recover their strength.

After we had been driving for three days, we encountered the main body of the caribou! Herds numbering thousands came grazing along toward the east. It was indeed ironical to see the plains now literally alive with the very hosts we had talked of and dreamed of so many times on the way out, when the plains had lain cold and lifeless. And bitter was the thought that, had we made our journey but a few weeks later, we should have lived on the fat of the land and, in addition to this, reaped a golden harvest of white-fox pelts on the banks of the Thelon.

But I had seen the head waters of this mighty river!

One afternoon, as we were gliding across Nonacho Lake and had only about twelve more miles to go, we made a fire and settled down to rest for the remainder of the day and night. To come driving into camp in the dark was neither fitting nor proper. On the following morning we literally raced across the lake. Even so, our pace quickened when we caught sight of the women. They were standing on a hill, their wide skirts and dark shawls whipping in the wind, as they stared off at the procession of sleds which, to the steady music of the bells, was twisting its way along through sun and snow. As we pulled up in front of the tepees, they thronged together — these women and children — and there were smiles and welcomes home for the far-faring hunters.

The Camp of the Caribou-Eaters

I PITCHED MY TENT IN THE INDIAN VILLAGE AND SOON FELT perfectly at home amongst the Caribou-Eaters. I went about from tepee to tepee as I chose, and there was no longer anyone who looked wide-eyed at the white man, even though many a jest was uttered at my expense, because I was " as tall as a tree," because I had " feet like a bear's " and " a fist like two." I tried as well as I could to adapt myself to conditions without going to extremes. The fact that I put on no airs because of my being a white man strengthened my position with the natives. More by instinct than anything else, the Indians appreciated my attitude of being on equal terms with them. They observed that I was thriving in their village, and that flattered them. But an Indian is an Indian. Many of his inborn traits are enough to set a white man's teeth on edge, and if the redskin is in a particular frame of mind, shamelessly and smilingly he will take advantage of the fact that a white man has established himself on a basis of equality with him. Rifts grew up between a couple of the Caribou-Eaters and myself. Our controversies were of short duration, however, and on the whole our relationship left nothing to be desired, this condition being exemplified by the fact that I was always invited to their village gatherings. I was accepted as a member of their society, or, as Antoine expressed it, " almost as good as a red man."

The Caribou-Eaters, who, as a general rule, spend most of the winter hunting in the Barren Lands, decided that, since the caribou were extremely uncertain this year, it would be wiser to remain for the time being in the woodlands. Thus the days passed with hunting and camp life. Early in the morning the hunters would start out with their dogs, each in a different direction. Sometimes we would make journeys lasting three or four days, setting our traps and shooting caribou. Occasionally we would all sally forth in a body. Then in the evening, when we would return with our sleds loaded to capacity, there would be merry-making in the village, followed by a grand feast. All that we shot was divided equally. One day Moose brought down eight caribou and gave away seven.

The Caribou-Eater women were for the most part younger-looking and more attractive than those of any other tribes I have seen. They did not indulge in idleness. From early morning till late at night their life was one of activity. There were dried meat to be cut up, skins to be tanned, moccasins and caribou coats to be stitched, the tepee to be kept in order, fresh spruce twigs to be strewn on the floor, food to be prepared for every hour of the day and night, thieving dogs to be cleared from the tent, and infants to be suckled. And in the midst of everything, with their hands full, they would have to drop everything, sling their youngest papoose over their back, step into their snowshoes, and betake themselves to the forest to chop firewood. Bowed beneath the weight of several logs of wood, they would return to the tepee and swing the ax like any man. And, even so, there was still time for a bit of faithlessness and a word or two of gossip with the squaw in the neighboring tent.

Some of the young girls of sixteen or seventeen were dangerously ardent and were easily worth a second glance.

[225]

But after observing them in the act of being deloused a time
or two, I soon lost all desire in their direction. A girl would
lie with her head in her mother's lap, permitting the latter
to negotiate a long and thoroughgoing hunt. The game she
managed to capture she would put into her mouth, crack
between her teeth, and swallow with seeming relish.

It was amazing how easily everything ordered itself in
this Indian society. The Caribou-Eaters might wrangle
amongst themselves, and that quite strenuously, but hostili-
ties would always break out in a fit of passion and would
never leave a feeling of rancor in their wake. Whenever a
man flared up, it was certain that a woman was at the bottom of it. One day shrieks and howls were heard from
Moose's tepee; he was pitching into his wife because she
had been untrue to him with Sitor. A few days later, when
Sitor was out hunting, his wife committed adultery with
Moose. So Sitor gave her a beating. But Moose and Sitor
remained as good friends as ever!

Some time ago the tribe had been in contact with Roman Catholic missionaries. On the surface, signs of this
contact were evident. But now and then I would catch a
glimpse of an entirely different realm of thought, a world
of superstition and ancient beliefs wherein wolves, moose,
caribou, bears, and the forces of nature were reincarnated
in the souls of men. What forest and lake and barren plain
had whispered into the ears of these Indian families for
past millenniums still found echo in their deepest souls.
But in regard to such matters — and these I shall discuss
in a later chapter — the Indians were extremely reticent.

Tijōn's three-year-old son was ill with a terrific headache
and such pains in his body that he was obliged to creep
about on all fours. Isep was called in to administer a cure.
Encountering him as he was busy preparing the medicine,

I asked him to explain what he was doing. His reticence knew no bounds. Later, however, when I informed him that I didn't feel quite well myself, told him I had great faith in his medicine, and asked him to try it on me, he melted somewhat. In the end he allowed me some insight into his realm of science. He even served me with a whole cup of powerful laxative, which had a bitter taste and a foul odor.

He prepared this medicine as follows: four small bundles of sweet gale (*Myrica gale*) and birch-root (in this case, the outer bark removed) were tied up in deerskin, dropped into a kettle of water, and boiled for thirty minutes. The resulting liquid was poured off and drunk by the patient. It was essential that the sticks of wood in each bundle should be of a certain number, and of a prescribed length and shape. If the patient failed to improve after such treatment, it was a sign that the medicine had been imperfectly prepared, or, as Isep said: " Evil sickness won't get out."

．．

Late in March a period of cold set in, the temperature being lower than any I had ever before experienced. Down on Slave Lake the Canadian police, as I later learned, took a thermometer reading of 76° below zero. I had my own thermometer, a rather crude instrument — my nose. When it became frozen, I knew that it was cold; but when, as in this case, it froze so often that I was obliged to rub it continually with the back of my mitten, I knew that it was colder than cold, and that was saying a great deal. Fortunately the air was still, as is usually the case when a cold wave settles over the country, but, even so, it was extremely uncomfortable for both man and beast to be out of doors. The fur animals crept into their lairs, and there was hardly a fresh trail to be seen in the snow. The caribou remained in the deep woods, and the few that appeared on the ice of the lakes kept constantly in motion. They never came within fair range, and it was a problem to bare one's fingers long enough to load and fire one's gun. At times I would be forced to beat my hands together just as some caribou were passing; at other times my fingers would freeze to the gun and I would have to stop and thaw them out in the snow.

During this period there were whole days when the Indians would remain home in the village. Otherwise they took little notice of the cold. Their hardiness has many times astounded me. In a biting blast they can haul in a net which they have set out under the ice, and actually sing as they occasionally dip their hands in the water to keep them from freezing. They can lie down to sleep under a simple caribou blanket wherever they may find themselves, and wake up next morning entirely rested. On their feet they wear two pairs of stockings; these and their moccasins are all that protect their toes. What factors determine their powerful resistance to cold I shall not even attempt to analyze. Suffice it to say that, unlike the Eskimos, they have no layer of fatty tissue to protect them from the cold; they are a slender, sinewy folk.

It is always a source of much smiling amusement on the part of the redskins whenever a white man begins to feel the effects of frost. My nose, thus, was the cause of no small amount of interest. Whenever it would take on a whitish hue, it was obliged to bear the brunt of many a clever witticism. But when, by dint of much rubbing on my part, it would come to life again and begin blossoming red and violet, my public was with me to a man. All such trifling drolleries appealed to the Indians' sense of humor. They saw everything, and with the slightest disturbance of the usual order of things, they would swoop down like hawks and allow no opportunity for amusement to escape them. If Jonas happened to lace up his moccasins in a way differing but slightly from the usual, he was obliged to endure their laughter. If I chanced to push my fur cap back from my forehead, it was my turn to be laughed at. Every type of ill luck gave rise to their huge enjoyment. Once Isep's dogs came trotting into camp alone; they had run away with the sled whilst he was out hunting. Isep had been obliged to tramp home on snowshoe, a distance of between fifteen and twenty miles. It was not until late that same night that he put in his appearance, tired and hungry. The disagreeable experience he had gone through during the fore-part of the day was nothing compared with the ridicule he was obliged to endure when the other hunters undertook to comment upon the incident. Once a cache packed with frozen caribou carcasses broke down when Moose was beneath it, and he escaped a broken neck by a hair's breadth. As he limped, stiff and sore, back to his tepee, he was followed by ringing salvos of laughter!

After a time the caribou began to thin out, but by dint of much assiduous hunting we were able to procure all the meat we required. Along in April our task became more difficult; the game seemed more and more to shun our region, a situation probably due in part to the wave of intense cold. The result was that we now had fewer and fewer marrowbones, caribou heads, and other good things to eat.

Earlier in the winter, whenever a band of caribou would unexpectedly turn up on the ice right outside the camp, an old squaw who had her tent up on a hill where there was a good view of the lake would utter a cry of warning. Whatever hunters were in camp would promptly harness their dogs and race off after the deer. But such episodes of home hunting had, of late, become few and far between.

Then came the day when I was the only male left in camp. One corner of my sled had been partially broken off by striking against a tree, and I had been obliged to repair the damage before setting out with the other hunters. Just as I was standing there in the act of binding it up with babiche, the old squaw came racing down the hillside as fast as her legs would carry her, waving her arms and howling at the top of her lungs: " *E-then! E-then!* " In a flash, women and children poured out of the tepees and began gaping out over the lake. Far out, there was a band of some twenty caribou. What a disturbance then took place! Before I could utter a word, I was surrounded by a regular crowd of squaws. One tugged at my right arm and begged me for two caribou heads, another grabbed my left arm and put in her reservation for three. Then I felt an iron grip on my shoulder and was jerked sharply about face by the heavyweight, Phresi, demanding tongues and half a caribou carcass, as a mere detail, to go with them. At length even little Kachesy ingratiatingly fingered my jacket and made the whole thing even more difficult. All in all, these women demanded of me more meat than a hunter, under ordinary circumstances, would be able to shoot in the course of a week. I attempted to make a few meek objections, but was silenced at once. And, after all, what reply could I make, surrounded by all these women and children who looked trustingly upon me as the only available man and who were giving expression to such blind faith in my prowess as a hunter?

Since my sled was laid up, I put on my snowshoes, the entire party of women meanwhile stationing themselves on a hilltop from whence they could view the hunt. Whether it was this gallery of the fair sex that disturbed my mental poise and caused my hand to shake, I cannot say for sure. Suffice it to mention that I took uncertain aim at long range and succeeded in but slightly wounding one buck. Terrified by the shot, it raced off down the lake, mile after mile, pursued, unfortunately for me, by all its fellows. In a short time they all appeared as pin-pricks on the horizon. As they were fleeing, I sent a few pot-shots flying after them, but not a single creature fell.

My return to camp was anything but triumphant. I had contemplated sneaking up to my tent in silence, but nothing came of this notion. The massed ranks of the women stood in my path. Their scorn was unendurable. One asked me how many animals I had slain, another asked me for the head I had promised her, a third stated that she was already boiling the water for the tongues I said I would bring her, so now I could give them to her, she said. Only Phresi was well-meaning in her way; she took me aside and, in a motherly voice, explained to me the reason why I had failed to bring down any game: it was because I had remained behind while the hunters were off on an expedition. "For it is something which everyone knows, that he who hangs back in camp and shows too much interest in the women loses his luck as a hunter." I accepted this criticism without opening my mouth.

The cloud of opprobrium which hung over my head was not soon dispelled. To disgrace oneself as a hunter is, in this Indian society, no less serious than scandal affecting lawyer, doctor, or priest in a civilized community. There is no defense of one's failure; there are no extenuating circumstances, absolutely none. That the caribou had been within range and that not one had been slain were two hard, cold facts, which were highly aggravated by a third: the

[231]

whole affair had taken place just when there was something
of a food shortage. Such was the judgment I suffered. Furthermore, it had not been pronounced by a court of law;
worse than that, it was made known in the insulting attitude
of these Indians toward me and in the painful allusions
they made to me. This was their form of justice. In the
end there was only one thing for me to do: I would have
to make amends. So I harnessed up my dogs and departed
into the forest, with the determination that I would keep
going until I had felled some kind of game, even were it
to take me a week. I would not return until I could do so
with my sled loaded down with meat, my name and prestige re-established.

I knocked about for two days without coming within
range of a single wild creature. The few I sighted dashed
off in mad flight as soon as they saw my sled. I then
adopted a new stratagem, often chosen by the Indians on
biting cold days when it is downright impossible to creep
up on one's game. I established myself on an island, in
the vicinity of a narrow sound through which the caribou
would be likely to pass, and prepared to wait them out.

During the afternoon they arrived — four powerful
bucks! Sighting the smoke from my fire, they started a bit,
but continued, undaunted, along their chosen course. I
brought down three of them. The fourth was wounded, but
I followed it on snowshoe in through the woods and at last,
after an exciting chase, got home a shot. So far as I could
determine, all four of these deer were woodland caribou,
which have a more lofty crown of antlers and are considerably larger than the Barren Ground caribou. If so, these
were the first of this species I had shot in this region.

It was pleasant indeed to return home to the camp that
evening. Proudly seated on my load, I swung up in front

of the tepees, and shouted such an imperious " Whoa! " to the dogs that the occupants of even the remotest tents appeared. With that, I threw the meat out of the sled and arranged it in a large pile, making no great ceremony of the act, and, as casually as I possibly could, I said that there were two or three more carcasses out in the woods and suggested that it would be wise to cart them in before the wolves got at them.

That evening there was a banquet at the home of Tijōn. Two tallow candles were lit, and we all sat about in a wide circle. The choicest morsels were then passed round: first, the marrowbones and the roasted heads of the beasts I had slain, then round patties made of dried meat chopped up and mixed with fresh fat, a large wooden bowl of fried marrow, a pile of selected dried meat, inch-thick slabs of dried fat, and a bark cup full of otter-fat.

When the meal was over, Isep began to beat on his tom-tom. Immediately everyone picked up whatever object he could reach — knife, pipe, or snowshoe — and began to hammer out the rhythm on the stove-pipe, frying-pans, or meat-kettle, whilst they all burst out at the top of their lungs with that wild, monotonous festival song with its refrain of " *Hi-hi-he, hi-hi-he-ho, hi-yi*," uttered in screeches in every pitch and in every key. A most weirdly intricate orchestra of sound.

Then followed the dance. I remained in the background, for I could do nothing with this Indian dance. Furthermore, the roof was too low for my head. Great slabs of dried meat hung in rows from the tent-poles and I had to bend almost double every time I wished to cross the floor. But when the Indians crowded around me and insisted, I took my life in my hands and threw myself into the dance.

The effect was as I had feared. I leaned over so far that

[233]

my back ached, I ducked my head like a boxer, but no matter which way I turned, I ran afoul of dried meat. Dried meat cuffed at my neck, dried meat came raining down from above, and dried meat lay beneath my tramping feet. At length there were but a few slabs left hanging in their place, while on the floor there must have been the flesh of many a carcass. Then I threw up both hands and quit. But it was a long time before the Indians recovered from their hearty laugh. They simply lay down on their caribou blankets, held their sides, and roared. Oh, the white man! . . .

· ·

It was late in May, and spring was at hand. The caribou were trekking far off to the east in the direction of the Barren Lands, and in our section of the country there were very few of them left. Were a man to be dependent upon his luck in the field, it would not be long before he would find himself in dire straits. It happened that one hunter was without game for eight full days. On the other hand, some hunters might spasmodically run into a streak of splendid luck. Thanks be to the socialistic basis on which the Indians governed their society, we were able to keep going. We shared all we had and, although we lived no life of luxury, we did not experience any immediate want.

I had now definitely identified myself with the Caribou-Eaters. It was as though I had been one of them for years. Their daily life in camp and on the trail now seemed quite natural to me. If, early in the morning, I should sling my gun over my shoulder, go about amongst the tepees, stick my head in the door, and say good morning to the hunters, squaws, and youngsters, sitting half-dressed about on the floor as they chewed down pieces of dried meat, it seemed no more an unnatural thing for me to do than, in the past, it had seemed to stride jauntily down the street to my office, my legal portfolio under my arm, as I greeted acquaintances along the way. All that lay beyond the bounds of everyday life in the forest seemed remote and irrelevant. As I rode along in my sled behind my trotting dogs, I experienced no feelings of envy when I thought of all the good burghers living in civilized communities. I was getting along fine and time passed so rapidly that, in the main, I had no worries for the future. To be sure, I had no intention of living the life of an Indian for the rest of my days, but I gave no thought to a possible change, until one day something happened.

It began with Phresi, Kachesy's mother. She had always been straightforward and helpful, but of late she had been showing me attentions quite out of the ordinary. One day, out of a clear sky, she presented me with a brand-new pair of moccasins; on another occasion she surreptitiously took my deerskin coat and edged it from top to bottom with a dashing embellishment of wolverine fur. Then, whenever there was a dearth of food in the village, she would always manage to present me with a toothsome marrowbone or a bit of dried meat. There seemed to be no limit to her regard for me. All this attention from fat old Phresi was at first highly mysterious to me; then I began to smell a mouse and kept my eyes and ears open. I began to notice one thing or another, slight innuendoes and suchlike. Whenever I would enter a tepee, the squaws would put their heads together, begin whispering and giggling in such a manner as to produce a certain unpleasant effect upon me; the hunters, for their part, were constantly after me with jibes of the most insipid variety. Something was up, and then one day, blind as I had been, the last shred of doubt vanished. The whole village was simply taking it for granted that Kachesy and I were contemplating matrimony. The only one ignorant of the situation had been the bridegroom!

Kachesy (Little Hare) was seventeen winters old. She was quite different from the others. When quite young, she had spent some time in the Roman Catholic mission in the south, and there she had learned something about religion, as well as other matters. But she was still far from being tamed, even though she seemed mild enough at times. The very abruptness of her transitions from savagery to moods of dreamy peace was perhaps her most noticeable Indian trait. For there was something of the wilderness itself in Kachesy, no more when she was racing along on snowshoe than when she sat in the candlelight, her head bowed over her agile little hands, flying through their work, her black hair streaming down over her shoulders.

More than one dark-skinned hunter had gazed upon her with enterprising eyes. And Kachesy herself — yes, she had a bewitching gleam in her eye for one and all and was never wanting when it came to the use of the small devices common to women the world over, regardless of their color. At one moment she was a troll, at the next something quite different, but, taken altogether, neither better nor worse than the white members of her sex. Furthermore, she would kneel down on her sleeping-bag every evening in the candlelight and pray to the Virgin Mary. So there were many things about her which were anything but dangerous.

No, there was nothing to be said against Kachesy. Worse things could befall a man than to return from the hunt to a tepee in which she was waiting, so for that matter . . . But to be a " squaw-man " ! . . .

Quietly and alone I took stock of the situation. I fully

realized that since, without consulting me, it had been decreed that I was to receive the honor of being taken to their bosom, so to speak, by the Caribou-Eater tribe, the most tradition-loving of all the Indians up north, I was confronted by a consideration of the most practical nature. I was regarded as a good match. Not that there was the slightest indication that should lead them to suppose me a man of means — dogs, gun, ammunition, and the clothes I wore on my back constituted my entire stock of worldly goods — but the redskins still indulge in a mystical faith in the white man's resources. He is regarded as able to procure " heap of food," which is the greatest fortune conceivable in the forests east of Great Slave Lake. To marry one's daughter to a white trapper is considered by the Indians as a certain means of support, and the natural consequence of this belief is that the poor trapper marries not only the daughter, but her entire family as well.

My situation was not enviable. It was a long way back to Great Slave Lake, and the snow lay deep on the ground. If I were to attempt the journey alone, I should be obliged to break trail all the way, and wretched indeed would be my progress. I should have to figure on being a long, long time on the road. I could manage this all right, however, were it not for the difficult question of providing food for the dogs. To set out with an empty sled and to rely upon wild game exclusively would be sheer foolhardiness, judging by the recent paucity of venison. At best, I should have to carry with me enough provender to last myself and the dogs for at least the first couple of days. But there was already a food shortage in the village, and no relief in sight.

There I was, virtually a prisoner in that Indian village! Hard up as I was, I should have to bide my time and hope for a lucky kill, if not soon, at any event later, when the bucks should come trekking through the woods on their way north. Until some means of retreat could be assured me, I should have to remain on and maintain a poker face. Being the only white man amongst these Indians in the depth of the wilderness, I recoiled from the thought of putting my foot in it by telling them straight to their faces that I declined the honor they had offered me. They were odd fish, those redskins; they had their own way of looking at things, and were I to spring such a bomb-shell as this, it was not easy to tell where things would end. It was certain, in any case, that they would ostracize me socially, and this would be fatal at such a time of food shortage as the present. Although none save the Indians themselves had produced these complications for me, I felt quite bad about the double role I was obliged to play. "Mother-in-law" treated me with ever-increasing familiarity, and soon there were no limits to the pleasantries exchanged by the hunters at the expense of the "betrothed." Kachesy, in the meantime, spent her entire day at work upon the most charming pair of moccasins imaginable, embroidered as they were with red and blue flowers. Judging by the size, there was no doubt whatever as to whom they were intended for.

During the four years I spent knocking about in northern Canada, it was many times my fate to look anxiously forward to the arrival of the caribou. But the keenest anxiety of all — and I do not exclude those periods when my larder was utterly exhausted — was that which I experienced during my imprisonment in that Indian village when, with marriage hanging over my head, I waited for the bucks to come trekking north through the forest, thus giving me an opportunity to escape.

After a time the first small bands appeared and it was not long before the village food-supply had been restored to normal. Thereupon I bundled up a goodly amount of dried meat, went to my friend Antoine, and told him that I was going west to visit some white people on *Tu-de-theh-chō* (Slave Lake). Apparently he found nothing strange in my plan and merely asked me when I should return. I answered truthfully that I couldn't exactly say, but that likely enough we should be meeting again before long. He said that he himself was planning to come down to the trading post some time during the summer, and that he would surely run into me then.

A tremendous task lay ahead of me. One must have been through it himself to realize what labor it entails to plow along on snowshoe, clearing a path for the sled, at the same time keeping an eye on the dogs. There were no trails to follow, and I had only a notion of the general direction. Great was my relief, then, on the eve of my departure, when Antoine came over to me and said: "*Si, nen, beth-chinny, kli — mush!* (I, you, sled, dogs — march!) " It turned out that he intended to accompany me for three days, helping me to break trail. He was my friend to the last, that Antoine!

"*Oré-liōn* (Fine weather)," said Antoine, grinning up at the sun that morning as we stood outside the tepees, ready to begin our journey. White and gold lights were playing over lake and forest, and the air was so cold and still that the smoke from the tepees rose straight up into the blue like a series of slender pillars. The sleds were loaded, the carioles laced up tight, and up in front the dogs were snatching forty last winks, as they lay there all curled up, their noses buried under their tails. About us crowded the Indians. There was Phresi in all her might, there was Tijōn with his crafty, wrinkled face, Moose, clean-cut and straight, Jonas, leaning on his crutch, and all the others with whom I had shared joys and sorrows for nearly a year. The little Indian boys, almost lost to sight in their heavy caribou coats, formed a group by themselves. One of these was Batis, a little hunter of four. Several times I had taken him hunting with me, for that was the best entertainment one could offer him. Whenever the dogs would light out in a top burst of speed after the fleeing game, he would kneel as far forward in the cariole as he could, his small arms encircling the curved nose of the sled, and cry: " Hoi! Hoi! "

As they stood there in a little circle about me, there was something pathetic about these children of the wilderness who were clinging to the old life of their forefathers there in the forest, but who would soon have to go down beneath the wheels of fate, inexorably approaching from the land of the white man. Poor Caribou-Eaters — here were the sorry remnants of a once proud tribe — a little band of human beings on the shore of Nonacho Lake — the lake " with a string of islands."

I took my leave of each of them individually — all save Kachesy, who was standing apart outside one of the tepees. As I approached her, she fled into the woods. She was wearing her new caribou parka, edged with wolverine fur and embellished with broad red fillets. As she ran, her hood fell back from her head, and the last I saw of her was her black hair flowing out behind her.

With a crack of our whips, we trotted away from the camp. Just before we rounded Caribou Point, I turned to look back. The tepees were already hidden from sight; only the smoke which rose through the tops of the spruces bore witness to the existence of human life back there. At the very moment we were rounding the point, a fraction of a second before it shut off my view, it seemed as though someone appeared at the edge of the woods, someone who waved. But of course I couldn't be sure. . . .

The moment we left Nonacho Lake and began to pick our way through the forest, our tedious labors began. I broke trail, leaving Antoine to guide the dogs. Every step of the way was a task. The snow came well up to our thighs and lay like a heavy load on our snowshoes. The dogs had to wallow through as best they could. Antoine cursed.

After driving for three days, we came across a herd of caribou on a large lake. We chased them and brought down two of their number. Antoine then announced that he thought he had accompanied me far enough and would turn homeward as soon as we had eaten. We set up our last camp together in the lee of the roots of an upturned tree, on the sunshiny slope of a snug little hill. There we held a splendid farewell feast of rich kidneys, marrowbones, and caribou heads. After we had stuffed as much into us as we could hold, Antoine lighted his pipe, uttered a curt farewell, jumped into the cariole, and was off in the blink of an eye — every move like lightning, as was characteristic of him. I stared after his sled, watched it grow smaller and smaller as it proceeded out over the lake. The top of his deerskin hood, which was visible over the cariole's backboard, was all that I could see of little Antoine, but his shrill " *Taislini! Taislini!* " to his dogs, sounded clearly out over the ice until his sled disappeared in the woods across on the other side.

So the remainder of my journey I should have to make alone. We did our best — both I and my dogs — but how slowly we traveled! If we managed to cover six miles during the course of the first two days, this was the limit. At length I arrived on a long, narrow lake, formed by the Snowdrift River just before it breaks into a series of turbulent rapids. Ahead of me now lay the hardest stretch of all, an expanse of rugged country, almost devoid of lakes and covered with a maze of scrubby growth.

I was just about to leave the ice when I heard a shot. Startled, I gazed about me and discovered far out on the lake two sleds headed straight in my direction. Who in Heaven's name could it be, I wondered. Probably some of the Caribou-Eaters who had taken advantage of my freshly broken trail whilst out hunting, I thought to myself; for the possibility of running across anyone else in this God-forsaken neck of the woods seemed remote enough to smack of a fairy-tale. But, by George, how tall and bushy those dogs' tails were, as they danced along through the air! And how high the dogs held their heads, as they seemed fairly to hew their way along through the snow — white men's dogs!

Two huge fellows hopped out of their sleds, gave me their paws, and said: " How are you? "

We scrutinized each other. Confronting me stood two men, their faces overgrown with stiff, frost-bedecked beards from which lumps of ice were dangling. Who the dickens can these ferocious wild men be, I wondered, entirely forgetting that my own tattered clothing and year-old facial decorations might also be the cause of no small amount of wonderment.

Not many words had passed between us, however, before we were able to identify each other. One was Price, the big shot amongst the trappers east of Great Slave Lake, a splendid chap with whom I had made friends the summer before. The other was queer old Pehrson. They were returning from a point far east in the Barren Lands where they had encountered the same conditions we others had this year. Things had finally become so badly off with them that they had been obliged to find their way all the way down to Otter Sound in the Taltson River, where they were just able to make ends meet by fishing through the ice. Now they were cleaned out of everything and were trying to get back to the trading post on Slave Lake. Nor did they fail to express their surprise to find me paddling about in the woods alone. Price shook his head suggestively. It is anything but pleasant to contemplate how our journey would have ended had not a friendly fate brought us three together there in the remotest corner of the wilderness.

Not one of us knew the way in. We set a course due west, thus reckoning that we were bound sooner or later to strike Slave Lake. From there we could always find our way along.

We set out and in the course of two weeks covered as many miles as a dog-team under more favorable conditions could accomplish in a couple of days. We took hourly turns at breaking trail, for after an hour of this gruelling task both man and dogs were utterly worn out. Nor were there any limits to the brushwood through which we were obliged to hew our way.

But in spite of our toil by day, we had splendid times together in our tent during the evenings. Each of us had been wandering about in his own corner of the wilderness for nearly a year, and now it was a relief to talk about it. For me, after having identified myself with a tribe of Indians, limited myself to their narrow realm of thought, and adopted a childish medium of speech which was the worst kind of jargon imaginable, it was like entering a marvelous new world simply to see white faces again and to hear once more the luscious sounds of the English language.

We did not have much to eat during the first few days, but as we proceeded westward we managed to bring down

a caribou every now and then, and this sustained us splendidly. It was with intense anxiety that, later, we began
scanning the horizon for Great Slave Lake. Luckily we
found it at last, and then it was not long before three
bearded fur-hunters pulled up in front of the trading post
at Snowdrift. There stood the factor in front of the cabin
to receive us. He smiled from ear to ear as he shook hands
with us in a brotherly fashion, and well did he play the
hypocrite, for he stole many a sidelong glance at the sacks
in our sleds, all the time simply wondering how many
white-fox pelts we had brought in and what price he ought
to offer for them. For such is the mind of a fur-trader; he
thinks merely in terms of skins.

The Barren Ground Indians

THE INDIANS NATIVE TO THE CANADIAN NORTHWEST TER-
ritories belong to the Déné nation, and are subdivided into
the following tribes: the Hares, the Loucheux, the Yellowknives, the Slaves, the Dogribs, and the Chipewyans. Their
languages have a common root in the Athabaska language-
group.

We know but little of the history of these tribes. By
means of a number of dissociated and incomplete sources
alone are we able to trace through the general thread of
their story. As a rough outline, indicating something of
their earlier modes of life, a few facts must be mentioned:
First and foremost, these peoples were hunters and nomads,
the majority of whom were constantly migrating with the
caribou. Their weapons consisted of spears and arrows
tipped with flint, and various trapping devices, such as
snares and nets of animal hide (the latter also of bast)
and primitive deadfalls. Fire they obtained for the most
part by striking sparks from pyrites. Their shelter was a
tepee of caribou-skins, their means of transport dog-sleds,
snowshoes, and birch-bark canoes. These were poor
weapons with which to conduct a struggle for existence in a
land where the Arctic winter lasts eight months of the year.
Considering, then, the constant warfare waged amongst
themselves and with strange tribes, as well as those periods

when wild game was scarce, it is evident that these people lived a difficult life.

The advent of the fur-traders opened new possibilities to these natives. A rough choice of the goods of civilization was then accessible to them, and the price for these was pelts. The Indians no longer found it necessary to keep wandering about the country in quest of game in order to remain alive. The doors of the trading stores stood open to anyone who had a beaver, fox, lynx, or marten to offer in exchange. There were not only food and tools to be had, but weapons which were more effective than the old. This introduction of white civilization meant that the Indians, in addition to their ancient form of hunting, could undertake, if they liked, the harvesting of pelts and thus make a livelihood in a more limited field.

The majority of northern Canada's Indian tribes yielded, to a remarkable degree, to these new conditions. This marked the beginning of a new era. Hunting in the wilderness still constituted the most substantial and the most perfect form of existence, but it was no longer essential to life in the same way it had been in the past. Their society began to take on a different tone when, with a safer mode of existence open to them, they were no longer obliged to pursue their own more exacting struggle for food, wherein all was risked upon one mad dash, good luck, and their own alertness. Necessary adjustments were made, for weal as well as woe, but, in any event, the result for them was a life more insipid than their old.

One may find branches of the Déné nation, however, which still retain their ancient heritage — the Barren Land Indians. A few of the goods of civilization have filtered through to them, via the channel of fur-trading, but the primitive impulse which guides their daily lives is as firm as ever, and outside influences have altered to but a slight degree their original culture. Their existence follows the lines set by their ancestors, whether it be symbolized by their perpetual expeditions through forest or over barren plain in search of the wandering caribou, by their battle against blizzard and winter's cold, by their feasts and general gormandizing when the country is flooded with deer, or by their dark hours of need and starvation when the country lies empty about them.

The term " Barren Land Indians " includes the people of several tribes. Their hunting-grounds are the lands which follow the timber-line from Hudson Bay northwest to the Mackenzie delta, where the river empties into the Polar Sea. In its broader outlines, a common culture here exists. My statements apply in particular to the peoples east and northeast of Great Slave Lake, the peoples amongst whom I have lived and whose life and activities I have already mentioned in some detail in earlier chapters. In the following pages I shall attempt to include a number of facts which I have heretofore failed to mention or but loosely touched upon.

The Indians I shall treat of in this place may be divided into two groups. First, the " Fond du Lac Indians " who reside at the eastern extremity of Great Slave Lake and whose hunting grounds lie essentially off to the northeast (the Barrens surrounding Artillery, Aylmer, and Mackay lakes); second, the " Caribou-Eaters," who roam the region lying between Slave Lake and Lake Athabaska, and even farther north. Both groups depend, for the better part of each year, upon the caribou for their livelihood, but, as I have elsewhere mentioned, the name " Caribou-Eaters " has fastened itself upon the latter group by reason of the legends which deal with their isolated existence and their prowess as huntsmen.

Regarding the tribal connections of these peoples — numbering a couple of hundred individuals in all — it is commonly supposed that the Fond du Lac Indians are a close mixture of Chipewyan and Yellowknife stock. The Caribou-Eaters, on the other hand, are an ancient branch of the Chipewyan tribe who have maintained a comparatively pure strain.

It is difficult to estimate at just what period in the past these Indians, originally residing in regions farther south, established themselves in the Barren Lands. When the fur-traders first pushed their way north, the Yellowknives were a powerful people ruling over the greatest section of the country and the best of the caribou ranges. Their domain was the whole of that enormous region extending from Slave Lake north to the Coppermine River. Some time about 1830 the Dogribs rose against them and delivered them so severe a blow that it crushed all chances of their future development. The conquered peoples were driven farther south, where they have remained until this day. Later the Dogribs in turn relinquished the eastern portion of the territory they had conquered, and settled in the regions just south of Great Bear Lake. It is not out of the question that they were driven thence by the Fond du Lac Indians or the Caribou-Eaters. There are legends concerning a great battle, but little indeed is certain.

A culture such as has been ascribed to the Iroquois or Algonquins has no counterpart amongst these northern peoples. The bare struggle for existence has claimed their entire attention, and their mode of living has followed far simpler lines; particularly is this true of the Indians east of Great Slave Lake. Their social structure is extremely loose in outline. During the winter hunting period, groups of families cluster together, whereas during the summer

[248]

they meet only for an occasional banquet on the shores of some large lake in the forest. The socialistic impulse in their mode of living is strongly marked. He who owns more than his fellows must divide. This principle has developed spontaneously and is absolutely essential for a people entirely dependent upon the variable luck of the hunter.

Their society is based upon unwritten laws: in case of a dispute, the eldest member of each family group decides the issue, or, during the large summer gatherings, their common chief. However, there are remarkably few cases of friction in their society. Each problem which arises seems to have an obvious solution. He who has obtained authority to hunt in a certain territory can insist upon having his rights respected. He who first sights the game has the first right to shoot it, a rule which does not apply, however, when there is a shortage of food. The hunter who fells an animal, upon division of the meat, is entitled to the head, the layer of fat about the entrails, and, in spring and autumn, the back-fat. When working together at a common task, each man seems to know in advance exactly what his duties are to be, according to his age and social standing. If a man borrows a sled, he is in duty bound to return it, but is not responsible for damage during the time he is using it. In making an exchange, each party must take his own risk; he has no recourse in the event of future dissatisfaction. This rule applies, for example, in the case of swapping a dog which later reveals a tendency to bite itself out of the harness at every opportunity, a condition which renders the animal worthless, though it be excellent in every other respect. The rules governing property rights come seldom into use amongst these people who own practically nothing, aside from the bare essentials of life. The fact that furs now bring high prices has altered the situation but little. No lasting profits accrue, so far as the Indians are concerned, for most of the moneys they receive are immediately spent for foolish purchases. In spite of their splendid harvests of pelts, the majority of the Indians are in debt to the traders. Their obligations are treated almost with nonchalance; they will pay a certain amount on account whenever it is necessary to do so to maintain their credit, but they have no compunctions against running into debt with one trader and selling their pelts to another. When a red hunter dies, his debt is regarded as having died with him.

Naturally, it may occasionally come to pass that these unwritten laws of the tribe are broken, but this does not often occur. Stealing, for example, is an exceedingly rare occurrence. Two or three instances have been recorded of Indians' having robbed white men, but these cases are the exception. For my own part, I have left pelts hanging in my tent for weeks whilst I myself was out hunting, and have yet to miss a single skin, though a number of passing Indians stopped in to spend the night there. Amongst the Indians themselves I know of but one example of stealing, and in that case kleptomania was involved.

Law-breaking, where the natives are concerned, knows no punishment in the formal sense that we understand the term. Sometimes the person outraged may give way to righteous indignation and take the law into his own hands to the extent of administering a sound thrashing, but ordinarily the fact that the culprit is considered as an outcast by the others of his tribe constitutes sufficient punishment.

The language of these Indians — Chipewyan — is harsh and guttural in its pronunciation, in contrast, for example, to the more southern Cree, which is distinct in its utterance and is full of tonal color. One of the most difficult things

about the former is the fact that there is only a slight difference in pronunciation between a whole series of words sig-
nifying totally distinct ideas, as, for example: *tsa, tha, sa,
sas,* being native words for " beaver," " marten," " sun,"
and " bear," respectively.

No authentic written language, so far as I know, has ever
been developed by these people. If it is a fact that the in-
scription on the face of a cliff in the Taltson River district
can be identified with these Indians, there is a possibility
that they may once have employed a simplified picture-
writing. But until this fact has been established, one must
continue to assume that their symbols were far more primitive in character, such as marks upon trees, certain ar-
rangements of sticks on trail or camp-site, coupled with
smoke signals. A few of these still remain in use, but they
have given way for the most part to an effective written
language. This was invented by a missionary in the middle
of the nineteenth century. It consists of seventy-three char-
acters, each representing a different syllable. For example:

＜ = ba	∨ = be	∧ = bi	＞ = bo
⊏ = da	⊔ = de	∩ = di	⊃ = do
⊐ = ka	⊏ = ke	⊐ = ki	⊐ = ko
⊏' = t ta	⊔' = tte	∩' = ttî	⊃' = tto

The device is ingenious in its simplicity, and, as a result,
it is now possible for an Indian to master the art of writing
in a few weeks.

In the field of art, the culture of these Indians is most
backward. Their embellishment of skins, for example, is
far inferior in beauty to that of the Eskimos. Their adornments are often accomplished by the use of moose hair and
porcupine quills. From the white breast of the lemming

they make small pouches. Bags braided from fine strips of animal hide, with fringes and colored adornments, constitute some of their most attractive work.

When the caribou are thick on the plains, and the meat-kettle is full, the Indian sings his wild songs of rejoicing, with the characteristic refrain — " *Hi-hi-he, hi-hi-he-ho.*" When he is paddling along in his canoe and all is going well with his journey, he sings another song, like a weird *andante.* But when he is far out in the forest, far from his woman, and his heart is pierced with longing, the notes that he sings are plaintive. Song is a natural outlet for his emotions. Most of the Indians are musical. Their songs are inherited, learned by each son from the lips of his father. Everyone knows them, and everyone sings them. But in the way of instruments they have none save the tomtom — *hali-gali,* as they call it. This is employed mainly to accompany their dances, as described in a foregoing chapter.

STANZA OF THE HUNTER'S SONG TO HIS SWEETHEART:

SETZŌNIAZÉ
(*Love-song*)

Poco sostenuto

Chorus

THE BARREN GROUND INDIANS

In the society of these Indians, there is a rigid apportionment of all labor. Upon the man fall the duties of hunting, fishing, and dog-mushing, and all matters related thereto; upon the woman fall all others.

Of man's work, caribou-hunting comes first of all. Today, as much as ever before, it is upon this that the Indian's very existence depends throughout the major portion of each year. Trapping is an activity which engages him, *if he has time*. If he succeeds in harvesting enough pelts to exchange for necessities, such as ammunition, sled, dogs, and harness, he says " heap of skins " and is satisfied with these. If there is enough meat cached beside his tepee, thus permitting him to stretch out on his caribou-skin in the tent, he will smoke, eat, and sleep, and experience not the slightest prick of curiosity.

Of caribou-hunting as it is carried on today I have already spoken; I shall here set forth briefly a few points covering the older methods. Not more than thirty years ago these were in general use, although fire-arms must surely have been introduced into the regions east of Great Slave Lake prior to this time. The older Indians still recall the days when the caribou were slain by means of spears and bow and arrow. Old Chief Marlo once told me about his hunting experiences with weapons of this type, and stated that with a three-foot bow of good stout birchwood he could bring down a caribou at a range of between seventy-five and a hundred yards. Nor had he forgotten even then the art of shaping flint. He once showed me an arrow tip he had made, a remarkably fine piece of work.

[253]

In former times hunting was carried on mainly in the narrow passes and at the habitual swimming-places of the caribou during the great spring and fall migrations. In the water the beasts were speared from birch-bark canoes, on land they were sometimes speared, sometimes shot. Mass slaughter was common. The Indians would slay as many caribou as they possibly could, cut out the tongues, and leave hundreds of full carcasses behind to rot. The senselessness of such wanton destruction never seemed to enter their heads. They were following in the ways of their fathers, they reasoned, and the country had always managed to feed them.

When the herds had scattered, other methods of hunting were employed. To a large extent this took the form of hunting by dog-sled. By means of much shouting and howling, the game were driven either past an ambush of bowmen or into huge corrals. In accomplishing these devices use was frequently made of primitive fences — hedgerows of spruce or pine brush planted in the snow, coupled with stone barriers which would tend to deflect the fleeing game in the desired directions. Snares to entrap the caribou were also common up until comparatively modern times. The snares were made from thongs of caribou hide and were placed in the regular game trails in the forest.

During this period the musk-ox was also preyed upon by the Indians to a considerable extent. This species was plentiful and maintained its numbers as long as the natives had only their own weapons to use against it. The effect was otherwise with the introduction of fire-arms, for then the Indians' lust for killing was given full play. The mentality of the musk-ox was such that it refused utterly to flee from danger. As robust as a mountain, it challenged everything, and for the purpose of defense it had its " hollow square "

— side by side, with lowered heads, these animals would form a fortress of powerful horns which no beast ever dared to attack. But the hunter armed with modern weapons could stand within easy range and mow these creatures down. A fair number of these rugged warriors of the Barren Lands still remain in existence, but theirs is a dying race, considering their original numbers. The musk-ox now enjoys complete protection, and a large region has been reserved for them in the Thelon Game Sanctuary.

Compared with caribou-hunting no other quest for game, now as formerly, is of the least significance. During the long winter months there is no other food problem save that of venison. During the remainder of the year moose, ducks, swans, geese, muskrats, et cetera, come to the fore. And the Indian seldom allows a year to go by without tasting a beaver tail. Beaver-hunting sometimes calls for stalking, sometimes for the art of decoying. The Indian's ability to imitate the calls of the various animals is almost inconceivable. I have seen one of them cause a flock of wild geese to swerve from their course and alight on the surface of a lake directly in front of the hunter.

The staple food of the Indian during the summer months is fish, but he finds this variety of diet acceptable only when no other is available. Hunting is his most honorable pursuit, and meat his proper food. All else seems to dwell on a lower level. It would be an easy matter for the natives to place a greater safeguard upon their existence by fishing beyond their immediate needs and storing up a reserve supply during the autumn. But such a type of activity is alien to their nature. The fish can swim by in solid phalanxes right under an Indian's nose, but he will do no more than throw out a couple of lines. He neither shifts nor disturbs his nets, merely pulls the ends far enough out of water for him to lift out what fish he can reach. There lies his seine week after week, drifting in wind and stormy sea, whilst slime collects in the meshes. All is well as long as he is able to make a fair catch from day to day. And what about the future? Good heavens, when the fishing season is over, the caribou will have arrived!

The dexterity of the Indian is of a high order; with his long, nimble fingers he is apparently able to make all that he needs from materials of the poorest sort. The birch-bark canoe, snowshoes, and the toboggan are all instances of how far he has progressed in this direction. His tools are the ax and the curved knife; the latter he holds thumbs down and wields with inward strokes.

The true lords of creation are the menfolk, and as a consequence they confine themselves to the noble profession of hunting. When a hunter arrives in his dog-sled in front of the tepee, his work has been completed and he is ready to reap his reward. He hops out of the sled, blusters into the tent, and seats himself upon his caribou rug, ready to be served with food. God pity the squaw if he must wait! It is her duty to listen for the bells of the dog-train and to put the meat-kettle on the fire the moment she hears them. As the hunter is chewing down his venison, one of the youngsters removes his father's moccasins, the others running outside to take care of the sled and the dogs. Having eaten his fill, the hunter then lights up his pipe and prepares to take life with genuine ease, and if he is of a mind to nag at his wife as she sweats over an endless variety of tasks, he does not hesitate to do so. Why should he feed a woman if she doesn't work for him? This has been the Indian's view-point ever since the day when a hunter's position was determined by the number of wives he had. Today the hunter has but one wife. She is no longer obliged to haul the sled, as formerly, for the Indians now have many more dogs than before, but otherwise her position is little changed. She must labor early and late and is likely to be thrashed if she shirks. The following is significant: the hunter is first to be served with food, after him his children; whatever is left goes to his wife and dogs.

The hunter drives up to the tepee with a carcass of venison. Here you are, old woman! It now becomes the squaw's duty to make use of every last scrap of edible meat, including even the skin, according to the methods traditional to the tribe. The entire carcass, with the exception of the lungs, is put to some use. The latter are hung up in a tree, and not even the dogs are allowed to touch them. Indian superstition has it that any dog chancing to eat the lungs of any wild game will suffer from short-windedness ever afterwards.

In the tanning process, the brains of the caribou are used to rub the skin. Later the hide is dried out, washed in warm water, dried a second time, and scraped with a chisel-shaped bone. The hair is scraped off, unless the skin is to be used in the making of outer garments. If it be intended for use in the making of moccasins or mittens, it is put through a smoking process; after tanning, the skin is basted together in the shape of a long tube and placed over a bowl in which a heavy smudge is produced by covering a fire with moss and straw. Babiche is the name given to the thin strips cut from untanned, unsmoked caribou hide. It is rolled up into balls and is the Indian's form of rope. Babiche is used in making the web of each snowshoe and in binding the boards of the toboggan together; otherwise it is a convenience always kept within reach.

Sewing-thread is made from the large bunches of sinews running along the spine of the caribou. These are dried out, split, and rolled back toward the rump.

I have already spoken of the ways in which the edible portions of the carcass are prepared. I have mentioned how the fundamental principle is to seek first the fattest and most nourishing parts, and how the necessary variety of food is achieved by making use of marrow, heart, kidneys, liver, fat, stomach contents, cartilage of the larynx, brain, tongue, tooth-nerves, nose, blood, teats, horns in velvet, unborn calf, et cetera, boiling or roasting the above to no more than a superficial degree. Meat and every other kind of food are prepared and eaten *without the addition of salt*. The food is washed down with unsweetened tea. As a supplement to fresh food, there are dried meat and fat. The dried meat is often ground up between stones and preserved in pulverized form; when this is mixed with fat, the result is " pemmican," a product of modern Arctic research.

Here, in a nutshell, is the secret of all Indian cuisine. These foods, as developed by a primitive people, not only make it possible for one to endure an exclusive diet of meat throughout eight months of the year, but also keep the Indians in excellent physical condition. During the meat months fresh cases of sickness seldom break out (I have never heard of a case of scurvy), and even the undernourished seem to regain their strength.

Nowhere have I been able to discover that this excessive meat-eating has developed in the Indian a need for other forms of nourishment. If his meat-supply is adequate, for example, he will never go to the trouble of making a journey merely to procure flour; but it is a different matter if he finds himself running low on tea or tobacco! If it so happens that he is invited to partake of a civilized meal, he will eat a few mouthfuls and seem to enjoy the change. But on finishing he gives it no further thought and makes straight for the nearest kettle of steaming fragrant venison.

The Indian people must have adopted an exclusive meat diet a great many years ago, and it may well be that their physical constitution has, to a certain degree, been modified by it. My own experience has been that the food of these Indians is both adequate and satisfying to the white man as well. The year I spent with the Caribou-Eaters, I nourished myself during about eight months of the winter by confining myself to the eating of wild game according to their principles. So long as I had venison enough to supply me with plenty of fat, I found myself in high spirits and noticed not the slightest indication of any kind of illness. On the other hand, whenever I was short of fat, I soon began to run down, could eat no end of meat without feeling satisfied, and became more susceptible to cold. I should like to mention in this place that, unlike most other white trappers, I neither used any salt nor missed it; I ate dried meat, dried fat, and raw marrow whenever I had the opportunity. This was food which I felt gave me ample and lasting strength to work, and on a cold winter's day a piece of bread and butter, smeared with cheese, was not to be compared with it. Naturally, one may have moments of weakness when one's thoughts wander off to a heavily laden dining-table, but these are probably due to nothing more than the remnants of old habit.

It is a custom of the Indians to devour untold quantities of food during a meal, but, on the other hand, it is possible for them to endure hunger and terrific hardships for long periods of time without experiencing dire effects. This the Indian holds in common with the Eskimo dog. In this particular the difference between the Indian and the white man, and between the Eskimo dog and the more civilized breeds, is strongly marked.

I have already spoken of the many fatiguing tasks which the women must perform in the preparation of wild game. In addition to these, it is their duty to attend to all the many other matters which camp life involves. These include everything from the chopping of firewood and the trapping of hares to child-birth and the nursing of infants. Childbirth does not drain too heavily upon the native mother's strength. In the course of a few days she is able to return to her work. The infant is placed in a pannier of caribou-skin, at the bottom of which is a layer of reddish moss. The latter fulfills the purpose of both cradle and swaddling-clothes.

As soon as a youth is able to care for himself, he enters the hard school of life. He must carry wood and water, care for the dogs, the harness, and the sled, and in other ways make himself generally useful, with no reward save a good word. When he is thirteen or fourteen, his father takes him along on expeditions, which are many times strenuous indeed for so young a hunter, the more so when all the heavy disagreeable tasks fall to his lot to perform. He must break trail through the deep snow in front of the sled, he must do most of the work of setting up camp, must chop and carry in spruce boughs, and must be the first up in the morning to make the fire. Thus he is trained, thus he is gradually imbued with all the instinctive technique which is essential to life in the wilderness, and thus he acquires, one by one, the secrets of a hunter's existence. Then, at length, comes the day when he is given his own dog-train and is treated as an adult.

The young girls, too, have much to do; they must prepare themselves for the married state. During early youth a few of them acquire a good deal of beauty and charm, but they lose this shortly after their twentieth year, and in time, as their duties increase, they become quite large and flabby.

In their seventeenth year the girls are ready for marriage. When the hunter is confronted with making a choice, his first consideration is a girl's capacity for work. His success in winning his choice depends upon whether the girl's parents look upon him as an able hunter. If the suitor proves acceptable, he at once moves over to reside with his future parents-in-law. He is then betrothed, or, more accurately, married on trial. The only difference between this state and that of true marriage is that he may not as yet live with his bride in a tent of their own. Nor can the groom be absolutely certain of his bride. In the event that the old people discover that their son-in-law loses something of his glamour through closer contact, they show him the door, and with that the marriage is dissolved. Later, however, there is nothing to prevent the spurned lover from making further proposals, and, if he be energetic, it is possible for him to regain favor in the eyes of the elders. I myself knew one hunter who was accepted and cast out two or three times before his affair was permanently consummated.

When the hunter and his bride move together into their own tepee, the marriage becomes an actual fact. Of late, however, it has become more and more of a general rule for the young people to content themselves with "trial marriage" in the home of the bride's parents until such a time as they are able to make a journey together south to the mission, where they are wedded by the Christian Church.

A pronounced eroticism is noticeable in all these people. Though the man is more or less indifferent as to the physical appearance of his life's companion, this is not because he is immune to womanly charm, but because he is *obliged* to give precedence to practical considerations. On a cold winter's day it is but a pale joy to have a beautiful wife if she fails to provide one with moccasins, dried meat, and the reasonable necessities of life. And in the event that a hunter is wedded to a hoyden — well, there are surely other women to be had, for the married woman, on her side, does not regard with exaggerated conscience her moral obligations. When the hunter departs on an extended journey, there are many who have their way with her back home in the village. Of this her husband is fully cognizant, but so long as her affairs are kept secret, he allows them to continue. If, on the other hand, she becomes too open about them, and her reputation begins to suffer, her liege lord and master rises up in all his might and gives his wife the beating she deserves, and a bit more for good measure.

Sometimes it happens that a deeper feeling enters into the relationship between man and wife. If this feeling does not exactly fit the description of what civilization terms " love," it is nevertheless something strongly akin to it. But the man who is prey to this grand emotion soon discovers, to his woe, that he has fallen amongst thieves.

The Indians seldom live to a ripe old age. It is their custom to bury the dead and erect a circle of tall pointed poles about the grave. If the death takes place in the winter-time, the corpse is preserved in a wooden coffin, and later, when the frost has gone out of the ground, the relatives provide it with burial, even though they must make a long and arduous journey for this purpose.

Formerly the aged and others unfitted to make the long journeys were left behind in the wilderness. This custom is no longer adhered to. Even so, it is as pathetic today as before for an Indian to become old and infirm. By and large,

THE BARREN GROUND INDIANS

he receives full sympathy from the others, but he who must remain at home with the womenfolk, whilst the hunters are afield after the caribou, no longer enjoys the respect of his fellows, and this is indeed a bitter fate for men who rank the honor of the hunter above all else in life.

In olden times the Indians were susceptible to various illnesses; amongst these may be mentioned the plague of boils. The malady still occurs, although to a lesser extent. The boils often appear on the hips and buttocks and I have seen them as large as clenched fists. It takes quite a long time to effect a cure.

The ancient illnesses are of little significance contrasted with the diseases derived from the white race. Thus tuberculosis has wreaked havoc with the Indians east of Great Slave Lake. Spasmodic epidemics of "flu" have broken out in their ranks and have brought death to many. Venereal diseases, on the other hand, are anything but common. In an earlier portion of this book I have spoken of the epidemics of coughing which break out in the spring of the year and often continue all through the summer months, disappearing as soon as cold weather sets in. These colds can hardly be due to infection from the outside, since they afflict even the Indians living in entirely isolated regions.

Like other primitive peoples, the Indians are lacking in physical resistance to the diseases of the white race. There are other factors, too, which play a definite part in the spreading of disease: the habit of spitting incessantly and the general uncleanliness of the Indians, to which may be added their spirit of resignation when illness begins to assume serious proportions. On the whole, the people east of Great Slave Lake have fared better than the tribes which, to a varying degree, have given up a healthy tepee-life and

[263]

the food which the wilderness provides, in exchange for a life indoors and a diet of flour.

Ever since ancient times the Indians have had their own medicines prepared from weeds, roots, and bark, often administered to the accompaniment of certain rites. From an old Indian I once received the information that he knew about thirty different kinds of medicines, amongst these a poison which could kill a human being in the course of five minutes. Further than this he would say nothing, for an Indian guards his medical knowledge with the most scrupulous secrecy. How great a part mystic rites and possible frauds play in the cure it is, consequently, difficult to determine. One matter of significance in this connection is worth mentioning, however: the Indian is a most apt subject for all forms of suggestion.

In spite of the fact that the *materia medica* of the Indians is so frequently cluttered up with superstition, there are reasons to suppose that a number of their medicines have various effects. It is a known fact, for example, that they have a practical means of abortion. For diarrhœa they use dried rushes. For urinary ailments they drink a broth made from the inner red bark of the willow. For scurvy they boil the needles of the dwarf spruce in water for a short time and drink the liquid. By boiling the inner bark of the larch they obtain an antiseptic, which is then placed upon the ailing part as hot as the patient can stand it. It seems not only to kill infection, but also to cause the wound to heal more rapidly than otherwise. For frost-bite they use the inner bark of the pine. This they chew into a pulp, which they then plaster over the frozen part. May I add that, after writing the above, I allowed an Indian to doctor one of my great toes which had become frozen, but that the inflammation had gone so far that perhaps the treatment of my medicine-man was not wholly to blame? In any event, the result was that Williams of the Royal Mounted Police was obliged to cut away a goodly portion of my toe.

The Indians' world of ideas is extremely limited and is confined, as it is reasonable to expect, to hunting and wilderness life. They know little about anything that lies outside their immediate sphere of existence, and they have not the slightest interest in improving their knowledge. It has therefore been extremely difficult for the spiritual impulses of the white race to make any impression upon these people.

The ancient heathenish conceptions are combined to form an implicit faith in spirits resident in the various beasts of the forest, in the sun, wind, stars, et cetera. In many instances the exact influence of a particular spirit is somewhat vague. When a person falls ill, it is a sign that a spirit has got into him. The spirit must therefore be expelled by means of divers rites. In other cases it is important that one should avoid doing anything which might invoke the displeasure of a certain spirit, lest its vengeance be visited upon the entire tribe. Ideas of punishment and reward beyond the grave have no place in the belief of these Indians. The origin of man is interpreted. in terms of legends dealing with animals and spirits. There are further indications of a myth concerning a deluge which, at the dawn of time, inundated all the land.

The Indians of today are moved by teachings of the Roman Catholic Church, whose rituals find great response in their souls. How deeply rooted their faith has become is another matter entirely. It is possible that the Indians, even with the advent of the new teaching, remain faithful to their old superstition; the following will possibly throw some light on this subject.

Presumably the old rites are continued in secret. I do not make this statement from personal experience, but from the observations of white men who, for certain specific purposes, stand in direct contact with the natives.

The old belief in souls incarnated in the bodies of animals may still be traced. The Indians thus believe that misfortune will result from the killing of such creatures as the raven, the wolf, the wolverine, and the dog, and they avoid such killings whenever possible. It would be a simple matter for them to harvest wolf pelts in the same quantity as do the white trappers, but they refuse to slay a wolf, although a bounty of thirty dollars per head is offered for these creatures. There are Indians farther west who will even go so far as to throw away their rifles in the event of killing a wolf. This same superstition is probably responsible for the ancient custom of abandoning the old and infirm in the wilderness as sacrifices to the beasts of prey.

The common rule is that the bear, too, must be preserved. But here another thought appears to be involved, a thought based upon the conception of guardian animals, in whose bodies reside spirits responsible for man's well-being. No guardian animal must ever be slain, and no use whatever may be made of its pelts, above all by women, if misfortune is to be avoided. It is a known fact that the bear is not preyed upon east of Slave Lake. It is slain only when there is a definite food shortage or in self-defense.

In this connection, I once heard a story of a white man married to an Indian woman. The wife had been poorly for some weeks and was showing no signs of improvement. She could not understand what ailed her, until one day the thought came to her that perhaps her husband had a bearskin somewhere in the cabin. She set about to look for it. Sure enough, up under the rafters she found the pelt of a bear cub. The manner in which these married people reached a final agreement, we may just as well skip over, but the result was that the bearskin went out the door, and the wife recovered the very next day from her illness.

Amongst the tribes living along the Mackenzie River guardian animals are determined in a particular manner. When a young boy or a young girl attain a certain age, they betake themselves unaccompanied into the forest. There they build a fire and lie down beside it. Without taking any nourishment whatever, they sit there keeping themselves awake for two or three days, until at length, from sheer exhaustion, they fall into a deep slumber. The first animal they see in their dreams becomes their guardian beast throughout their lives.

In connection with their belief in spirits incarnate in animals and in the elements, the Indians also have their legends. These are handed down from one generation to the next whenever the Indians are gathered together for some special occasion. The legends often have to do with the characteristics of the various animals and are fantastic explanations of how these characteristics came into being — how the beaver came to have a flat tail, how the lynx came to have a spotted coat, et cetera. As an example, I shall repeat the story of the man who snared the sun:

One winter a hunter and his squaw were roaming about after the caribou. They had packed everything they had to their name in a deerskin which the squaw was dragging along behind her. Farther and farther north they proceeded, but the caribou were nowhere to be seen. At last they found themselves in the *Land without Trees*. Here it was bitterly cold and this cold increased as the sun sank lower and lower until at length it had almost reached the edge of the world. " Now we are losing the sun, and that means we shall

freeze to death," they said to each other. In one way or
another they must prevent the sun from disappearing altogether. So the squaw took the deerskin she was dragging
along, cut it up into long strips, and made an enormous
lasso. The man then cast the noose about the sun, drew it
tight, and fastened the nether end to a huge stone. The sun
was ensnared. That was the end of the cold, but in his haste
the hunter had drawn too hard upon the lasso, so that now
the sun was right over their heads like a glowing ball of
flame. They had been on the point of freezing to death before, but now they were in danger of burning up. Their experience was so limited that they didn't know how to cut
the rope, for the rock to which they had fastened it was
directly under the sun, and it was so scorching hot there that
no living thing could get near it.

At this point a shrewmouse came up to them and asked
why they were wailing so. They explained to the shrew their
difficulty. " Could be worse," said the shrew, which then
left them and dug a deep tunnel through the earth right up
to the rock. There he poked no more than the tip of his nose
up through the ground and gnawed the lasso in two. With
that, the sun sailed off into the blue. But the shrew's front
teeth were badly scorched and have been brown ever since
that day. . . .

The Indians give expression to their superstition in divers
other ways. Often their notions have to do with hunter's
luck, which must be safeguarded at all costs. Here the influence of woman is of the utmost importance. In many
different ways she is supposed to drive the game in the direction of the hunter or to drive it away.

Women are not permitted to have anything to do with
hunting or trapping; they are forbidden to touch the family
gun or to set foot in the hunting-canoe and under no cir-

cumstances may they paddle over a seine set in a lake —
they must paddle *round* it. Even an article of dress which a
woman has made use of may, in certain cases, bring about
misfortune. For example, a hunter must be careful to refrain from placing himself beneath such an article and
must under no circumstances accept such an article as a
present. Once upon a time a starving Indian asked a white
man married to a squaw for some clothes in place of the
rags he had on. The white man felt sorry for the poor fellow,
dragged a fine woolen blanket from the bridal bed, and
handed it to him. Instead of thanks, the benefactor received
no more than a volley of abuse for having been wicked
enough to wish misfortune upon another's head. Strangely
enough, the same Indian would not have hesitated an instant
to come in contact with the same woolen blanket had the
white man's squaw under a different set of conditions been
alone beneath it.

Since ancient times women during their period of men-
struation have been considered as unclean and obliged to
maintain a separate existence. Even today traces of this
custom are observable east of Slave Lake, but, in so far as
my own experience has determined, the custom is more
general amongst the tribes living along the Mackenzie
River. In certain localities women during this critical period
are forbidden to use the door of the cabin. There is a hole
in the wall just beneath her bunk, and through this aperture
she must crawl in and out. Nor is she permitted to follow
along the common trails. A trapper once told me that he
had come across the tracks of one of these " unclean "
women. Mile after mile they went through the deep snow
alongside a well-packed sled-trail.

Thus the Indian's world of ideas reeks with mystical
superstitions, as is always the case with those striving to

maintain their lives in the wilderness. Just how their mental outlook came to develop will be perhaps best understood by those who have themselves tried living up there in the north. When the sun stands shedding its warmth over the snow-fields for the first time after a long winter, and when the caribou begin by the million to flood the wastes which formerly lay empty and desolate, it may then well happen that each and every one feels within himself a sudden wave of that same heathenish feeling which first caused the Indians to bow down before the sun and offer up their praise to the god of the hunters.

The Trail to Solitude

THE MONTH DURING WHICH THE CANADIAN, FRED, AND I together did our best to conquer the Snowdrift River was in the nature of a prelude to the year I spent knocking about alone.

The Snowdrift is the most turbulent river east of Slave Lake. Between steep granite walls it races toward the lowlands in a series of rapids and cascades. It is no river for a canoe. The fact remained, however, that a party of Indians had once chosen this route into the interior of the Barren Lands, and we refused to be outdone. So, with our winter equipment and our dogs packed snugly into our canoes, we set out.

" Small lake near big river, fine for canoe," Batis Lockart had told me, drawing on a piece of bark a series of figures resembling a string of sausages. We discovered no lake; instead, we fell upon mile-long portages up over steep rugged country swarming with mosquitoes. Up the only stretch of river which could be called navigable we had to track and wade. This tracking was not always so pleasant, for the current was swift enough to capsize our canoes on the slightest provocation. More than once we were prepared to say farewell to our winter equipment. After a week in the water, wading along as best we could, we heaved a sigh of relief, for it had indeed been a week of nerve-racking suspense.

To put it tersely, the Snowdrift had balked us at every turn, but this would not have been so bad, had it only provided us with something to eat. Less than a month before, its waters had been teeming with whitefish; now they were as empty as could be. The dogs were hungry and the pups, in particular, were in a most pitiful condition. We ourselves kept going on oatmeal.

Since there were no fish at the foot of the rapids, they must be up above. This thought seemed logical to us, so we agreed upon one last advance upstream. Leaving Fred to make camp and care for the dogs, I was to proceed east until I encountered still water. There I would drop in a net. If I were to catch some fish, all well and good; if not, there would be no point in our continuing, for the dogs were already too weak to carry packs.

My fishing trip up the rapids of the Snowdrift River forms one of my darkest memories. It was late evening when I finally came upon a comparatively still stretch of deep water. There I knocked together a raft, threw the net aboard, grabbed a good stout pole, and started out from shore. I whistled softly and confidently, for here I should have things going in a jiffy. The meshes of the net got caught every now and then in the bark and branch-stubs of the raft, but I did not take this too seriously; I simply picked the net loose and went on poling myself along.

I had succeeded in paying out most of the net when it suddenly struck me that my craft was not going the way it ought. It was swerving in a semicircle from the point where I had set out from shore. I now had a back-eddy to contend with! I clutched the pole, but the water had suddenly become so deep that I came within a hair's breadth of pitching head-first overboard. With that, I began paddling; I paddled for dear life, that wretched vessel of mine listing first to port and then to starboard. But the back-eddy persisted, and it was a hopeless battle I was waging. In a short time I had sailed completely round in a circle, and, buried in the folds of the net, like a spider in its web, the raft was now lapped by the ripples in the identical spot where I had first set out from shore. The only thing for me to do was to free the net — this took me some time — and to begin all over again. Thus it went hour after hour; I poled and I swore and I sweat and I swore, trying to get that net into the water. I was soaked to the skin and continually tortured by mosquitoes. The moon rose and piloted its pale disk up over the forest; still I struggled with the net. The back-eddy swirled round and round, and I swirled with it. And I didn't even have a dog to scold!

But there is an end to everything, even to a hungry trapper's patience. When the end came, I heaved the whole net overboard in a tangle and went ashore, where I lay down and fell asleep on the spot. The next morning there was *one* miserable trout in the net. I stuck it out one day longer and had somewhat better luck in a different place: there I caught *another* trout, one somewhat fatter than the first. . . .

Two weeks later:

We were sitting in front of a smoky fire as we ate our oatmeal and blinked our eyes in the rank smudge which was all that prevented the mosquitoes from doing away with us entirely. A short distance upstream roared a waterfall. Round about us lay twelve dogs who, with large pleading eyes, followed every move we made. Mechanically we brushed the layer of mosquitoes from our bowls of oatmeal and ate spoonful after spoonful. Neither of us uttered a word. There was nothing to say, for we had at last reached the point where we were obliged to turn back. All our striving had been in vain.

A spoonful of oatmeal was on its way to my mouth when it suddenly struck me that a certain black shadow in amongst a patch of whortleberries as high as a man's head on the other side of the river *was moving*. In a flash I had thrown aside my spoon and was on my feet. " A bear! " I said. Fred did not even bother to turn his head, just coolly kept on eating his oatmeal. " Devil take me if that isn't a bear! " I repeated warmly. Then Fred gave me a look as much as to say that this was hardly the time to pull a joke like that. He did not take me seriously until I stood there with my rifle in my hand. It was then that a big black bear received the surprise of his life. There he was, shuffling down to the river flats on his usual nocturnal rounds. Unsuspectingly he shuffled along, nibbling a few whortleberries along the way, enjoying himself immensely in this evening hour, with the music of the waterfall in his ears. And then — a series of shots! At the first shot the bear raised his head in surprise. At the second he began dancing round in a circle. At the third he stared stiffly across in our direction, shook his head, whirled about, and was off like the wind, finally disappearing behind a gravel knoll. He was gone.

In silence we laid aside our fire-arms. In silence we returned to our oatmeal. It tasted just as usual.

After a time Fred cautiously asked: " Have you ever seen a bear shake his head? "

I admitted that this was the first bear I had ever observed to behave in such a manner.

" Well," said Fred, " do you think he would have shaken his head without some good reason for it? "

" Hardly," I replied.

[274]

"There you have it," concluded Fred, with conviction. "That bear is badly wounded."

At this, I passed the jocose observation that a shake of the head might also betoken disgust for such unbelievably poor aim as we had taken.

But Fred ignored my remark and stuck to his point: "That bear is ours. One of us ought to paddle across and follow the trail of blood."

Risking life and limb, I set out across the rapids. For a half-hour or so I searched high and low for signs of blood on the ground, but without success. What I did find were the quite ordinary tracks of a quite ordinary bear which was enjoying the best of health and which had put miles between itself and the river. On my return with the report that my hunt for telltale blood stains had ended in failure, Fred was at a loss to understand the whole affair. He added that it was just as well, since it was a gruelling job to skin an autumn bear like that one!

Thus our one last opportunity had gone up in smoke. It was now merely a question of how we could best manage the return trip down the river. Were we to wade the long hard way in the water as before, or could we take a chance and shoot the rapids? The canoes would not stand much buffeting; they had no more than a hand's breadth free-board, and that was something to be considered. But there we were, both of us in a suitably ironical mood. What, wade? Never in all this world!

A kindly fate must have kept watch over our canoes as they danced down those frothing rapids, for we succeeded in reaching still water with both boats on an even keel.

It was at this point that Fred and I agreed amicably to part company. He would remain in the woods, whilst I, with the Barren Lands still in mind, had decided on another route which led to them. I took Slave Lake as far as the east end of Fond du Lac Bay. Here I put packs on the dogs, slung the canoe over my shoulders, and started out over Pike's Portage, the summer route of the Indians.

From then on it was the old toil of packing from lake to lake and the same eternal battle with the mosquitoes. I did manage to make fairly good time eastward, for I did not have so much equipment to hold me back. I had not brought a great deal with me. My provisions consisted of a small bag of oatmeal and a few slabs of bacon. But then, in addition to this, I had a fish-net and a remarkably fine rifle. With the coming of the caribou, there was sure to be " heap of meat," as the Indians say, and after a year of close contact with the Caribou-Eaters, I myself had become something of an Indian in my thinking.

At last I stood beside the forest's last outposts — century-old spruces, gnarled and bent. Ahead lay the North American tundra. When last I had viewed the Barrens, it had been winter, and they had lain beneath a carpet of snow. Now they wore a friendly smile for me, covered as they were with moss and brown grasses and scored with countless small lakes and shimmering ribbon-like rivers. In the shelter of each hollow the grass grew lush and green; here and there shone bright patches of red and white saxifrage and blue lupine.

Just what would be the best thing for me to do at this point was still somewhat of a quandary to me. It was after the fifteenth of September, and winter would soon be along. Thus far there was no sign whatever of the caribou. All in all, I decided it would be wisest were I to remain for a time, at least, at the edge of the woods. For that matter, one place was as good as another for me to pitch my tent; I was my own master and I had no irons in the fire.

THE TRAIL TO SOLITUDE

Up to the present, I had experienced no difficulty in catching enough fish to satisfy the needs of myself and the dogs, but in the lakes near the spot I had now chosen for my camp the fishing was as poor as could be. I was thus obliged to feed the dogs from my own stock of provisions, which began to disappear with discomfiting rapidity. No, there was nothing else for it but to try my luck elsewhere. I struck camp and made off west through the woods, keeping my eyes peeled for anything which might serve to maintain life in our bodies, prior to the arrival of the caribou. One day I shot a " chicken," a fowl resembling a grouse, which will often remain perched on the limb of a tree until one has blown its head off. Another day Tiger managed to capture a polar hare after a wild chase. Thus we were able to pick up a few odds and ends which the forest had to offer, but in the main these signified little and I was somewhat depressed in my mind.

Then came an evening when, with my dogs in the canoe, I was paddling across a long lake. Far off on the opposite shore I observed what appeared to be a series of pin-pricks. " Just stones," I said to myself in order to fortify myself against possible disappointment. But, at the same time, I paddled in that direction to have a closer look at those stones. Half-way across the lake, the last shred of doubt was removed from my mind — *they were caribou!* In an endless procession the animals came streaming out of the woods, followed along the beach for a long stretch, and disappeared behind a crag.

Now for it! The sun was hanging low over the hills. In ten, possibly in fifteen, minutes it would set, leaving the dark to rush in and render all shooting impossible. Could I make it? Could I win this race with the sun? I paddled as I had never paddled before. The canoe cut through the water with a good-sized bone in its teeth, whilst that glowing red disk sank lower and lower into the tree-tops. Then, all at once, it was gone. But I still had a few priceless minutes left before the afterglow died out of the sky. . . . There! At last, directly in front of the bow, and well within range, stood a husky caribou buck! I picked up my rifle. But, alas, at this point my dogs, previously curled up in the bottom of the canoe, unexpectedly woke up. In a flash they were on their feet and staring ahead at all that lovely meat which was parading by under their very noses.

Although I may pardon my starving dogs for the event which immediately took place, I shall never wholly forgive them. Sport made a sudden leap to starboard, Tiger to port. Once in the water, since they were held fast by the chains attached to their collars, all they could do was splash about. Meanwhile the other dogs stood with their fore-paws on the gunwales and set up a barking as though the devil were loose. From opposite sides Sport and Tiger did their best to crawl back aboard, whilst the other dogs tugged at their chains and hurled themselves against the gunwales with uncontrollable joy. The canoe careened first to one side, then to the other. The muzzle of my gun was pointing in all directions, and the caribou buck was never once in danger.

The whole affair was hopeless. I gathered up the dogs, paddled ashore, took my gun, and headed into the woods. Naturally, there was no sign of life on any hand, for such a terrible commotion would certainly have frightened away even the tamest kine.

Then darkness fell.

I carefully set up my tent on the very spot where the buck had stood, crept into my sleeping-bag without any supper, and fell asleep. Early next morning I was up prowling through the woods. Yes, there had been caribou here, thousands of them. Everywhere I found the marks of their hoofs. But had they all forsaken these parts? It appeared so.

After pottering around for half a day without glimpsing a living thing, I clambered up a barren ridge and sat down for a consoling smoke. It was a sparkling autumn day. Far off in the distance lay the subdued green of the forest, alternating with the glittering surface of small lakes. Beneath where I sat, white birches were growing in the lee of the ridge, the sunlight dancing in and out amongst those snowy trunks and caressing with its rays their foliage of pure gold.

I thought at first that my eye had fallen upon two huge caribou bucks, but then I saw that they were moose. Sedately they were stalking along through the birches. I threw myself down on the ground, crawled forward and fired. One moose tumbled head over heels. On my running up to it, the other simply stood there looking at me, so I shot it, too.

An enormous quantity of meat. It was almost unbelievable. Here was food for hungry dogs, and here were marrowbones, fat, kidneys, tongues, and all manner of good things — enough so that I could eat as much as my belly would hold. Had I suddenly inherited a fortune, I could not have felt more wealthy. Fate, in spite of everything, had kept a friendly eye upon this solitary trapper, wandering about through the wilderness.

I immediately moved my camp over to the place where I had felled my game. This marked the beginning of a busy time for me, for to transform two moose carcasses, each weighing approximately nine hundred pounds, into dried meat required slightly more than a wave of the hand. Day after day I sat outside my tent and cut off slab after slab of meat. The piles grew. The knack of cutting the meat off in broad thin slices I had acquired from my friends amongst the Caribou-Eaters. First you must cut the muscles, one by

[279]

one, then, grasping each one in turn in the left hand, roll it over the wrist whilst a large meat-knife cuts it loose from the flesh. It is otherwise with the rib meat, which must be cut off and dried in its entirety.

Outside the tent I had erected a good stout scaffold from which I hung the meat to dry over a slow fire. The hides I stretched as tight as a drum across two four-cornered frames made from spruce poles, at once proceeding to flesh them and prepare them for tanning. It was my thought to get some of the Indians to tan them for me later, a service they would gladly perform in return for half the finished leather. Moose hide is both warmer and stronger than caribou.

As I was busy with my various duties, the forest about me suddenly came to life. Ranks and files of caribou began to pass unconcernedly in close proximity to my camp. They paid not the slightest heed to the smoke from my fire. They were all coming in from the northwest and were making a bee-line for some point to the southeast; they went tramping along with such self-assurance and at such a rapid pace that it was apparent they were bound for a general rendezvous. They had already acquired their winter pelage, and it was a weird sight to see those gray-white hosts against the green background of the forest. This was in the fore-part of October, the rutting season directly at hand. The necks of the bucks had swollen to be very large, and the beasts were strikingly fat. In a week's time the migration had passed by and, for the next five or six days, it was silent there in the forest, until a number of emaciated bucks came wandering back from the southeast. No pausing to rest for them; they kept right on at a steady trot, making straight for the hills beyond. Frequently it was amusing to see them jogging along behind a rise of ground which completely shielded the beasts themselves, whilst their antlers appeared like moving trees above the crest of the hill. These were, no doubt, the unfortunate bucks which had been eliminated during the rutting combats and which were now experiencing love's bitter anguish.

Both the dogs and I agreed that it was worth all our former hardships to be so handsomely rewarded later. With dried meat hanging in thick rows in front of the tent, our camp had assumed a homelike atmosphere. Our spirits brightened and the wilderness, which before had seemed so bleak and oppressive, now wreathed itself in smiles for our benefit.

The autumn season dragged out. It was toward the very end of October, and the lakes were still free of ice. One day of sunshine followed another and the black flies continued at their work with midsummer enthusiasm. My preparations for winter were well out of the way. Sled, harness, and clothes were all in perfect order. I was ready to start out across the Barrens the very moment there should be snow. The period of waiting went by like a dance. When one keeps house without the help of a servant, there is always plenty to do. And if ever, by chance, I became fed up with domestic duties, I would simply pick up my gun and start off into the woods.

During my excursions off to the east, I regularly came upon the tracks of moose. No small number of them apparently maintain their existence as far north as the timber-line. Their grazing-grounds are small and scattered, but the animals keep wandering from one snug birch or aspen grove to another. It is stated that the moose go south when the caribou arrive. They do not get along together, some say.

In a bottom land close beside a large lake, I came across

a level piece of ground tramped down by many hoofs; the earth was dug up in many places, and everywhere the ground was strewn with broken tree-branches. The battle-field of the bulls, an ideal spot for one of a mind to call the moose Indian-fashion. There are two methods of decoy. One is to reproduce the sharp scraping sound of a large animal rubbing its shoulder-blade up and down against a bush or tree-trunk; another is to imitate the call of the moose by uttering a kind of groaning sound through a little trumpet made from bark. I had had some experience call-ing other animals, but never calling moose. It was worth the attempt. So early one evening I betook myself to the spot in question and threw myself down on a little birch-clad knoll by the side of the lake. From this point of vantage I had a good view up the valley and along the beach as far as a point of land where there was a bend in the lake. There I wrapped myself up in the sled-cover — a large piece of canvas — as a defense against the black flies, and raised my trumpet to my lips.

I was highly pleased with myself. The lowing sound I made was perfect, its vibrations echoing delicately in through the forest. It was inconceivable that a genuine moose could do better himself. Enthusiastically I kept at it, meanwhile staring about after the game I expected any moment to see loping in my direction. For fifteen minutes I kept on bellowing; for a half-hour. No game. The same breathless silence over lake and forest; there was not even the stirring of a leaf to break the stillness of this evening hour. Perhaps it wasn't such a simple matter, after all, to call a moose. I drew a deep breath. " Maybe I ought to bel-low more in the bass," I said to myself. " Or else it wasn't the right time until now, when the twilight is really beginning to fall." Once more I cupped my hands and sent one of my better calls out upon the evening air.

" Errk! " came an answering call suddenly from far down the lake. Death and tarnation, there he was! I tried it again and listened. " Errk! " The sound which came back to me was as clear as could be, there was no mistaking it. I called and I called. Each time the answer was more distinct than before; the moose was drawing near. A unique and nerve-racking form of hunting! I was luring the game right to me; soon it would be mine. In a moment or two the moose would come racing across the point off there by the bend in the lake. I uttered one last languishing love-call, picked up my gun, and began peering through the semi-gloom, meanwhile experiencing that same thrill of rapture one always feels when preparing to shoot big game.

" Errk! " came the answering call, vibrant with desire, from the direction of the point, and then — a small canoe came gliding into view. In it an Indian was kneeling, in his hands a bark trumpet exactly like my own. At this point he laid it aside, listened for a moment or two, made a couple of delicate strokes with the tip of his paddle, then gripped his rifle and began staring eagerly about him, as his canoe came drifting straight in the direction of my hiding-place.

" Hey, you! " I cried, running forward. " Don't shoot! " I swung my arms and waved my strip of canvas in the air in order to convince him that I could not possibly be a moose.

The Indian started, his rifle slipping out of his hands. Just what thoughts passed through his head I shall never know, for he turned his canoe sharply round and began paddling off down the lake as though the devil were after

him. I don't believe I ever saw an Indian paddle a canoe
so fast. . . .

.·.

The snow arrived. I harnessed up the dogs and drove off
into the east. I had no particular goal. Temporarily it was
a question of cruising about at random. Later, were I to
discover an especially inviting spot in on the Barrens, I
should likely enough settle down there. Permanent winter
quarters always give one a sense of home.

The dogs were overjoyed to be back in the harness, and
the pace they set left nothing to be desired. After driving
for several days, we found ourselves on the Barrens, with
caribou grazing on every hand. For the time being, I had
sufficient meat and refrained from shooting any game, a
failure the dogs seemed never able to understand. They
would prick up their ears, stare off into the distance at the
caribou, and flash many a resentful glance in my direction.

After a time I came to the narrow belt of woods bordering both sides of the Snowdrift River's northern arm. There
I ran across an old sled-trail, followed it some distance,
and finally arrived at an Indian village.

Here I was met by a whole flock of squaws. I looked
around for some of the hunters, but failed to discover a single one. The only male representative of the tribe was over
sixty years of age. Then I learned that all the hunters had
set out upon an extended expedition after white fox and
had been gone for weeks. The latter fact was as plain as
could be; the women were devoid of all coyness and, with
no beating about the bush, gave me distinctly to understand
that they were enjoying the rare sight of a man, white
though he was. Their attentions were most flattering — but

still! Women singly and alone are one thing, but when they
appear in droves. . . !

Before I could so much as unhitch the dogs, one enterprising squaw had grabbed me and towed me into her
tepee. There she dished out more dried meat, fat, and caribou tongue than a starving trapper could possibly consume
in a week. I ate, offered my thanks, and went outside to
take care of the sled, but hardly had I left the tent when I
was captured by another squaw. So then I was obliged to do
honor to her table as well. When I finally succeeded in
chaining up the dogs and unloading the sled, I found myself back in the tent of my original hostess, surrounded by
a circle of squaws. The older and more ugly ones stood
nearest me, leaving two or three young girls, who were
really pleasing to the eye, far in the background. Some of
these women were chewing tobacco, and every now and
then they would spit a sizzling stream against the red-hot
stove which served to heat the tepee. Others were smoking
pipes, an act which likewise called for profuse expectora-
tion. The only squaws unable to enjoy themselves to the
fullest in this regard were those who were suckling their
infants; they had their hands full and were obliged to leave
their pipes hanging out of the corners of their mouths.

There I sat, feeling like a veritable curiosity. How they
stared at me! How they talked and jabbered! After all
these weeks a man at last! The furore I had apparently
created weighed somewhat heavily upon me, but I lit my
pipe, drew my legs up under me, and attempted to appear
nonchalant. This was by no means an easy matter for me.
Every now and then the squaws would put their heads together, do their best to flirt with me, and laugh significantly.
Whenever shame directed me to utter a word or two, casual
though my remark might be, the entire assemblage would

burst forth into the wildest merriment, just as though I had said something extremely clever, a most remote intention on my part, considering my mood.

At length it was bedtime. One by one the squaws filed out through the flap of the tent. I was not entirely clear in my mind just what I was to do with myself, but, to be on the safe side, I, too, moved toward the door. I had not gone very far, however, when I was given clearly to understand that my place for the night was there in the tent. Giggling amongst themselves, the last of the ladies departed, the tent-flap fell back into place, and there I was alone with three small youngsters, ranging from one to four years of age, and an unattractive squaw of perhaps forty. Spending the night in an Indian tepee was nothing new to me, but such overpowering hospitality as I was now obliged to accept made me feel decidedly ill at ease.

Fully dressed, the squaw rolled herself up in a caribou blanket. The children followed her example, and at length I crept down into my sleeping-bag. Out went the candle. . . . Darkness and restful quiet, broken only by an occasional sputter from the stove. . . . Then I heard a suggestive cough. . . . This was repeated twice in succession. A long pause, and then another cough, sharp and imperious. With that, I drew the sleeping-bag up about my ears so that, were there to be further coughings, I, at least, should not be obliged to hear them. Tired as I was, I soon fell fast asleep, and I doubt not in the least that I also did some snoring.

The next morning no caribou tongue, no dried meat, and no fat were set before me for breakfast. A few dry over-boiled scraps of meat, hardly fit for a dog to eat, were all I drew. . . .

I took a chance and continued eastward, at length coming to a little bottom land in which there was a scattered growth of dwarf spruce. Soon I had left all trees behind and henceforth had only the Barrens about me.

Then it was that I fell upon my oasis in this vast snowy desert — a hollow through which flowed a river and a lake. A hundred or so full-grown spruces had survived all the winds of the tundra in the shelter of the surrounding hills, but, aside from this sign of growth, the naked plains stretched forth in all directions. Driving in across the Barren Lands, I did not suspect the existence of this hollow until I was fairly upon it. Quite suddenly it smiled up at me like a veritable scene from fairyland.

It was here that I pitched my tent, and it was here that the dogs and I had our home until the coming of the long spring days.

Alone on the Barrens

Down in the hollow near the little lake formed by the river, I pitched my tent. About it stood tall shelter-ing spruces. Indoors the tent was so spacious that I could stretch out, like a lord, full-length and stand up almost without bending my back. And it was cosy inside, too, for I had reinforced the walls of the tent with caribou-skins. This was necessary, for otherwise, though I had chosen a sheltered spot, storms sweeping in off the Barrens would drive their swirling snow right through the naked canvas. Darkened ax-marks indicated that a party of Indians had camped in this very clump of trees some time before and had carted away what dry wood they had been able to find. There was not a sliver of dry wood left now, and I was obliged to haul fuel from the nearest strip of forest, a day's journey away to the south.

Outside the tent stood the dogs, straining at their chains each time I came near them. Tiger, the train-leader, was the handsomest of all the dogs; he was yellow and white, and as massive as a wolf. The finest leader in the world! He would respond to " you " and " cha " in a manner to delight one's heart, and, hearing the cry " whoa," he would come to a dead stop, even though he were in the very midst of a herd of caribou. But Tiger was not alone obedient, he likewise used his intelligence. He was forever examining the lay of the land with those sharp eyes of his, and there was no convenient passage through rugged country which Tiger failed to spot. Dashing along at a furious pace in pursuit of a herd of deer, he would never lose his head and go plumb crazy, like the others. Always, by careful calculation, he would cut in ahead of the caribou and bring us up as close on the heels of the game as possible. In addition to these qualifications, there was Tiger's love for work, which he transmitted to the entire train, to say nothing of his ability to understand my wishes, whether I spoke or held my tongue. On odd occasions it might be that his wolf blood would surge up through his veins, resulting in a sharp conflict between us, but, in the main, Tiger was a quiet intelligent dog I could rely upon in the traces and a dog it was a comfort to have round the tent. But he simply detested Indians.

My two pups, Trofast, Jr., and Spike, Jr., who had been born in the forest the previous year whilst I was living with the Indians, needed no instruction in the art of drawing a sled. They had it in their blood. To pull in the traces was the grandest sport they knew, and even before it was time for us to start out in the morning, they would be ready and pawing up the snow in their eagerness to be off. Body and soul, they were exactly like two little boys. They had no end of fun, tumbling about in front of the tent. Occasionally they would fight until the fur flew, but the rest of the time they were the best of friends and would hit upon the oddest things to do together. But whether they fought, hunted ptarmigan in the willow swamp, or stole a caribou head away from me, they were priceless pups none the less. Spike was the brighter of the two, and I had trained him as a reserve train-leader, to the utter exasperation of Tiger, who, every time I removed him from the place of honor, would be insulted and sulk for the entire remainder of the day.

Sport was the team's unruly element. I could never seem to direct his superabundance of vitality. The moment I considered that I had succeeded in making Sport over into a good, steady-going dog, some odd fancy would strike him and he would be impossible again. Here I stand, for example, by the side of the sled, ready to fire into a herd of caribou, when suddenly Sport takes it into his head to do a bit of hunting of his own. The very moment he knows I am not watching him, he worms his head out of the collar with the aid of his fore-paws, crawls out of the belly-band, all in the twinkling of an eye, and then — one, two, three, go! — in a burst of joy he is off across the Barrens on the heels of the terrified deer. This was simply one of his vices; he had plenty of others, each one of which was enough to make a musher's blood boil. But it was utterly impossible ever to hold a grudge against Sport, for whatever he did was prompted, not by evil intentions, but merely by the wantonness of youth.

The responsible position of butt-dog was occupied by Skøieren, whom I had received from the old Indian squaw as a reward for my assistance, the time her people were ill with " flu " on one of the islands off Snowdrift. From the time I started out in the morning until the time I arrived back in camp at night, it was never necessary for me to speak a single word to Skøieren. He worked like a machine. How distinctly I can still see him trotting along in front of me, his tail standing straight up into the air, his head bowed beneath the weight of that shaggy coat of his, which shifted from side to side in time with his twinkling gait! People always smiled a little when they looked at Skøieren, and it was surely true that this dog had a most whimsical appearance, practically lost as he was in the depths of his hircine coat of fur. But out of that shaggy mass shone a pair of eyes which fairly glittered with animation; slanting like the eyes of a wolf, they were set at a quaint angle to his pointed snout. Furthermore, Skøieren was gifted with a special ability: he could talk! During our conversations together he would throw back his head and express himself clearly and unmistakably by means of a whole series of specific sounds. Oh yes, we understood each other perfectly, Skøieren and I.

We were not the only ones living in this sheltered hollow; others there were who had made their homes here long before we came. But there was plenty of room for us all. By tacit agreement we remained good neighbors, each with respect for the domain of the others. The flats down by the river belonged to me, but only as far as the big spruce. Beyond that lay a marshy osier thicket, and this belonged to the ptarmigan. Scores of them lived in this quarter, parading sluggishly about in the snow. Their phlegmatism was such that they paid not the slightest attention to me, whether I happened to be chopping wood or driving by in my sled. As for the lake, I was granted an easement for my sled-trail across the lake, but this was all. The lake belonged to the caribou. In a snug bay directly opposite my tent, they had their beds on the ice, and toward evening two or three of them would always swing down from the Barrens to enjoy a quiet rest, dozing and chewing their cuds. The surrounding slopes were outside my proper province, so long as I could drive across the lake, but I did acquire title to a sled-trail into the north as well. This the polar hares were obliged to put up with, especially since they had more room to move round in than all the rest of us. Theirs was a large family, numbering twenty or more, were one to reckon in the young ones, and this could not be denied; but, on the other hand, they had three slopes in all on which to romp and any number of dwarf spruces and other forms of vegetation to gnaw.

Thus the valley was in reality fully populated and the snow-birds and squirrels could almost be considered in the light of extra boarders. As for the snow-birds, it made no difference whatever if they did encroach upon the domain of others. There was, to be sure, a whole flock of them, but they were in turn so quiet and unobtrusive in their ways that one would be utterly ignorant of their presence until, like a white cloud, they would start up from the ground. But the squirrels were quite another matter. They were our *enfants terribles*. They respected the rights of no one and did their best to make life wretched for us all. One might take its place up in a tree-top and indulge by the hour in such nerve-racking chatter as would try the patience of a saint. Another might throw the whole hollow into con- fusion by taking it into its head to tease the dogs. It would scamper like lightning across the snow and up and down the trunks of trees. When it had succeeded in rousing the dogs to a high pitch of fury and in creating such a general hubbub that I came racing out of the tent and the caribou rose to their feet and moved on in disgust, the squirrel would chatter triumphantly and appear to be marvelously well pleased with itself. This was not all; the squirrels would never let an opportunity go by to disturb the peace. Once, when I had been away from home for several weeks, they had gnawed a hole in my roof and had filled the legs of my overalls with remnants of food and other rubbish. No, there was little to be said for the squirrels there in the hollow!

If, during the course of the winter, I did not fire a shot

at any of these creatures, the main reason was that in other ways and without much trouble to myself I could procure all the food I required. All I had to do was to drive a short way out across the Barrens, and there I was in the very midst of a huge herd of caribou. They would be marching in battalions up and down the rolling hills, lumbering across the lakes, or lying down in vast numbers to rest. Thousands upon thousands of them had apparently settled down in my immediate vicinity. There was hardly a square yard of plain which did not bear the marks of hoofs; the lakes were trodden as hard as city streets, and when shedding-time came, the whole region was littered with antlers. In a short while I had slaughtered all the meat I needed, sledding the carcasses into camp and piling them up in a huge mound in front of my tent. From time to time it might be that I slaughtered a calfless doe which was certain to be extremely fat, but other than this I saved my ammunition for the wolves.

There existed a friendly relationship between all these creatures, and, whether it be my conceit or not, it seems that they gradually came to regard both me and the dogs as safe neighbors, as phenomena which belonged with them there in the wilderness. On days of bright sunshine, as I drove across the waste, occasionally by necessity straight through a band numbering a hundred or more caribou, the animals would barely make way for me to pass. They would look up for a moment, then resume their grazing, as much as to say: " Oh, it's only that fellow! " In the course of the evening a party of hares might appear on one of the surrounding slopes, where they would sit in pairs, washing their faces with their paws and every now and then glancing down in the direction of the tent where smoke was rising into the air and the dogs and I were busy fussing about.

The thought of roast hare or ptarmigan offered no great temptation here where meat was served at every meal and where a caribou head or tongue proved a most satisfactory variation in the menu.

In the very beginning the dogs were delirious with excitement. But, receiving all the food their bellies would hold, and discovering that the caribou were an everyday occurrence, their hunting-fever cooled. Whenever, on rare occasions, I gave chase to the herd, the dogs would be overjoyed, but they had learned that unless I gave the word, they were to make no demonstration. And when the caribou out on the lake in front of the tent began to move about, it might be that the dogs would prick up their ears and show great signs of interest, but that was all. The scent of wolves, on the other hand, was a horse of a different color — then their canine natures would burst forth in a mighty flame.

. .

In order to make the most of my opportunities for hunting the wolf and white fox, I established a trap-line to a spot on the Barrens, two days' journey off to the east. There I slept in a small double tent which I pitched each evening. Here is a record of one of my days on the Barrens:

It is dark in the tent when I awake in the morning and poke my nose out of the sleeping-bag. A cold gust of wind strikes my cheek. No matter; I must be on my feet early today if I am desirous of reaching my main camp before nightfall. After lighting the oil-lamp I peep at my watch. Six o'clock, it shows by its hands. With my toes I fish up moccasins, socks, and stockings from the bottom of the sleeping-bag, where they have lain overnight to dry. The act of dressing takes place within the sleeping-bag. I am cramped for space and find it difficult to move round, but elsewhere it is too cold for me to dress.

At length, fully clad, I spring up, throw some sticks of wood and shavings into the stove, and put a kettle of snow on to thaw. It takes a short time for the stove to warm up and, in the meantime, I throw my fur coat about me, draw on my mittens, and stamp up and down to keep from becoming stiff. It grows warm in the tent. Then I rattle the dishes and drive my ax into the meat, which is frozen so hard that it splinters into loose fragments. Breakfast out of the way, my lighted pipe in my mouth, I creep out of the tent. Overhead, in a distant blaze of glory, arch the starry heavens, and on every side the barren waste stretches forth in the definitely greenish semi-gloom. About the tent, each curled up in his own snug hole in the snow, his nose buried under his tail, lie the dogs half-covered with drift. I dig the sled out of the snow, haul it up in front of the tent, and lay out the harness. With that, the dogs awake. Tiger, Skøieren, Spike, and Trofast are on their feet at once; they shake the snow from their fur, stretch themselves until their spines crack, and yawn voluptuously, as much as to say: " It's a hell of a thing to do to wake us up like this, but here we are." One by one I strap them into the harness. But where is Sport? He hasn't budged as yet! With one half-open eye he is following our movements from his nest in the snow. Observing him, I walk over to him, whereupon he snaps his eyes tight shut and pretends to be lost in profound and innocent slumber. " Sport! " I cry. With that, he buries his nose still farther beneath his tail. A good-natured slap on the rump, and he looks up at me with a deeply injured look in his eyes." Hasn't he any heart left in his body that he feels he can break up an honest dog's hard-earned night's rest? " they seem to say.

All are in the traces, shivering and bucking the air, whilst I wrestle with tent and sleeping-bag. Then we are off.

I have covered quite a distance when the gray light of dawn finally awakes in the sky; another interval, and there flames the sun. It seems then as though thick blinds have suddenly been thrown open on the world. The caribou at once become visible, some close at hand, others like pin-pricks off on the horizon. Away into the distance stretches this great land, dotted with muskegs, lakes, and hills decapitated by the wind; off into the distance it billows like some great white sea, the delicate, flowing lines of its outermost rim melting into a blue haze.

On a lake directly ahead a band of some hundred or more caribou are lying. Here L decide to have a little fun and try one of my old tricks. About a hundred yards away I halt the dogs, light my pipe, and snuggle down into the cariole. The caribou have already caught sight of the sled, but not until this point do they stand up. One by one they deliberately rise to their feet. The snow which has clung to their sides slips off, but a white covering of it still remains on their backs. All stare in the direction of the sled and study it intently. What in the world can it be, that object which is one moment moving along and the next has stopped stock still? At length the calves and the young bucks can no longer restrain their curiosity, they *must* go over and see. Right up to the sled come some twenty or thirty of them, at a ludicrous, sauntering trot, their legs swinging loosely out to either side of their bodies. The young bucks have antlers of at least two points, and it is apparent that, in the company of the calves, they feel themselves decidedly grown-up. The latter seem little more than woolly heads to which four inconceivably long legs are attached and for which there hardly seems room. Barely six months ago it was that they first saw the light of day on the shores of the Polar Sea. Everything is strange to them, and there seems to be no end of weird things to be sniffed and examined in this odd new world into which they have been born. A short distance from the sled they come to an abrupt halt, their eyes popping out of their sockets.

The dogs stand with ears erect, Sport every so often shooting me a glance, as much as to say: " Good heavens, can't we do a little hunting? " But I am cold to his query and order " Mush! " in the direction in which we are headed.

The very moment the dogs strain forward in their traces, the caribou bolt in terror, humping their backs in the air and making straight for the main herd, which immediately dashes off up a hillside. On the summit they halt abruptly, recover their poise, and at once fall to grazing as though nothing at all had occurred.

We proceed on our way. Every now and then I pause at a trap. An occasional white fox finds its way into the cariole. I reset the traps yielding me furs together with most of the empty ones, which, in the course of a day or two, have been sprung by the hoofs of the caribou.

The dogs are now trotting along at a beautifully even pace, the breath from their lungs trailing out upon the air, their fluffy tails waving on end. What splendid dogs they are!

About me a sea of endless white dotted with grazing caribou. Peace dwells over the wasteland. Somewhere off to the north a wolf is howling. The Lord only knows why he should be howling now, right in the middle of a day of glittering sunshine!

Close beside Wolverine Lake I have left a caribou carcass, and it is high time for me to haul it into camp. I'll soon be at the spot. My way lies in between a number of rolling eskers. In the narrow passes between them, huge slate-stones rise like obelisks. About these I must thread my way. Now I can see the lake — but what's that?

I lose no time in tying Tiger's head fast to the tail of the sled and creeping stealthily forward. Wolves; four in all, dark gray and sleek. With their fore-paws resting on that caribou carcass of mine, they are ripping into it with their fangs, every now and then tearing off a huge slab of meat.

As my shot rings out, three wolves scoot off across the plain. The fourth lies on the ground with stiff sprawling legs, its upper lip curled back from its gleaming teeth in a ferocious sneer. Blood trickles from its mouth.

In a half-hour now we shall be back home. For a time I attempt running along on snowshoe behind the sled in order to keep warm, but I cannot keep up the pace set by my galloping dogs. They are thinking of the pile of meat in front of the tent in the hollow. A cold wind whistles about my ears, and I am forced to shield my face with the back of one mitten. That devilish nose of mine is frozen again!

At last we arrive in the hollow where the tent is pitched in the shelter of green spruces. It is fine to be back home. As the sled swings headlong down the slope into the hollow, I catch a last fleeting glimpse of the Barrens, now tinted with shades ranging from red to white in the sunset's afterglow.

Then evening comes; the dogs have been cared for and we have all eaten well. I light my pipe and get busy stretching and fleshing my wolf-skin. This task requires hours to perform, for the beast is as fat as a pig. He must have had many a caribou on his conscience when he died. Finishing this job, I now have my mending to do. Sewing of this type soon gets on a man's nerves. One is never through with it. See this; not so many days ago I put a splendid three-cornered canvas patch on the seat of these pants of mine, and now I'll be dashed if here isn't another hole! So it goes, patching and patching until there is hardly anything left of one's breeches save patches! And then one must patch the patches. . . . Nevertheless, I am rather proud of my needlework. It even once happened that an old Indian squaw, watching me skillfully threading my needle, nodded her head approvingly, and, though my seams are not likely to start a new fashion, they do hold, for I use a double strand of very thick thread and pull each stitch as tight as I can. The art of making moccasins I acquired from the heavyweight, Phresi, and I have no cause to be ashamed of my footgear.

Now for a bit of dried meat. I still have loads of it hanging from the roof of the tent. Nothing like dried meat when a man is up and doing. I now bite off a piece and chew it. Then it is time to chop wood. Outside, the moon has risen and the aurora has just begun to spray the northern sky with iridescent light. The night is so sharp and clear that it would be possible to bring down a wolf at fair range.

"Hello, lads, how goes it?" The dogs wag their tails and fall all over themselves jumping up. We converse a bit together and soon I am finished toting firewood.

A quiet smoke before I turn in. It is peaceful and cosy inside the tent. The stove crackles, and every now and then a puff of wind bellies in the walls of the tent.

There, now it is beginning! First one wolf, far off to the south, utters, in a thin voice, a tentative howl which ends abruptly half-way up the scale. But an answering howl comes immediately. A wolf on the slope directly behind the tent raises his voice, and immediately there is a grand howling from every quarter. Ah, there go the dogs, first Sport, then the pups, and then all five of them! Good Lord, what a howling! Now and then they pause to hear whether the wolves are keeping up their end of the conversation; then they burst forth again. Strange that you should care to take part in such a dismal serenade, my lads, but if it's so much fun for you, why keep at it!

Along one wall of the tent hang my white-fox pelts — delicate masses of long silken white hair. I let my eyes linger upon them for a time and feel like a veritable capitalist, though the majority of these furs are doomed to find their traditional way into the warehouse of " Hudson Bay " to balance my indebtedness.

One fox-skin in particular stands out from the others; it is larger and more luxuriant, a perfect cataract of white. Where will it finally come to rest? In Paris, perhaps? I permit my fancy to roam. A gleaming limousine draws up in front of l'Opéra in Paris; a young lady steps out and glides up the steps to the door. About her bare throat and shoulders floats a billowy mist of white fox . . . mine! Lucky white fox. . . .

· ·

Many of my days in the heart of the Barren Lands were much like this. But then, there were also days I should like far less to remember, times when icy winds blew in across an implacably cruel wasteland.

Once I set out on snowshoe, without the dogs, to slaughter a few caribou. It was a simple matter and I thought nothing of it. But the game kept moving away, and I followed them farther and farther into those barren wastes. In the very midst of the hunt night fell and I became lost. Aimlessly I went tramping about there in that biting cold. The moon rose and the night became freezingly clear and unreal. The mountainous snow-drifts cast long, black shadows, and the pale yellow surface of the lakes stretched forth into the endless distance. Occasionally I almost stumbled against caribou asleep in the snow. In terror, they would scramble up and, like ghostly shadows, float off into the moonlight. I came to a river and decided to follow it downstream. But in which direction did the river flow? Its frozen surface at this point formed a part of a level plain. Here and there a number of rocks rose above the surface of the ice and I immediately dug away the snow to feel whether the current had worn them down on either side. They were all as round as could be! Every other telltale sign lay buried beneath the drifting snow. Trusting to luck, I walked along the river in one direction until I came upon several lakes which appeared to empty into the river. So I was obliged to retrace my steps. Hour after hour I tramped down the river, hither and yon, as I followed its divers twistings, never daring to attempt a short cut, for the moon was now hidden behind clouds and I had lost track of the north star.

At length I came to a sheltered spot where there was a wretched growth of dwarf spruces, and there I made what might pass for a fire. Bending over a thin, smoky flame I sat as the hours dragged by.

Then the howling of the wolves began. On all other occasions I had listened to this sound with perfect composure, but on this particular night it inspired me with anything but a feeling of *gemütlichkeit*. The wolves appeared to be on all sides of me and extremely close at hand. I therefore set up a hedgerow of dwarf spruce behind me in the snow and sat with my rifle on my knee. If only my fuel would hold out until this crisis were past! I scraped together all

I could find and fed my fire sparingly, stick by stick, just often enough to keep the flames alive. As I sat there staring into the darkness, pierced every now and then by a shaft of moonlight which had eluded the scudding clouds, the howls of the wolves suddenly ceased. Shortly afterwards I thought I saw a dark shadow pass in front of me, followed by several others. With that, I discharged one shot, two shots, then the entire magazine.

With the coming of the dawn, there were no wolves to be seen; but I did discover a trail of blood in the snow. I followed this downstream to a little lake formed by the confluence of this and another river. There I caught sight of the skeleton of a huge caribou buck which had been slaughtered by the wolves. The angle at which the head was turned struck me at once as familiar. Then I knew! I had passed this way a couple of times before, whilst out hunting for wood. I was directly south of my camp; the way back home lay upstream along the *other* river. Thus luck was with me again and I reached camp suffering no ill effects from my experience.

After this affair I seldom went anywhere without the dogs. Were I to get lost again, the chances would be against my ever returning alive. And the danger of becoming lost is forever present there on the Barrens. Most trappers have, at one time or another, found themselves in my predicament. The Barrens are not to be relied upon, for their appearance is never the same. Contours are constantly shifting, so that one's conception of distance is forever disturbed. One may arrive at a certain locality he has visited countless times, and swear he has never been there before.

Amongst the dogs, there are certain train-leaders who are able to find their way home under any set of conditions. Tiger turned out to be such a dog. The first time I tried him

out in this direction, I was somewhat skeptical. Darkness
and a blizzard of wind-swept snow overtook me some distance out on the Barrens, and I had my choice of digging
myself into the snow or of taking a chance on Tiger's sense
of direction. I made the latter choice. Hour after hour we
drove along. I entrusted the dogs with the entire problem
of finding the way, and lay there in the bottom of the cariole
with my mittens in front of my face to ward off the stinging
snow. It was so dark that I could barely see the dog nearest
the sled. But in Tiger's mind no shadow of doubt existed;
at a steady pace he kept following the course he had chosen.
Once we ran into a band of caribou, and the dogs swerved
off to give chase. But I had only to utter a single command,
and Tiger, without a moment's hesitation, turned his head
sharply back in the original direction. At length the sled
halted with a jerk. I looked up — and there was the tent!

"You're some dog, you are!" I said to Tiger, patting
his head.

But Tiger merely looked at me with a supercilious expression on his face, as much as to say: "Shush, that's
nothing to what I really can do!"

. .

One day, on driving out along my trap-line, I discovered
that some of my white foxes had been stolen from the traps,
and that the plain round about was strewn with dead caribou, with only their rear quarters eaten away. Then I knew
that the killers — the big wolves of the north — had arrived. Right along, there had been sparse packs of wolves
in the neighborhood, but now the real fun would begin.

I actually saw but little of these big wolves. By twos and
threes they would race along to the east, keeping up such a

steady pace that they allowed themselves barely enough time to eat a square meal, in spite of all they had slaughtered. But toward the end of December, two or three weeks later, the main wolf packs came hurrying out of the west, and from then until the end of February the country was alive with them. In February the main army of them moved off into the east and I saw no more of them until the following April, when, shortly after the rutting season, they came jogging north from the woodlands.

The hollow in which I lived was directly on their line of march, and straight across from the tent, on the other side of the river, the wolves would pass. Most frequently they would go by in the night. Scenting them, the dogs would sound a lusty alarm, bellowing at the top of their lungs, pulling and tugging at their chains, and breaking up my good night's rest. Occasionally I would rush outside and take a few shots at the wolves, but shooting in the moonlight is difficult enough in itself, to say nothing of having a moving gray shadow for a target.

The hullabaloo set up by the dogs did not appear to awe the wolves very greatly; on the contrary, the latter often displayed a keen interest in these animals which bore such a familiar scent. Sometimes their tracks in the snow revealed the fact that they had approached fairly close to the dogs, and at other times that they had circled the tent several times before moving on. Their interest in the dogs was proved by another fact as well: it was a common occurrence for a wolf, on coming across my sled-trail out on the Barrens, to turn and follow it back into camp. In this instance I cannot flatter myself by supposing that I, too, formed a part of their interest.

There had always been excellent concerts of wolf-music before in the evening, but these turned out to be no more than chamber musicales compared with the symphonic demonstrations which followed. On nights of clear cold moonlight the orchestra would assemble for its ritual song of the wasteland. Far off in the distance it would begin like the wail of a dismal flute; voice after voice was added, the music growing in volume, until, from the slopes surrounding my tent, it would blare forth in a mighty crescendo which gathered into its web of sound all the doleful misery in the world and hurled it aloft at the moon. I grew to enjoy this dismal music and could sit by the hour listening to the howls as they rose and fell through the night, so much so that on the rare occasions when silence prevailed over the wastes, something seemed missing from my life and I might wonder to myself: What in the world has happened to the wolves tonight?

These Canadian wolves are enormous, considerably larger than their European brethren. In weight they vary from 80 to 120 pounds, and in size they compare favorably with a St. Bernard dog. Judging from the struggle I many times had to lift one into the sled, one might estimate their weight to range from 140 to 160 pounds. The wolf is an agile, wiry beast, built for endurance in the chase and speed in the final attack. Its backbone is as straight as a bar of iron, its breast sharply curved, its legs long, its paws broad and heavy. Its pelage is thick and often silky, occasionally shaggy about the withers. The gleaming white teeth, contrasting with the bright red tissues of the mouth, and the sharply slanting eyes complete the picture of a perfect beast of prey in all its beauty and brutal strength.

There is a wide variation in color. There are the totally white wolf, the reddish brown, and the gray, the latter ranging from very dark to very light, sometimes even bluish in tone. Most common is the grayish white, with black

[305]

markings. As a rule, wolves of all different colors journey in one pack, though on occasion it appears that wolves of the same color hold together. One trapper, in the course of a single month, in a specific region, took thirty wolves all of which were dark gray.

After the wolf-rush took place, I experienced no want of entertainment during my daily journeys by sled across the Barrens. The animals were difficult to distinguish in this environment, and the ones I did observe thus actually constituted but a small minority of the vast numbers which infested the region; even so, I saw no end of wolves. Sometimes I would surprise them feasting upon dead caribou; on other occasions I could see packs of them jogging across some lake. One day I came as near colliding with a wolf as possible. I was driving along from the south with a load of wood, was sitting there high on the load, my pipe in my mouth, as the dogs went trotting along. Just as I was rounding a hummock, I came face to face with a shaggy gray wolf, who, absorbed in thoughts of his own, was ambling round the base of the hill in the opposite direction. It was a rude awakening for both of us, and our confusion was mutual. I am sure, however, that the wolf showed the keener reaction. He was completely astounded — I still have a clear picture of the look in his eyes as he glared at me. He then crouched in the snow and did his best to get me to flee in a zigzag course. But it was too late; that evening the pelt was hanging in my tent, whilst the carcass lay behind in the snow as a solemn warning to others of his race not to go wool-gathering in the heart of the Barren Lands.

Ordinarily the wolves ran together in packs numbering from three to seven, though at times there were as many as twenty hunting together. Interesting it was to study their

methodical co-operation when felling their game. First
there was the marathon chase, when the caribou stormed
like an avalanche out across the Barrens with those gray
shadows in hot pursuit. The very moment the deer paused
in their flight or swung off on a new course, the wolves
would dart in and attempt to separate one or two victims
from the main herd. Then there was the still hunt, when
the wolves would stealthily approach their game, quite as
a lynx would do. Once I was an eyewitness, at comparatively close quarters, to one of these still hunts. Three
wolves were creeping up the slope to a plateau where a
band of caribou were grazing. Hugging the ground, they
slunk forward, step by step, until they came to an overhanging snow-drift at the very top. There one lay down in
the snow, whilst the other two slipped round to one side
and disappeared. Shortly afterwards I saw them bob up
some distance beyond the caribou, which had already
showed signs of restlessness. Suddenly both wolves threw
back their heads and uttered a most harrowing howl. This
threw the caribou into a mad panic and put them to flight
immediately. The two chasers took stations, one on either
side of the herd, and drove the frantic beasts straight in
the direction of the wolf which lay in ambush. I watched
how the latter shifted his paws and gathered himself up
ready for a spring. At the very instant the caribou swept
past, he darted out. The events which followed occurred so
rapidly that my eye failed to register them clearly. I caught
a glimpse of the other two wolves as they raced in like
streaks of lightning. For a moment there was a wild chaos
of stampeding deer, dancing backward and forward; then
the herd went storming out across the Barrens. Three
wolves remained behind, ripping and tearing with their
tushes the bowels of a caribou buck which was casting

about with its head and kicking up the snow in a last un-
even battle.

In regard to me the wolves behaved somewhat differ-
ently. Sometimes they would flee at the sight of my sled,
but for the most part they were not over-timid. Once a
pack of five followed my sled for hours. At first they remained a fair distance behind, but gradually they crept
up on me, until at length the pack formed a column and
visibly quickened their pace. I turned and blazed away
at them, killing one and frightening away the other four.

Of my other adventures I shall mention only one which
was somewhat out of the ordinary. One night I was awakened in my tent by such a commotion of barking dogs that
it seemed as though it came from the nether regions. The
strident annoyance in their voices indicated that Sport had
again twisted his head out of the chain and was now running about free, thus making the others green with envy.
I ran out of the tent just as I was. Angry and frightfully
sleepy, I hoped to set things to rights in a jiffy. Some distance away from the tent I stared about in the moonlight.
On the very top of my tall pile of caribou carcasses stood
an animal gorging itself with meat. Oh, that Sport! I
thought to myself, fumbling around after a missile. Getting hold of an old gnawed-off bone, I threw this as hard
as I could. With a metallic sound it caught the miscreant
right between the eyes. The animal crouched and uttered
a low growl. It was a wolf. Discovering this, I lost no time
in running back to the tent after my rifle, and just at the
right moment, too, for the wolf was at me with so little
delay that I was obliged to fire from the hip.

One day I brought down a wolf which was in a most
pitiful condition: it was almost without fur on its body.
Save for a little tuft of hair on the tip of its tail and a col-

lar of fur about its neck, its back was as bare as could be, the skin being black and stretched taut over its body. How this creature had ever been able to survive the cold was a mystery to me. The disease which had robbed it of its fur was a kind of mange, found also among dogs. It will attack men as well as animals.

There is another and a more dangerous disease which afflicts the wolves — a kind of rabies. Presumably it is this disease which reduces the wolf race at such times as, in numbers, it reaches the crest of a cycle. The Indians always speak of good and poor years for wolves, and it is said that there are times when the wilds are strewn with their dead. When this disease smites a dog, the animal must be shot immediately.

I have had numerous opportunities to study the mutual adjustment between dogs and wolves. It is so truly representative of the relationship existing between animals of allied species that I believe it worth while to dwell for a moment upon it. In the present case there is a strange mingling of hatred and mutual understanding. My own dogs — they were all males at the time — were ready to murder a wolf anywhere at any time, save in the event it should be a she-wolf in heat. When in bondage outside the tent, they would bark at the fair interloper, for they felt it their duty to challenge any and all who might approach our castle, but they would not harm her were they free to get at her.

On one occasion I surprised Tiger eagerly exchanging courtesies with a wolf-bitch. Nose to nose they were standing in the middle of a frozen lake. Similar situations have been discovered by many other observers, especially by the Government wardens in the newly established Thelon Game Sanctuary. Unless it be during the wolves' rutting season, any dog — male or bitch — running afoul a wolf pack will be promptly torn to pieces. During the rutting season, either dog or bitch is likewise doomed should it fall in with wolves of the same sex, though they may otherwise pair off together. As previously mentioned, the dogs of the Northland have a good measure of wolf blood flowing in their veins. This comes out in their general appearance — their pelage, their sharply slanting eyes, their pointed muzzles. In their dispositions, too, this wolf blood many times manifests itself. Certain dogs are so intractable by nature that it is next to impossible ever to teach them anything, and on many occasions they have been known to tear a human being to pieces. A case in point is that of the wife of one of Canada's Mounted Police officers.

Ordinarily the wolf is not considered satisfactory as a work animal; it has strength and endurance, but the wildness of its nature is difficult to cope with. Even a first-generation product of dog and wolf is almost unmanageable. When the ratio of wolf blood stands at one to three, one begins to find good work animals.

Naturally, much depends upon the dog-musher's individual knack. One may consider, for example, such a trainer as Slim Campbell. This very day, I believe, he is driving a full-blooded wolf-bitch which is superior to any sled-dog at the east end of Great Slave Lake. Several winters ago he caught her, when quite young, in a trap. Slim hog-tied her and drove home with her to his tent. Later she was harnessed to the sled along with his regular dog-train, and she fitted in all right. She no longer wears a muzzle, and, although at night he must tie her up with a double chain, she is as even-tempered as a wolf can be, whenever her master handles her. Others, however, had best keep their distance. " Wolf " strains in the traces like an experienced

dog today, but, whereas her companions of the trail hold
their tails like feathery plumes in the air, she carries her
own on a stiff level with her spine. . . .

. .
.

The months flew by and my life was anything but boring.
My hands were constantly busy keeping things in order,
and something new was forever happening. Often came
days of glittering sunshine and sharp cold. Driving across
those fields of snow dotted with grazing caribou, I would
feel that I was the lord of some vast estate and that these
were my herds of kine. And in spite of the many hard spells
of blizzard and cold, it was remarkable how quickly I
could forget the dreariness outside when the stove began
to crackle and the meat-kettle to send up its clouds of steam.
The dogs were my companions, and in many diverse ways
they kept me in high spirits. At one time they would fight
amongst themselves and do all they could to tear each other
into shreds; at another they would hit upon the most amusing things to do. I learned to comprehend their mental
world, whilst the dogs, on their side, had a pretty good notion of mine; even though they might subtly try to fool me
now and then, and even though we had many a wild set-to,
we had great respect for each other.

Oh yes, my life on the Canadian tundra was entertaining
in many ways. I had given but small thought to humanity
when, one day, people suddenly arrived. Toward dusk I
swung down into the hollow and was astonished to see sleds
in front of my tent. Inside were five Indians, who had
stopped in to break their journey. They had spent some
time off to the east and were now on their way home to their
main village, south in the forest. Their sleds were comfor-

tably filled with white fox, and one of the Indians had with him a caribou hide which, without a single dark blemish, was as white as the driven snow. In the party was my old acquaintance François, who was planning to return in a fortnight to the same district where he had been hunting before. We agreed that he was to stop off and pay me a visit, after which we would hit the trail together.

François kept his appointment, and, although he arrived two weeks later than the time agreed upon, this was pretty good for an Indian. We set our course in an easterly direction, followed along the narrow Sandy Lake, crossed the divide near Zucker Lake, passed the large lakes forming the head waters of the Thelon, and entered a land of eskers and maze-like lakes.

After continuing our journey for a week, we ran into a blinding snow-storm. For three full days we lay side by side in the tent. When we awoke on the fourth morning, the storm was still raging and our meat-kettle was empty. François mentioned that he had seen a dead caribou killed by wolves a short time before we had pitched camp. To this I replied that it would hardly do us much good, for in such fiendish weather as this it would be impossible to lug in the meat. But this was wind in François's sails. " Storm nothing for Indian," he said superciliously. I then asked him why, if this were so, he didn't start out after the meat, to which he replied that, since he wasn't hungry himself, the matter didn't interest him — unless *I went, too!* He could always guide the way, you see. The chance of my taking him up on this offer seemed to him quite remote, I suppose, considering the way in which the storm was howling about the tent, so, from his cosy corner indoors, he now began to hold forth in dead earnest on the ability of an Indian to

[312]

cope with any blizzard! At length, reaching the end of my patience, I threw on my deerskin parka and made for the door. François followed me with his eyes, then reluctantly joined me.

Outside, the storm barred our way like a wall of white. The driving snow stung our faces and blinded us. Our garments clung to our bodies and we were obliged to bend forward as we walked to avoid being blown over by the wind. François went first to lead the way. He had not taken many steps before he stopped and asked: " Maybe you cold? " But I smelled a rat and swore to myself that if he were of a mind to turn and go back, he should not use me as an excuse; therefore I yelled through the storm at him: " *Ni sentilly!* (I'm all right!) " After we had plowed along another short distance, François again halted to inquire whether I was cold. " *Ni sentilly!* " I cried, rubbing my nose, which was already frozen stiff. Shortly afterwards I was asked for a third time if I were cold, and although I had never been so cold in my life, I again screeched my " *Ni sentilly!* " in François's ear. With that he halted and remarked doubtfully: " Big wind, maybe go home."

Luckily we had not gone very far, and, with the wind propelling us from behind, we had no trouble returning to the slope where our tent stood. Only the tips of the tent-poles stood out above the snow, but we discovered the place without difficulty.

Before digging our way indoors, we went out to visit the dogs. I couldn't find Skøieren anywhere. I hunted high and low for him, until at length I caught sight of something black on top of an enormous drift. It was Skøieren's tail. He himself stood in an awkward position deep down in the heart of the drift; he was unable to move and was hardly able to breathe. As the drift had continued to pile up, Skøieren had crawled along until he had reached the end of his chain.

These four days indoors in the tent gave ample opportunity for afterthought and speculation, which for François began more and more to revolve about one thing only: his beloved Tha. He asserted that she was absolutely loyal to him and that she cared nothing for the other hunters while he was away from home. But he reiterated his point so frequently that it was apparent some doubt dwelt in his mind. When, on the fifth day, the blizzard had passed, François reported to me that he already had " heap of skins " and that he didn't need any more. Then he harnessed up his dogs and started out west for his home village, where his loyal Tha awaited him.

Alone once more, I wandered about for another month, hunted, trapped, and saw much new country. When, late in April, the caribou began to retire into the north, I thought it wise to return to my main camp, where I had laid up a copious supply of dog-feed. Furthermore, the wolves' rutting season was on and the second big rush could now be expected at any time.

It seemed good to see once more my old home-place in the hollow. All was just as I had left it, save the door-yard, where the snow now lay in huge drifts, and where wolf, fox, and hare had been cavorting about to their hearts' content.

The End of the Adventure

I TAKE MY USUAL ROUTE IN ACROSS THE SNOW-FIELDS, now bathed in a sea of light. Behind my swiftly trotting dogs the sled goes dancing along over the hardened drifts. About me bands of caribou are grazing; they scrape away the snow and stoop to nibble at the blue-white lichens beneath. The sunlight on the snow is a blinding glare and I give my fur cap an extra downward pull.

And now something occurs which I have long anticipated, but which dawns upon me with all suddenness — *the sun gives warmth!* Through my deerskin coat I can feel its rippling caress. Then it is true that winter cannot last forever! There really can be a time when I shall not be riding in a sled or running on snowshoe, when my clothing will be other than a heavy parka and mittens, and when these snow-fields will vanish into a fairyland of tinted moss and waving grasses, the brownish gray of rock and the gurgling blue of lake. Yes, there can really be such a thing as springtime!

Month after month I have gone wandering here alone. The mere struggle for existence has occupied my entire attention, so that I have almost failed to note the passage of time. One winter day has drifted into the next, and the spirit of the wilderness has filtered into my manner of thinking. My monotonous existence together with my dogs, whether in camp or *en route* to some distant point, has become the normal for me, and all there was of my life prior to my sojourn in the wilds has drifted off into a distant haze, permitting me but occasional faint remembrances of those once proud realities. But now spring is coming, and things are otherwise.

I halt the dogs and peer in all directions. What a power of light over all this whiteness! I shield my eyes and take stock of these familiar stretches of country. Off there in the distance lies Wolverine Lake with its strangely irregular coves, now strewn with loafing deer. Over there is Hog Ridge, from the summit of which the wolves always howl at night. Close in beside Hog Ridge lies the trail which leads south to the forest. Hundreds of miles of silent forest, then cities and people! Down there spring must be well along by now — green lawns, dry sidewalks, women in light gauzy dresses! People thronging the streets, greeting and talking with one another, wiping away the perspiration which beads on their brows. Men swinging in through café doors, sitting at tables, calling: " Psst! Waiter! " Some are eating potatoes, others cauliflower, asparagus, or tomatoes. They may have all four if they wish. None of them are chewing on caribou meat!

" Tiger," I say, " perhaps the time has come. I'll never have another dog like you, and there probably will never come days such as those we have spent together. God knows why I should move on when I have everything I want right here, and when I know that home-sickness will forever assail me! But it can't be helped — restlessness is astir in my blood and I must give in to it. . . . Five wolves more, Tiger, and then we shall head due south and go as far as we can by sled."

I succeed in taking two more wolves, and now I cannot

[316]

bring myself to delay another single day, even could I be assured of hundreds. I am filled with a burning desire to get away.

So one morning, just as the sun is coming up, I stand in front of my tent and look about me for the last time. Then I lace up the sled, hop on top of the load, and urge the dogs down the valley at a brisk trot. I sit there looking back. My clump of spruces stand nodding a friendly farewell from their hollow in the heart of these glittering snow-fields. In the tree-tops the squirrels are chattering after my vanishing form. On the sunny slopes the hares are sitting in pairs, and down in the osier thicket the ptarmigan are perched on the leafless bushes like fabulous white fruits. Crossing the lake, I find one doe and her calf idling on the ice. They do not move in their tracks, merely turn their heads and stare off after the sled with a look of surprise in their large eyes. Here, too, is a last farewell.

My road lies over wide plains and countless lakes. Here it is not a question of knowing the way, for the country is like one landscape endlessly repeated; but my course lies directly southwest and I use the sun for my compass. After a time I sight the distant landmark named by the Indians " White Mountain," which rises some six hundred feet above the plain. Now I know where I am. It is not long before I encounter the forest. How good it is to see it again! After those naked wind-swept wastes, it is like returning to a land of mild green summer. I peer about me, to right and to left, let my eyes drink in the green of pine and spruce, stroke with the palm of my hand the bole of a tall jack pine. We are like two friends, meeting after a long absence. . . . In the forest I find loose snow and must run along on snowshoe ahead of the dogs. How close they keep to me! Tiger burrows his way through the snow so close on my heels that once my snowshoe strikes him under the chin as I lift it, taking a step. No need to ask if the dogs realize that we are now bound for the place where winter's toil will be over and where a summer of loafing in the golden sunshine awaits them!

At the east end of Slave Lake I arrive at an Indian camp; here a band of natives, on their way out from the edge of the Barrens with furs, dried meat, and fat, have raised their tepees. They are now busy getting out their squaw-boats, left here during the previous autumn, and binding them fast to the sleds. In a day or two they will strike camp and head south for the post at Snowdrift. A number of the Indians must have started out already, for out across the lake runs a glossy white trail, cut through the snow by sled and snowshoe.

Here I learn some news. I meet Corporal Williams of the Royal Canadian Mounted Police, the man who enjoys power and authority over so wide a territory that it would elsewhere pass for a kingdom. He tells me about Hornby and his two young colleagues who, two years ago, disappeared into the Barren Lands. . . . Near the confluence of the Hanbury and Thelon rivers a cabin and three corpses were discovered. It was the old story: the caribou had disappeared and the three had died of slow starvation. Hornby and the elder of the two young men had perished early in the winter — wrapped up in canvas, they lay in front of the shack. The youngest member of the expedition had kept going on scraps of leather and the few bones he was able to dig up from beneath the snow. He lived several months after the death of the others — was alive when the ducks flew by from the south. Nor did he go mad — soberly and conscientiously he kept up his diary until he was too weak to write any more. The last lines read something like this: " There are definite signs of spring and I have already seen ducks. Sit by the door of the shack with my rifle across my knees. Am too weak to walk, but still hoping."

I take leave of Williams and set out south across the lake for Snowdrift. The sun streams down upon the lake, sharply contrasting the glittering white of the snow which stretches off into infinity and the green of spruce-clad islands. The sled glides lightly over the hard-packed trail, and the journey is matchless sport for both man and dog. Suddenly we drive past a number of dead dogs in the snow beside the trail — other dogs are floundering helplessly round in the snow. There has evidently been an epidemic of rabies.

After driving along for some time, I overtake several families of Indians. They are obliged to make slow progress, as the canoes, lashed to the sleds, are filled with various trappings. In a long column they are trailing along on snowshoe behind the dogs — hunters, squaws, and young children. All smile as I pass by; in spite of my beard they still recognize me. One of them is a sixteen-year-old girl named Marie. She seems to be floating along over the snow, so lightly does she tread on her snowshoes; and her skirts, wide and altogether too long for her, do not seem to hamper her in the least. Her deerskin coat is wide open in front, her hood is pushed back from her head, and her black hair bristles about her neck. As I drive up, she stops and smiles. I do not hesitate a moment before inviting her to ride in the sled with me, for I have long known that Marie is the prettiest Indian girl east of Great Slave Lake.

Hour after hour we go driving along together with absolutely no traffic of sleds to pester us. Then, about noon, we catch sight of a black speck on the horizon far to our rear. It draws nearer and nearer until we are able to make out that it is a dog-train with a man seated high on a loaded sled; he is wielding his whip like a lunatic.

" Bessami," says Marie.

So! The end of our idyll already! That Marie is engaged to Bessami everyone knows. That he is a madly jealous lover and that he is a tough customer are also facts pretty generally known.

The devil gets into me. He is still some distance behind us; well, then, if he wishes to recapture his bride-to-be, he must be given a chance to pursue her! So deciding, I speak a few words to Tiger, who immediately pricks up his ears and breaks into a breath-taking trot. I encourage him with my voice and make it clear to his mind that the chase we now have on our hands is more interesting than any we have had before on the trail of wolf or caribou. He comprehends, and that long, supple body of his seems to cleave its way through the air.

The race is on. Mile after mile slips by beneath our speeding sled, and Bessami hasn't a chance. I can see him lashing out with his whip more frantically than ever before, and every now and then I hear his hoarse cry of: " *Taislini* (The devil) ! " But his efforts and his profanity are of no avail; slowly and surely I am pulling away from him. Marie, sitting beside me, does not utter a word, but her eyes are sparkling, and there is no doubting the fact that she is enjoying the tense excitement of the race.

Then a harness strap breaks! Helplessly the sled slithers from side to side, and, before I am able to repair the damage, Bessami pulls up beside us. "*Nen nézōnilly!* (You bad man!) " is all his wrath permits him to say. I am ready to settle matters with him, when Marie hops out of my sled and into the other. Bessami swings his team round and is off across the ice as fast as his worn-out Indian dogs can

drag him. I am left alone to repair the broken harness.
Meanwhile Tiger and I have a serious talk together and are
finally agreed that one ought to stick to caribou-hunting
and let other types of chasing go by the board, especially
where engaged people are involved. . . .

Snowdrift is the same old place, tepees pitched at the
edge of the woods, the entire post swarming with Indians
and dogs. Naturally, I must go about greeting everyone individually, for it is at least a year since I saw them last. A
number of white trappers are at the post, all of them acquaintances of mine. Furthermore, a rare guest has arrived
at Snowdrift — the Roman Catholic missionary. He is a
tall, husky fellow with a mighty beard which flows down
over his breast — a genuine " he-man." Now, the arrival of
the missionary is, for the Indians, an event of the greatest
importance, for he will be able to settle a great number of
matters for them. No small amount of work has been piled
up for this man of God. Years have passed since last he
called at Snowdrift to take part in weddings, christenings,
and other pious ceremonies, and much has happened since
then.

More fuss and feathers are made over the baptism of
children than over anything else. The squaws come trailing
down from their tepees to the post, each with her infant
under her arm. They are all attired in their choicest finery,
on their feet embroidered moccasins, and over their heads
long black shawls, heavily befringed. In the course of an
hour the procession wends its way back, each red-skinned
citizen of the forest properly registered on the books of the
Almighty. Then great feastings are held in the tepees,
where the squaws sit jabbering as women always will after
such affairs. The hunters who sprawl on their caribou blankets are utterly deprived of their usual peace and quiet by

[321]

these sounds of gabbling squaws. But the man does not shout at his squaw today. If the racket becomes more than he can stand, he quietly leaves the tepee. More than one defeated hunter comes down to join us at our fire on the beach.

Departure is in the air. A large party of us will make the journey together south to Fort Resolution — both factors, four white trappers, and a large number of Indians. One of the fur-traders has his entire family with him, the other his future bride. The latter are but recently betrothed, and they are to be married at Resolution. This is a deep secret which no one is supposed to know. We whites are going farther than the others, all the way to the city of roseate dreams — Edmonton, over seven hundred miles south. It has been a long time since some of us have set foot in civilization — eight years for Klondike Bill, four for each of us others. It is not strange, then, that we are filled with a wild unrest and can hardly wait until we are off. Our wanderlust infects all the others, and it is taken as a matter of course that this year no one, regardless of old habit, will wait over for June and open water in order to make the journey by canoe. In a grand body we shall start out for Fort Resolution by dog-sled.

But we are obliged to curb our impatience yet awhile longer. The spring thaw has set in, and it will be impossible to go anywhere until after the sun has melted the slush from Slave Lake, and the water has run off into the cracks. Whilst waiting, we prepare ourselves for the journey. Each sled must be put in perfect order and equipped with steel runners. Then for each team of dogs it is necessary to stitch together some hundred and fifty moccasins made from canvas or tanned caribou hide. Without seeing that the dogs

are properly shod it would be hopeless to think of covering the hundred and seventy-five odd miles to Fort Resolution over honeycomb ice, the points of which are so sharp
that a man can feel their pricks even through socks and
moosehide moccasins. . . .

The snow has disappeared from the surface of Slave
Lake, which is now one vast field of ice dotted with black
pools of water. Tonight, if the temperature drops and these
surface ponds freeze hard enough to bear up a sled in motion, we shall be leaving. Traveling by day during May or
June is unthinkable, for then one has not alone sledding
conditions to consider, but also the comfort of the dogs,
who, in their thick winter pelage, are unable to endure the
heat of the sun.

It is midnight. In small groups we are waiting down by
the lake. About us lie sleds loaded to capacity with pelts,
ahead of them long lines of dogs half-asleep in the traces.
A cool breeze blows in from the lake, where a frosty fog
still hangs thick and gray.

" She's all right," says Klondike Bill, testing the new ice
with his foot. With that, he cracks his whip, hops on top of
his load, and disappears into the fog. His action is followed by a general commotion; a farrago of cracking
whips, oaths, and dogs' whines sounds through the night as,
one by one, the sleds get under way — fifteen all together.

We drive along like the wind. The steel runners fly, as
though greased, over the ice, and every time the dogs come
to a stop, the sled coasts up on top of them. There are sleds
ahead and sleds behind. I can hear the muffled sounds of
their bells, but can see nothing, because of the fog.

The hours pass. Then I observe a reddish glow on the ice
ahead. Before long I arrive at a small island where a huge

[323]

camp-fire is flaming in amongst a clump of spruces. Near shore, sled after sled is drawn up, the dogs loafing about on the ice. The procession has stopped here to rest.

Soon we are all together, boiling and roasting our food. The Indians sit cross-legged about the fire, but the rest of us, for the most part, prefer to stretch out full-length on a patch of dry ground. The lovers have found a sequestered spot beneath a thick, overhanging spruce, whilst the priest sits scribbling in the firelight. Our conversation is expressive of a coarse-grained good-fellowship, for we are all in the highest of spirits, as who could help being on a midsummer sledding trip across Great Slave Lake?

Off we go again. The priest soon leaves us behind, for he has two teams of Indian dogs and can change from one to the other; furthermore he has in the Indian Abel a driver who can keep up a lively pace.

Gradually the fog lifts, and before long the sun announces its coming by tinting the hills to the east with ruby light. Forest and lake emerge from the shadows of night, and on all sides of me I see the sleds of my comrades turning in toward shore. Off to the west lies Red Cliff Island, and close beneath its rocky coast a band of caribou are strolling, the first rays of the rising sun upon them. Now and then the creatures stop to stare at the sleds, then resume their journey north.

With the first warmth of the sun comes a sudden uncontrollable drowsiness; it is almost irresistible. I yawn and every now and then must walk briskly along beside the sled to prevent myself from dozing off. Up ahead one of the sleds gradually slackens its pace. Soon I am close behind a team of dogs which are loafing along half-asleep and doing exactly as they please. Where on earth is the driver? I run up ahead. Over the top of the cariole lies a large piece of canvas, and through this comes a lively stream of gurgling sounds. I tear aside the covering and discover the bronzed face of the Indian Souzi. He is having a better time snoring here than he would at home in his tepee!

It is eight o'clock and the dogs are already panting with the heat. Time to find a camp-site. The fire is made, the dogs looked after, our meal stowed away under our belts, and now it is bedtime. Each with his sleeping-bag under his arm, we wander off into the forest to sleep in the shade of some tree.

The farther southwest we proceed, the more difficult we find the ice. The lagoons of open water inshore drive us far out on the lake. The coves and narrow sounds are now completely open, and in many places the ice is so rotten and full of holes that it bends beneath the weight of our sleds and sends water gushing up. Where conditions appear to be overly treacherous, two Indians run ahead to test the ice with their axes. We others do not proceed until we see them beckon. The worst problem of all lies in the form of broad rifts in the ice which completely bar our progress and sometimes project out into the lake for miles. Here we urge the dogs forward at a stiff gallop and let them plunge across. But much splashing and some swimming are necessary before they have safely cleared these obstacles.

Just what the snow-birds can find to do so far out from shore is somewhat of a conundrum, but flock after flock of them starts up in front of the dogs. We also suddenly encounter a party of muskrats, certainly far from home. They provide much entertainment for the Indians, who chase them and kill them with their whips. Wherever there is open water, there are ducks swimming, and here, too, the Indians must indulge in their lust for murder, even though there is no chance whatever of recovering their game. They

blaze away, with a perfect barrage of gun-fire, and giggle
sillily as they drive on their way, leaving their wounded
prey to flop helplessly around in the water. But over our
heads the gray goose is migrating in huge flocks north toward the Polar Sea.

The dogs are having a hard time of it, sore-footed as
they are by this time. We change their moccasins many
times a day, but it is not easy to tell just when the old ones
have worn through. The dogs cannot go far over this needle-
ice before their paws begin to bleed. A number of them are
unable to continue in the traces, and all of us have loose
dogs trailing along behind. A few of them, even when re-
lieved of the strain of hauling, are unable to keep up with
the procession, and far behind us there are those who limp
slowly forward and those who remain where they are.

Early one morning we arrive at Stony Island, a day's
journey from Fort Resolution. Directly ahead lies the Slave
River delta, and much depends upon whether the powerful
current of the river has destroyed the ice about its effluence,
for unless we can cross it on runners, we shall be obliged
to make a circuitous journey out into the lake. Our anxiety
leads us to investigate matters at once. But after ten hours
of hard driving, there must be a deal of inducement to lure
anyone into the mess of slush and pack-ice we sight off to
the west. We therefore club together and bribe a couple of
the Indians to go ahead and study conditions. Quite readily
they accept the bargain and are off. They return some time
later, soaking wet, and report: " Much open water, ice
good, maybe not so good. Heap mud and squaw-ducks see,
bad sign."

Receiving this enlightening report, the Indians and fur-
traders immediately decide to press on to Fort Resolution
without further delay. Although their dogs are dead tired,

these men are bound to continue their journey, as though
their lives depended upon it, regardless of ice conditions.
The one thought they have in mind is to hasten the grand
moment when, as travelers from far-distant parts, they will
come driving into the gilded town of Resolution to be met
by an astounded, inquisitive throng.

We whites are left to ourselves again; we take care of
our dogs and enjoy the relief of having for once no Indians
to share our camp-fire. At noon we clamber up to a little
grassy plateau on the very top of the island. There we creep
into our sleeping-bags and, side by side, in the mild
warmth of the sun, we sleep the sleep of the just. On awakening we set out for Resolution.

We set a direct course, prepared to take a chance on
crossing the delta. The Slave River growls beneath us; the
pack-ice and stretches of open water testify to the possibility that the river may at any moment burst its bonds,
but we go racing along over the danger spots and at length
heave a sigh of relief.

Now we are rounding Moose Island, and — there ahead
of us lies Fort Resolution, a cluster of houses and a white
frame chapel, whose windows are aflame with the sun. A
flock of swans whir by, so low over the ice that their white
bodies are almost one with the white of the lake. And now,
ahead of us, the racket begins, for they have already caught
scent of us — the eternal dogs of Resolution. . . .

• •

Glorious days of idleness while waiting for the river
boat! We wander about, meeting different people and listening to all the news. And what all hasn't happened during
the years we have spent in the wilderness! When last we

saw Resolution, it was during the days of dogs and fur-trading; today everyone is agog over prospecting and avia-tion. Down on the beach lies the wreckage of an aeroplane. Folks now speak of flying-machines as unaffectedly as they used to speak of dogs. And the Indians of the fort no longer flee terror-stricken into the woods when they see a "flying canoe."

The wilderness is in the process of being conquered from the air, this conquest being in the name of the yellow metal and radium. Giant corporations from the south send up whole fleets of aeroplanes carrying geologists to strategic points in the wilds. One region after another is being care-fully combed for deposits. There is talk of strikes up the Yellowknife River, near Great Bear Lake, near Baker Lake — in the remotest corners of the wilderness. In certain places the initial machinery, transported north by plane, is already operating in the interests of test mining. Even Resolution has experienced a rush of its own. On Pine Point, some miles west, enormous deposits of galena have been discovered. The necessary drilling apparatus arrived by air, and in no time the mine was going full blast.

But it has not been so easy to conquer the North, even by aeroplane — many times the wilderness has bared its fangs. More than one frisky flying-machine has come a cropper on the ice or against some comber-like snow-drift. Deep in the Barren Lands lie various masses of wreckage for wolf, fox, and caribou to rack their brains over. Millions have been invested to cover initial costs, it is true, but what do these amount to when one has faith in the country!

In such wise has the age of progress, with seven-league boots, assailed the strongholds of the North. The pros-pector no longer tramps about with his pan. He goes sailing through the air! The romance of the Klondike belongs to a bygone day. . . .

Two planes are due at Resolution any day now. They are coming from the north, are bound direct for Edmonton, and will carry any passengers who can afford to pay the price. This gives us something to think about. Shall we take the river boat, or shall we fly? We drape ourselves about the wrecked aeroplane not far from our tent to discuss the matter. Klondike Bill vows that before he will set foot in a noisy, infernal contraption like that he will make the journey to Edmonton on foot. Joe has heard of air-pockets which cause a plane to plunge straight down two or three thousand feet; he is extremely distrustful of flying. We others likewise have our doubts, not least because of the cash it will take to get us down to Edmonton. The fare is a couple of hundred dollars. But just think of it — to fly! " In two days we would be guzzling cool beer at some bar in Edmonton," says Jim, rocking against one broken wing, and staring dreamily out over Great Slave Lake. "Hm," we hear from Klondike Bill, and realize that Jim's reference to beer has made a deep impression on him. "But by boat and train it would take us two weeks," continues Jim. . . .

Naturally, we decide to fly!

. .

The whole of Resolution is aflame with excitement. All the men in town have invested in a grand sweepstake, the bets being on the hour the two flying-machines will arrive. Everywhere are people bending back their heads and staring up at the sky, or pricking up their ears for the sound of an aeroplane motor.

Two days pass; no planes. It is eleven o'clock on the morning of the third day. Klondike Bill is sitting out on a grassy hilltop, his watch in his hand, his eyes roving the clouds. In the sweepstake, he has drawn the hour between eleven and noon, a devil of a fine hour, he assured me. Then from the tent comes the cry of " *Mi-su!* " and unwillingly he comes in to eat. We have meat and bacon and peas for lunch. But Bill does not seem to relish his food; he merely takes it in his mouth and swallows it, his eyes all the while glued on the minute-hand of his watch, which shows the hour to be approaching noon. Then the dogs break into a howl. We listen. A faint roaring in our ears, the roaring of a motor. Bill lets out a yell, upsets his plate of food, and starts for the door. " My time! My time! " he bawls out at the top of his lungs, waving his arms and pegging it over the hill to the trading post as fast as his stiff old legs will carry him.

In the sunny blue sky over Fort Resolution two red birds are circling. Lower and lower they soar, whilst the dogs of the fort race hither and yon, giving voice to their terror. Then the planes float down behind the woods and vanish in the direction of the river. . . .

I step aboard with a small bundle carried under my arm. Whatever else I owned before will remain here in the North. Tiger, Trofast, Spike, and Sport I have sold to some friends of mine, but Skøieren — no one else shall ever drive him. . . .

We rise into the air. Beneath us the wilderness unfolds like a map — lake after lake, a network of rivers and channels, an endless expanse of forest. Like a silver ribbon the Slave River winds its way northward until it spreads out, like a glittering fan, to meet the misty blue of Great Slave Lake. We fly so low that I can see the muskrat etching with ripples the clear surface of a pond as he swims, and a flock of wild ducks starting up from the reeds. Off across a muskeg a moose is racing in terror.

Farther south we overtake the river boat pushing ahead of her two heavy scows, her bright-red paddle-wheel twinkling in the sun. Ponderously she fights her way upstream, seeming barely to move as we go sailing by. Staring back at the steamer as she splashes her way along, awkward and old-fashioned in every detail, I see two different ages closely contrasted. The Northland has been given her warning; civilization, expanding from the south, is seeking new fields of activity for her sons. Today she is still groping, but another day will come when, with full majesty, her will shall prevail: factories, smoke-darkened cities, milling humanity. . . . But the peace of the wilderness, the silence of these great forests, the Barrens where the wolves give voice to their dismal music, and the caribou graze by the million . . . and the Indians — the few small bands that are left, still pursuing the free nomadic existence of their forefathers, challenging the wasteland with dog-sled and canoe . . . what of these? I stare back at the river boat, whose twinkling red paddle-wheel is still visible far in the distance, and suddenly I pour out to it all the sympathy I have in my soul. . . .

In McMurray we land and stay overnight. The following day sees us soaring up the Athabaska. Farming country comes into view, the Saskatchewan River spreads out beneath us, and at length we alight on a small lake just outside of Edmonton.

We drive into the city, which harbors all we have spoken of on countless evenings in our tents or beside our campfires in the North. The city's bedlam assails our ears — automobiles and street-cars rushing hither and yon, roaring and screeching. Then the flash of confused colors and lights, swarms of humanity jostling each other on the streets as though the welfare of the entire world depended upon their efforts.

During our fourth day in the city, Klondike Bill comes over to me and says: " Lighting out for the north tomorrow. Got to get home to my tent, it's too lonesome out here."

A NOTE ON THE TYPE IN WHICH
THIS BOOK IS SET

This book is composed on the linotype in Bodoni, so called after Giambattista Bodoni (1740–1813), son of a printer of Piedmont. After gaining experience and fame as superintendent of the Press of the Propaganda in Rome, Bodoni became in 1766 the head of the ducal printing house at Parma, which he soon made the foremost of its kind in Europe. His Manuale Tipografico, *completed by his widow in 1818, contains 279 pages of specimens of types, including alphabets of about thirty foreign languages. His editions of Greek, Latin, Italian, and French classics, especially his Homer, are celebrated for their typography. In type-designing he was an innovator, making his new faces rounder, wider, and lighter, with greater openness and delicacy. His types were rather too rigidly perfect in detail, the thick lines contrasting sharply with the thin wiry lines. It was this feature, doubtless, that caused William Morris's condemnation of the Bodoni types as "swelteringly hideous." Bodoni Book, as reproduced by the Linotype Company, is a modern version based, not upon any one of Bodoni's fonts, but upon a composite conception of the Bodoni manner, designed to avoid the details stigmatized as bad by typographical experts and to secure the pleasing and effective results of which the Bodoni types are capable.*